June 2011
    Your energy & drive are
infectious. Keep your wonderful
spirit, your wit, and never
give up.
Mr. M°Kean

PIRATE HUNTER OF THE CARIBBEAN

ALSO BY DAVID CORDINGLY

Cochrane: The Real Master and Commander

Under the Black Flag:
The Romance and Reality of Life Among the Pirates

Seafaring Women: Adventures of Pirate Queens,
Female Stowaways, and Sailors' Wives

PIRATE HUNTER
OF THE CARIBBEAN

*The Adventurous Life
of Captain Woodes Rogers*

DAVID CORDINGLY

RANDOM HOUSE

NEW YORK

For Shirley

CONTENTS

Author's Note

The Juan Fernández Archipelago consists of three islands and a rocky islet. The largest island, which used to be known as Isla Más a Tierra, is the only one which has ever been inhabited and is the one which the buccaneers and later seafarers called Juan Fernández. In 1966 the Chilean government renamed this island Isla Robinson Crusoe, and the smaller, uninhabited island 112 miles to the west (formerly called Isla Más Afuera) was renamed Isla Alejandro Selkirk. The third island in the group was, and still is, called Isla Santa Clara, and the rocky islet is called Islote Juananga. I have followed the usage of the early seafarers and always refer to the large island by its original name, as in this quote from Woodes Rogers' journal, 'At seven this morning we made the Island of Juan Fernandez.'

During the course of this book I have used the terms 'pieces of eight', 'pesos' and 'Spanish dollars' depending on the source of the information. All three terms apply to the same silver coin which was worth eight *reales* and was the common currency used throughout Spain's empire in the New World for more than three centuries. One side of the coin had the Spanish coat of arms and the other side usually had a design which included the pillars of Hercules. The twin pillars symbolised the limits of the ancient world at the Straits of Gibraltar and these eventually formed the basis of the dollar sign used today. In 1644 one piece of eight (or peso or Spanish dollar) was valued in England at four shillings and sixpence. That would be the equivalent of about £18 or US $28 today.

In their books, Woodes Rogers and Edward Cooke usually anglicised the names of the Spanish ships which they encountered. I have used the Spanish names for Spanish ships and smaller vessels. However, I have retained the archaic spelling of *Dutchess* and *Marquiss* for the English ships because these are the names given to them by the privateers.

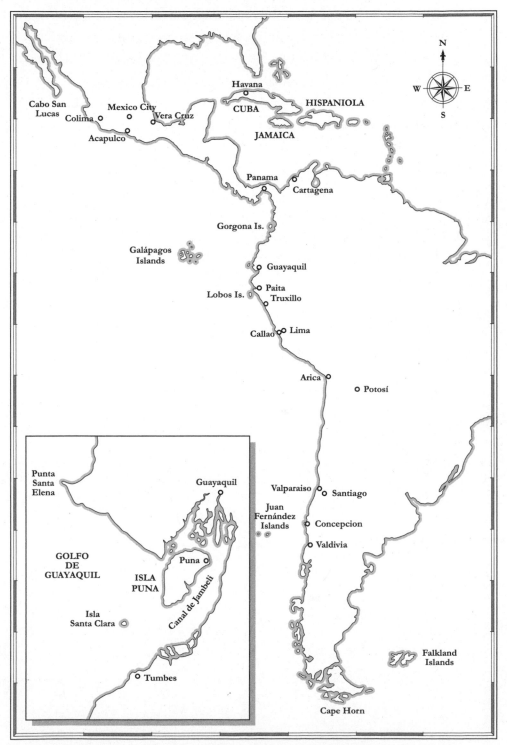

Map of the Pacific coast of South and Central America showing the places associated with the buccaneers and with Woodes Rogers' privateering expedition.

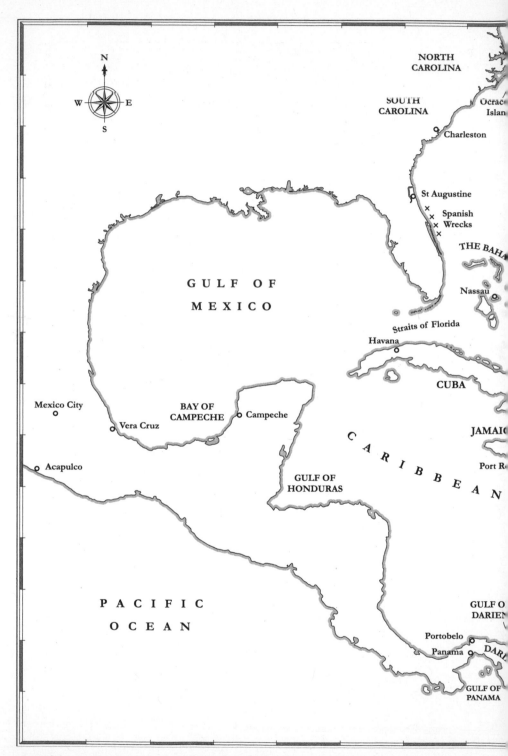

Map of the Caribbean and Central America during the time of the buccaneers, privateers and pirates of the seventeenth and early eighteenth century.

The Bahama Islands

ATLANTIC OCEAN

Grand Bahama Island

Green Turtle Key

Abaco Island

Bimini Islands

Harbour Island

Nassau

Eleuthera

Andros Island

New Providence

Cat Island

San Salvador

Green Cay

Rum Cay

Great Exuma

Long Island

Crooked Island

CUBA

Windward Passage

Tortuga

HISPANIOLA

PUERTO RICO

LEEWARD ISLANDS

Santo Domingo

St Thomas

St John

Anguilla

St Kitts

Nevis

Antigua

Guadeloupe

Dominica

WINDWARD ISLANDS

Martinique

St Lucia

SEA

Barbados

Grenada

Curaçao

Tobago

Trinidad

Maracaibo

Cartagena

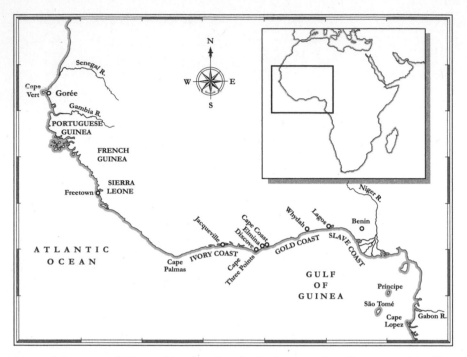

Map of the coast of West Africa showing the harbours and trading posts visited by the pirates of Bartholomew Roberts and naval ships sent to hunt them down.

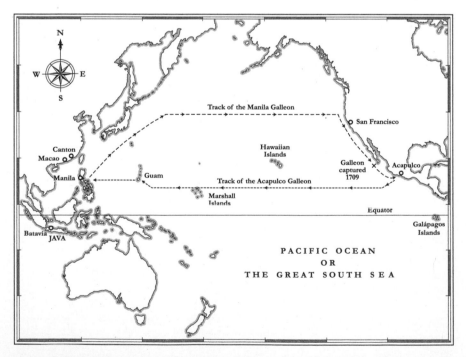

Map of the Pacific to show the tracks of the eastbound Manila Galleon and the westbound Acapulco Galleon.

PIRATE HUNTER OF THE CARIBBEAN

Prologue

In the autumn of 1717 the following item appeared in a London newspaper: 'On Wednesday Capt Rogers, who took the Aquapulca Ship in the South-Seas, kissed his Majesty's hand at Hampton Court, on his being made Governor of the Island of Providence in the West Indies, now in the possession of the Pirates.'[1]

Behind this brief statement lies an extraordinary story. It is the story of a tough and resolute sea captain who led a privateering raid on Spanish ships in the Pacific, rescued a castaway from a deserted island and then played a key role in the fight against the pirates of the Caribbean. It is also a tale of treasure ships and treasure ports, of maroonings and hangings, and the genesis of Daniel Defoe's most famous book, *The Life and Strange Surprising Adventures of Robinson Crusoe*. The story is played out against the background of fierce colonial rivalry between Britain, France and Spain; and it is linked with the fabulously rich trade in gold and silver from Central and South America, the trade in silks and spices from the Far East and the shipment of black slaves from the west coast of Africa to the sugar plantations of the West Indies. Many of the events centre on two groups of islands: the Bahamas and the remote archipelago of Juan Fernández in the South Pacific.

For several years the harbour of Nassau in the Bahamas was the base for a roving band of pirates which included many of the leading figures of the so-called Golden Age of Piracy – figures such as Ben Hornigold, Charles Vane, Calico Jack, Sam Bellamy and Edward Teach, otherwise known as Blackbeard. This nucleus of 'loose and disorderly people' produced a generation of pirates whose operations extended from the Caribbean to the east coast of North America as far as Newfoundland, and across the Atlantic to the slave ports of West Africa and beyond to the Indian Ocean. The usual explanation given for this explosion of piracy is the signing of the Treaty of Utrecht in 1713, which brought an end to eleven years of war and caused Britain, France and other maritime powers to reduce the size of their navies. This threw thousands of redundant sailors on to the streets of coastal towns and cities. Unable to find work elsewhere, some of these seamen turned to piracy. They were joined by the crews of privateer ships who had been legally authorised by letters of marque to attack enemy shipping when their country was at war but, with the declaration of peace, were tempted to exchange their national ensigns for the black flag of piracy.

Redundant sailors and privateers were certainly among the crews of the pirate ships but there were other events which sparked off the alarming surge in piracy following the Treaty of Utrecht. The first was the wrecking of a Spanish treasure fleet on the coast of Florida in 1715. This attracted sailors and adventurers from across the Caribbean to go 'fishing on the wrecks' for Spanish gold and silver. The second was the misguided action of the Spanish in expelling the logwood cutters from the Bay of Campeche in the Gulf of Mexico and the Bay of Honduras. Described by one observer as 'a rude, drunken crew, some of which have been pirates, and most of them sailors',[2] the logwood men alternated the laborious work of cutting down the valuable logwood trees with extended bouts of heavy drinking. When the Spanish seized the ships involved in the logwood trade, the cutters migrated to Nassau, which was already being used by the treasure hunters as a base for their operations. The sheltered harbour on the north coast of the island of New Providence in the Bahamas became a magnet for a motley group of seafaring men who found piracy to be an easier and more profitable occupation than life on a merchant ship or cutting logs in the steamy jungles of Central America.

Colonial governors sent disturbing reports back to the Council of Trade and Plantations in London. In 1718 the Governor of South Carolina asked for the assistance of a naval frigate to counter 'the unspeakable calamity this poor province suffers from pyrates'[3] and the Governor of Jamaica reported that 'there is hardly one ship or vessel, coming in or going out of this island that is not plundered'.[4] The situation was most critical in the Bahamas, where there was so little provision for the defence of the islands that most of the law-abiding inhabitants had fled, 'whereby the said islands are exposed to be plundered and ravaged by pirates and others, and in danger of being lost from our Crown of Great Britain'.[5] It would be the task of Captain Woodes Rogers to rid the islands of the pirates and to put an end to the raids of Spanish privateers.

The Juan Fernández islands were a refuge for generations of mariners who had rounded Cape Horn and survived the icy storms and mountainous waves of that bleak region. It was here that several buccaneer ships called in for wood and water in the 1680s. During one of these visits a Miskito Indian called Will was inadvertently marooned, his rescue three years later being witnessed and recorded by William Dampier. And it was on the same island that the most famous of castaways, Alexander Selkirk, was abandoned in 1704 after an argument with Captain Stradling, who had parted from an ill-fated privateering expedition led by Dampier. When Captain

Woodes Rogers dropped anchor off the island four years later he and his crew were greeted by 'a man clothed in goat-skins, who looked wilder than the first owners of them'.[6] On his return to London after his successful privateering expedition Rogers published a book entitled *A Cruising Voyage Round the World* which described his raid on the town of Guayaquil and his capture of a Spanish treasure galleon, and included vivid accounts of faraway anchorages and exotic native peoples. But it was his detailed description of how Selkirk survived his lonely ordeal on Juan Fernández which proved of more interest than anything else which took place during the epic voyage of the two Bristol ships under his command.

The driving force behind the early privateering expeditions into the Pacific, and the raids of the buccaneers and the pirates in the West Indies, was the age-old lure of gold and silver. Ever since the conquest of the Aztec civilisation in Mexico by Hernando Cortés in 1519, and the brutal overthrow of the Inca ruler in Peru by Pizarro in 1533, a constant stream of gold and silver bullion had been transported by mule trains across the mountains and through the jungles of South and Central America to the treasure ports of the Spanish Main. On the hot and humid waterfronts of Nombre de Dios, Portobelo, Cartagena and Vera Cruz the precious cargoes of gold and silver, together with spices, hides and hardwood, were loaded on to ships which sailed first to Havana in Cuba for refitting and victualling, and then across the Atlantic to Seville and Cadiz in Spain.

The treasure galleons were an irresistible target for British, Dutch and French privateers. In 1523 the French corsair Jean Fleury intercepted three Spanish ships off Cape St Vincent as they neared the end of their homeward journey. He attacked and boarded the vessels and found their holds filled with the treasure which Cortés had looted from the Aztecs. There were three cases of gold ingots, 500 pounds of gold dust, 680 pounds of pearls, coffers of emeralds and

Aztec helmets, shields and feathered cloaks. The quantity of treasure shipped across the Atlantic rose steadily during the sixteenth century and was given a spectacular boost with the discovery in 1545 of the silver mountain at Potosí in Bolivia (then part of the vice-regency of Peru). The great cone of the mountain known as Cerro de Potosí soared to 15,827 feet (4,824 metres) above sea level and proved to be one of the richest sources of silver ore in the world. By 1650 the sides of the mountain were peppered with mine shafts and at the base of the mountain there was a town of more than 160,000 people – larger than Amsterdam or Madrid. The Spanish were reliant on local Indians for extracting and refining the silver, but working at such a high altitude was exhausting and thousands died from the hard labour, the brutal treatment and mercury poisoning. Although there were 150,000 black African slaves working in Peru and the Andean region in 1640, it was found that the Africans were unable to work with their usual energy in the rarefied air of Potosí.[7]

The treasure ships which transported the silver across the Atlantic were so vulnerable to the attacks of swift, heavily armed privateers that in 1543 the Spanish instituted a convoy system with fleets of up to 100 vessels being escorted by warships. This measure proved so effective that it was rare for any ships to fall into the hands of predators. When they did so the rewards for the captors were enormous. In 1628 the Dutch admiral Piet Hein intercepted one of the treasure fleets in the Bay of Matanlas on the north coast of Cuba and captured four treasure galleons and eleven smaller vessels. The total value of the gold, silver and trade goods taken was more than eleven million guilders, enough to fund the Dutch army for eight months and ruin Spanish credit in Europe that year.

In addition to the treasure fleets or *flotas* making their regular crossings of the Atlantic there were treasure galleons which made annual crossings of the Pacific. In 1571 the Spanish had founded a trading settlement at Manila in the Philippines and this had become the focal point for a hugely lucrative trade between the Spanish Empire in the New World and the Far East. Once a year a consignment of silver from the mines of Central and South America was transported in one or two galleons from Acapulco on the coast of Mexico across the vast expanse of the Pacific to Manila. There the silver would be traded for silks from the Chinese ports of Macao and Canton, and for spices and other exotic goods from India and the Spice Islands. These would be loaded on to the galleons at Manila for the long voyage back to Acapulco. The galleons were known by the port of their departure, so the east-going galleon was called the Manila galleon and the same ship was called the Acapulco galleon on her west-going voyage.

Unlike the treasure fleets which crossed the Atlantic, the Acapulco and Manila galleons travelled alone and without an accompanying escort of warships. The Spanish had good reason to be confident in their ability to survive the journey unscathed. The ships themselves were among the largest merchant ships of their day, ranging from 500 to 1,000 tons. They were strongly built of teak, were usually armed with 50 to 80 guns and carried crews of up to 700 sailors and soldiers. Moreover, Spain jealously guarded her sovereignty over the Pacific, which, with some justification, had come to be known as 'the Spanish Lake'. Her warships patrolled the coasts of her empire in the New World and the crews of any foreign ships captured were subject to imprisonment, torture or death.

Before Woodes Rogers' expedition of 1708 only two treasure ships had ever been taken in the Pacific. On 1 March 1579 the British privateer Francis Drake, during the course of his circumnavigation of the world in the *Golden Hind*, had fought and taken the *Nuestra Señora de la Concepción*, which was en route from Lima to Panama.

She was not one of the Acapulco or Manila galleons but she carried a cargo which included 'a great quantity of jewels and precious stones, 13 chests of royals of plate, 80 lb of gold and 26 tons of uncoined silver'.[8] A few years later two British ships under the command of Sir Thomas Cavendish encountered the Manila galleon *Santa Ana* as she approached the American coast off Cape San Lucas. After enduring six hours of gunfire from the British ships she surrendered. Cavendish returned to England in September 1588 and in November he sailed up the Thames in style. According to a Spanish agent in London, 'Every sailor had a gold chain round his neck, and the sails of the ship were a blue damask, the standard of cloth of gold and blue silk. It was as if Cleopatra had been resuscitated. The only thing wanting was that the rigging should have been of silken rope.'[9]

The voyages of Drake and Cavendish provided a tempting glimpse of the riches to be found in the Pacific, or what was then known as the Great South Sea, but it is the exploits of the buccaneers which are the real curtain-raiser for the story of Captain Woodes Rogers. The buccaneers' audacious attacks on Spanish treasure ports and coastal settlements in the New World revealed the fragility of Spain's hold over her sprawling empire. And the adventures of one particular group of buccaneers are of direct relevance to Rogers' expedition. Known by their contemporaries as the South Sea Men, they cruised the same waters as Rogers, and they called in at the same islands to refit their ships and stock up on wood and water. Among the South Sea Men was William Dampier, whose published account of his voyages with the buccaneers brought him considerable fame when he eventually returned to London. As a result he was given command of a voyage of exploration to Australia, and later he led an expedition to capture the Manila galleon. Both voyages were abject failures but his reputation as a navigator, and the unrivalled experience which he had gained from travels that had taken him twice round the world, ensured that he was taken on as pilot by the sponsors of Rogers' expedition to the South Seas.

The term 'buccaneer' is generally used now to describe the privateers and pirates of the West Indies who raided Spanish towns and shipping in the Caribbean and along the coasts of Central and South America in the period from around 1600 to the 1680s.[10] But the word originally applied to the groups of men, mainly French, who lived off the wild herds of cattle which roamed the northern regions of the great island of Hispaniola. They became known as *boucaniers* or *bucaniers* from their practice of roasting meat on a *boucan*, a type of barbecue, in the manner of the local Indians. Armed with an assortment of weapons and dressed in bloodstained hides, these rough men were described by a French missionary as 'the butcher's vilest servants who have been eight days in the slaughterhouse without washing themselves'.[11] Driven off Hispaniola by the Spanish in the 1630s, they migrated to the rocky island of Tortuga and used this as a base from which to attack passing ships and particularly those of the hated Spanish. After the capture of Jamaica by the British in 1655 many of the buccaneers moved to the harbour and town of Port Royal, which soon acquired the reputation of being the wickedest city in Christendom. The successive Governors of Jamaica encouraged the buccaneers to base themselves at Port Royal and issued privateering commissions for their ships. The buccaneers' presence protected the island from attack by the French or Spanish; and the ships and loot which they seized were of considerable benefit to the island's economy.

It was from Port Royal that Henry Morgan, the greatest of the buccaneers, set out on his devastating raids on the Spanish Main. Born in the county of Monmouth in Wales, he always regarded himself as a gentleman's son. Two of his uncles were distinguished soldiers (one was a major-general and another was a colonel who was briefly Lieutenant Governor of Jamaica). Morgan himself was a soldier in the expeditionary force which had captured Jamaica. He took part in a number of raids on Spanish towns in Central America and proved to be a brilliant leader of irregular forces. In 1668, in a bold attack at dawn on the fortified town of Portobello, he used the element of surprise to good effect and with only 500 men he took the castle, forced the garrison to surrender and negotiated a ransom. He returned to Jamaica with a haul of gold and silver coins and bars of silver worth around 250,000 pesos. The following year he led a fleet of ships and attacked Maracaibo on the coast of Venezuela in the Gulf of Mexico, but his greatest feat was the sack of Panama City.

In August 1670 Morgan put out a call for men to join him in an attack on the Spanish Main. By September a multi-national fleet of thirty-eight ships and nearly 2,000 men had assembled at Isla Vaca on the south-west coast of Hispaniola. In December they sailed to San Lorenzo at the mouth of the River Chagres, captured the castle and commenced a gruelling march through the jungle to Panama. The army of mostly inexperienced soldiers and horsemen assembled on the plain outside the city were no match for Morgan's battle-hardened men, who swept them aside, and entered Panama. Within hours the great city was on fire and the buccaneers were looting the houses of any valuables they could find. The Spanish were outraged by the attack, which had taken place after a peace treaty had been signed between England and Spain.[12] Morgan, and Sir Thomas Modyford, the Governor of Jamaica, who had authorised him to carry out the raid, were both recalled to London. But just as Drake had been forgiven for his piracies against his country's traditional enemy and had received a knighthood from Queen Elizabeth I, so Morgan received a knighthood from King Charles II and was sent back to Jamaica as Lieutenant Governor to defend the island from any future attack by French or Spanish warships. He rebuilt the coastal defences but proved to have little appetite for the administrative duties of his post. In August 1688 he died of drink and dropsy on his Jamaican estate, attended by Sir Hans Sloane, the celebrated physician whose library and collections would later form the basis of the British Museum.

Morgan was followed by the South Sea Men, who roamed all round the coast of South America and far out into the Pacific. Most of them were British but there were Dutchmen, Frenchmen, New Englanders and Creoles among them. Although they were regarded as bloodthirsty pirates by the Spanish whose ships they captured and whose towns they pillaged, it would be a mistake to dismiss them all as barbaric raiders. Their letters of marque were often of dubious validity, but they regarded themselves as privateers fighting an old enemy whose right to the riches of the New World they were prepared to challenge. As Protestants they had no hesitation in looting the Roman Catholic churches in South America of their gold and silver plate, and while they were merciless in shooting and slaughtering any who opposed their raids, they generally treated defeated enemies with respect and, unlike some of the earlier buccaneers and many of the later pirates, they rarely resorted to torture. While the Spanish had a dismal record of enslaving the native peoples and working them to death in the silver mines and on the plantations, the British buccaneers were invariably welcomed by the native Indians, who were prepared to supply them with food and shelter and to act as their guides in a hostile terrain.

We know this because there were several educated men among the buccaneers who kept journals of their travels which were later published. Some of the journals reveal an intense curiosity about the little-known lands these buccaneers visited. They made maps and charts and included sailing directions for the benefit of mariners who might follow them, but they also recorded the appearance and customs of the native peoples, and recorded long, meticulous descriptions of the strange animals, birds, trees and plants they came across. The writings of William Dampier are deservedly the best known but he had several companions whose journals make fascinating reading, notably those of Lionel Wafer, a surgeon who spent three months living among the Cuna Indians of Central America, and Basil Ringrose, who fought alongside the buccaneers and frequently acted as their interpreter. William Dick, who also published his experiences, wrote that 'we made use of one Mr Ringrose, who was with us in all this voyage, and being a good scholar, and full of ingeniosity, had also good skill in languages. This gentleman kept an exact and very curious journal of all our voyage, from our first setting out to the very last day . . .'[13]

In December 1679 these buccaneer writers were among a miscellaneous crew of adventurers, logwood cutters, naval deserters and soldiers of fortune who had gathered on seven ships off the west coast of Jamaica. Under the leadership of captains Coxon, Sawkins and Sharp they set sail towards the Isthmus of Panama (then called the Isthmus of Darien), their aim being 'to pillage and plunder in those parts'. They looted Portobelo and then sailed south to Golden Island, where 300 of them landed and marched inland across the Isthmus. After nine days' march they reached the Spanish town of El Real de Santa Maria, which was situated at the head of a great river estuary. Warned of their coming, the Governor had despatched all the gold and valuables to Panama. El Real de Santa Maria was defended by wooden palisades and by a garrison of 200 men but the buccaneers had no difficulty in overcoming them. Disappointed to find a settlement of primitive houses with scarcely anything worth looting, they set fire to the church and the fort and set off downstream. Their next target was Panama.

I

Raiding the South Seas

The buccaneers arrived off Panama shortly before sunrise. It was the morning of 23 April 1680, a day of good omen because it was dedicated to St George, the patron saint of England. The men had been rowing since four o'clock the previous afternoon and had kept going through the night, following the coastline but staying a few miles offshore to avoid detection. As the light increased they could see the church towers and tiled rooftops of the great city. To the east were the ruins of the old town, which had been burnt down following its capture by Sir Henry Morgan. The wooden buildings had gone but prominent among the remaining stone structures was the old cathedral, 'the beautiful building whereof maketh a fair show at a distance, like unto that of St Pauls at London'.[1]

Of more immediate concern to the buccaneers were the ships lying at anchor nearby in the lee of the island of Perico. Among the smaller local craft they could see five large merchant ships and three Spanish warships. As soon as the leading canoes of the buccaneers were sighted, the warships weighed anchor and got under sail. The Spanish had been warned of their presence in the area and had orders to intercept them and to give no quarter to those they captured. The ships had the wind behind them and, steering directly for the canoes, seemed intent on running them down.

The buccaneers were exhausted after rowing more or less continuously for twelve hours and there were only sixty-eight of them, the rest having stayed behind at El Real de Santa Maria. Thirty-two of them were in a heavy piragua, a large dugout vessel made from the trunk of a cotton tree. The remaining thirty-six buccaneers were in five canoes commandeered from the local Indians. These were extremely unstable craft. Ringrose recorded, 'Here in the Gulf it went very hard with us whensoever any wave dashed against the sides of our canoe, for it was nigh twenty foot in length, and yet not quite one foot and a half in breadth, where it was at its broadest so that we had just room to sit down in her, and a little water would easily have both filled and overwhelmed us.'[2] His canoe had in fact capsized during their journey to Panama but somehow they had survived and managed to save their weapons.

While the buccaneers were aware that the odds were heavily against them, having come so far they were in no mood to surrender. As John Cox later recalled, 'we made a resolution rather than drown in the sea, or beg quarter of the Spaniard, whom we used to conquer, to run the extremest hazard of fire and sword'.[3] The Spanish forces bearing down on them were overwhelming. They had a total of 228 men on their three ships and they were led by experienced commanders. The leading ship was commanded by Don Diego de Carabaxal, who had a crew of sixty-five men. This was followed by the flagship, commanded by Don Jacinto de Barahona. He was 'High Admiral of those seas' and had a crew of eighty-six Biscay men, who were reckoned the best mariners and soldiers among the Spaniards. The third warship was commanded by Don Francisco de Peralta, 'an old and stout Spaniard, native of Andalucia'. His ship was manned by seventy-seven Negroes.

Although tired and outnumbered, the buccaneers were a formidable fighting force. They appear not to have been affected by the heat, the humidity and the swarms of mosquitoes and they evidently had extraordinary reserves of stamina. They had survived a gruelling march across the Isthmus of Panama during which they had had to cut their way through the jungle. They had crossed mountains and fast-flowing rivers and endured days of being drenched in tropical downpours. Most of them had a long history of raiding coastal settlements and they had recently captured two Spanish towns. They were armed with pistols and cutlasses but their most deadly weapons were their long-barrelled muskets.[4] These apparently unwieldy guns were made in France and came to be known as *fusils bucaniers*. They were extremely accurate in the hands of experienced sharpshooters and had proved deadly during Morgan's attacks on Spanish treasure ports.

In addition to their proven marksmanship the buccaneers had the advantage of being able to manoeuvre their canoes in any direction – unlike the Spanish ships, which were dependent on the strength and direction of the wind. As the first of the warships bore down on them the buccaneers simply rowed past and got to windward. Four buccaneers were wounded by a broadside from the ship's guns as she passed but a volley from the buccaneers' muskets shot dead several men on her decks. The admiral's ship now drew abreast of the canoes and this time the buccaneers managed to shoot the helmsman. With no hand at the helm the ship rounded up into the wind and lay helpless with her sails aback. The buccaneers rowed up under her stern and shot every man who attempted to take the helm. They also shot through the ship's mainsheet and the braces (the ropes controlling the sails), an astonishing feat to achieve with muskets from a moving canoe.

The third ship, commanded by Don Peralta, now headed towards the flagship, intending to assist the admiral and his beleaguered crew.

But before he could reach the admiral, Peralta's ship was intercepted by the heavy piragua with its thirty or more buccaneers led by Captain Sawkins, which came alongside, 'both giving and receiving death unto each other as fast as they could charge'.[5] By this time the first ship had tacked and come about and was also intending to come to the aid of the admiral who was observed standing on his quarter-deck waving a handkerchief to attract the attention of his captains. To prevent the two ships joining forces the canoe of Ringrose and the canoe commanded by Captain Springer headed for the first ship and let loose a murderous fire which killed and wounded so many men that there were scarcely enough left to sail the ship. Don Carabaxal decided to take advantage of the freshening wind to flee from the scene of battle and save the lives of the few men who had escaped the buccaneers' musket balls.

The canoes of Ringrose and Springer now joined the canoes besieging the flagship and, coming close under her stern, managed to wedge her rudder, preventing the crew from getting the ship under way. They also shot dead the admiral and his chief pilot, 'so that now they were almost quite disabled and disheartened likewise, seeing what a bloody massacre we had made among them with our shot'.[6] Having refused up till now to surrender, the few Spaniards who remained alive cried for quarter. Captain Coxon, who was one of the leading buccaneers, climbed on board, taking with him Captain Harris, who had been shot through both legs.

With one ship captured and the other having fled, it was time to deal with the ship commanded by Don Peralta, the 'old and stout Spaniard'. He and his crew of black Africans were putting up a desperate fight and had three times beaten off attempts by Sawkins and his men to board the ship. Two canoes were despatched and these fired a volley of shot as they came alongside. As they did so there was an explosion on deck which was so fierce that it blew men into the air, some falling on the deck and others falling into the sea. Ignoring the shots directed at him, Don Peralta dived overboard to rescue his men and succeeded in getting several of them back into the ship. While he was rallying his men to renew the fight, another barrel of gunpowder exploded on the foredeck, causing several more barrels to take fire and blow up. Taking advantage of the thick smoke and confusion Sawkins boarded the ship, which surrendered to him.

When Ringrose climbed aboard he discovered that 'not one man there was found, but was either killed, desperately wounded, or horribly burnt with powder. Insomuch that their black skins were turned white in several places, the powder having torn it from their flesh and bones.'[7] He later boarded the admiral's flagship and found that only twenty-five of the eighty-six Biscay men were still alive, and of those twenty-five only eight were still fit to bear arms, the rest being grievously wounded. 'Their blood ran down the deck in whole streams, and not scarce one place in the ship was found that was free of blood.'

The battle had begun half an hour after sunrise and ended around noon. Of the buccaneers, eighteen men had been killed and twenty-two wounded. The Spanish casualties could only be guessed at because it was not known how many had died on the warship which had fled, but the accounts of Ringrose, Coxon and Bartholomew Sharp (who missed the battle but rejoined the buccaneers two days later) suggest that the Spanish lost more than 100 dead and a similar number were wounded. In Sharp's opinion scarcely half a dozen escaped unharmed, 'the rest being either killed or wounded, or else sadly burnt with the powder'.[8] During his time as a prisoner of the buccaneers Don Peralta, who had himself been badly burnt during the fight, constantly praised the valour of his captors. The buccaneers in their turn were impressed by the fierce resistance they encountered, and Ringrose concluded that 'to give our enemies their due, no men in the world did ever act more bravely than these Spaniards'.[9]

To capture two warships and force a third to beat a retreat was a considerable achievement but the most useful outcome of the fight was the acquisition of the large merchant ship lying at anchor off Perico. Don Peralta tried to dissuade Captain Sawkins from taking the ship by telling him that it was manned by a crew of 350 but one of his men who lay dying on deck contradicted him. He told Sawkins that all the crew had been taken off to man the warships. When the buccaneers rowed across to the merchant ship they discovered that the dying man was correct and there was no one on board. An attempt had been made to scupper the ship by starting a fire and making a hole in the hull. Having extinguished the fire and stopped the leak, they found themselves in possession of a fine ship of 400 tons called *La Santissima Trinidad*. With her name anglicised to *Trinity* she served as a hospital ship for the wounded and then became the buccaneers' flagship. During the next two years she would be used for carrying out a series of raids up and down the coast of South and Central America. According to Spanish sources the cost of the damage inflicted by this group of buccaneers on their ports and shipping amounted to more than four million pesos. During the course of the raids at least 200 Spaniards lost their lives and some twenty-five ships were destroyed or captured.[10]

The *Trinity*'s cruises along the Pacific coast were frequently interrupted by mutinies and changes in the leadership of the buccaneers. Unlike the autocratic regimes on naval and merchant ships, where the captains ruled supreme, the buccaneers ran their ships on democratic lines. The loot was shared out equally; agreed sums of money were put aside to recompense men who suffered injuries in battle; and captains were voted in and out of office by all members of the crew.[11] When he came to write the introduction to his *Cruising Voyage Round the World* Woodes Rogers was scathing about the buccaneers' exploits and their democratic ways:

> I must add concerning these buccaneers, that they lived without government: so that when they met with purchase, they immediately squandered it away, and when they got money and liquor, they drank and gamed till they spent all; and during those revels there was no distinction between the captain and crew: for the officers having no commission but what the majority gave them, they were changed at every caprice, which divided them, and occasioned frequent quarrels and separations, so that they could do nothing considerable.

He was also scornful of the romantic accounts of their adventures and concluded that 'they scarce shewed one instance of true courage or conduct, though they were accounted such fighting fellows at home'.[12]

The first mutiny and change of leadership took place during an eighteen-day visit to the Juan Fernández islands. The buccaneers had been running short of food and water and so they left the coast of Chile and headed out into the Pacific, intending to renew their supplies, carry out necessary repairs and have some respite from coastal raiding. On Christmas Day 1680 they anchored in a bay on the south side of the main island – until a rising onshore wind caused the anchors to drag and they were forced to seek another anchorage. Ringrose was able to take a party ashore to hunt for goats and replenish their supplies of wood and water but was stranded when the ship had to put to sea again because her anchor cable parted. So rough was the weather that it was two days before the shore party could get back on board. The conditions continued to be difficult owing to fierce gusts of winds from the shore every hour or so. This may have contributed to the growing dissent among the buccaneers.

Captain Bartholomew Sharp had taken over the leadership following the death of Captain Sawkins but his authority was under threat. According to Dampier he was 'by general consent, displaced from being commander; the company being not satisfied either with his courage or his behaviour'. He was replaced by John Watling, a veteran privateer who was considered a stout seaman. On 12 January 1681, ten days after Watling had taken over command, three Spanish warships were sighted, heading towards the island. The buccaneers on board the *Trinity* fired guns to warn the men ashore. As soon as the shore party had got back on board they weighed anchor and stood out to sea. Deciding on this occasion that discretion was the better part of valour, the buccaneers did not engage the enemy but set a north-easterly course towards the coast of South America. They left behind on the island a Miskito Indian called Will 'because he could not be found at this our sudden departure'. He had been in the woods hunting for goats. He would be marooned on the island for the next three years.

Will was not the first castaway on Juan Fernández. While they were anchored off the island Ringrose was told by the pilot of the *Trinity* that, many years before, a ship had been wrecked in the vicinity and only one man had survived. He had lived alone on the island for five years before being rescued.[13] Will would have been sorely missed by the buccaneers because they relied on the fishing and hunting skills of the Miskito Indians to supply them with food. Dampier devoted several pages of his journal to a description of this remarkable race. He described them as tall, well-made and strong, with long, copper-coloured faces, lank black hair and stern expressions. They came from the stretch of the Caribbean coast of Nicaragua which is still labelled the Costa de Mosquitos on modern maps.[14] Brought up as hunters from a young age, they became adept in the use of spears and bows and arrows. So expert were they at catching fish and turtles that one or two Miskito Indians in a ship could feed 100 men. They were also bold in a fight, proved excellent marksmen if they were supplied with guns, and had 'extraordinary good eyes, and will descry a sail at sea farther, and see anything better than we'.[15] They preferred to offer their skills to ships with English commanders and crews, having no love for the French, 'and the Spaniards they hate mortally'.

Within a week of leaving Juan Fernández the buccaneers had decided that their next objective would be the coastal town of Arica. This was the principal port for the silver mined in the region, and in particular the silver from the mountain at Potosí, which lay some 350 miles inland. The buccaneers had planned a raid on Arica the previous year but had been foiled by heavy seas which had prevented them from landing, and by the defensive precautions taken by the inhabitants, who had been warned of their coming. This time they hoped to take the town by surprise. On 27 January they anchored the *Trinity* forty miles south of their objective and set off in canoes. They landed at sunrise on a rocky coast a few miles away from Arica, which was a modest settlement of single-storey mud houses defended by a fort. What the buccaneers did not know was that 400 additional soldiers had been despatched from Lima and the town was now defended by 600 armed men and the fort by a further 300. Having left a party of men to guard the boats, ninety-two buccaneers, led by Captain Watling, marched towards the town. Their initial attack was ferocious 'and filled every street with dead bodies' but they were soon overwhelmed by the defenders, who threatened to cut off their retreat to the boats. Watling, two quartermasters and twenty-five other buccaneers were killed and eighteen others were gravely wounded. Choking and almost blinded by the dense clouds of dust raised by the guns of the fort, the survivors beat an ignominious retreat, chased by horsemen who kept up a continuous fire until they had launched their canoes and put to sea.

The death of Watling enabled Bartholomew Sharp to resume command of the *Trinity* – until another mutiny took place. On 17 April they anchored near the Isla la Plata, a barren island on the equator not far from Guayaquil. Here the grumblings of the men came to a head. They were still divided between those who wished to abandon the privateering cruise and head home via the Caribbean, and those who wished to carry on with their coastal raids. The shortcomings of Captain Sharp as a leader continued to be a source of division among them. A council was held on board the *Trinity* and, in the words of Dampier, 'we put it to the vote; and upon dividing, Captain Sharp's party carried it. I, who had never been pleased with his management, though I had hitherto kept my mind to myself, now declared myself on the side of those that were out-voted.'[16] This resulted in a major parting of the ways. Fifty-two men, including Dampier and the surgeon, Lionel Wafer, opted to leave the *Trinity*. Under the command of Captain John Cook they headed north in the ship's launch and two canoes. They made for the Gulf of San Miguel, where they went ashore and marched across the Isthmus of Panama and back to the Caribbean.

The remaining sixty-five men, including Basil Ringrose, William Dick and John Cox, stayed with Captain Sharp and the *Trinity*. They headed south. On 29 July 1681 they captured the ship *El Santo Rosario*, which proved to have on board a prize arguably more precious than gold or silver. It was a volume of Spanish charts covering the entire coast of Central and South America from Acapulco to Cape Horn with 'a very accurate and exact description of all the ports, soundings, creeks, rivers, capes and coasts belonging to the South Seas', together with sailing directions on how to work a ship into every port and harbour.[17] The information contained in the volume was of such strategic value to an enemy of Spain that, according to Sharp, 'They were going to throw it overboard but by good luck I saved it.'[18] In fact the charts may well have saved the lives of Sharp and two of his associates.

Having sailed the *Trinity* round Cape Horn and along the coast of Brazil to the West Indies, the buccaneers separated and by March 1682 most of them were back in England. When the Spanish ambassador in London learnt of their return he demanded that they be put on trial for piracy and murder. On 18 May Bartholomew Sharp, John Cox and William Williams were arrested and sent to Marshalsea Prison in Southwark. Sharp had already contacted the chartmaker William Hack and arranged for him to make copies of the Spanish charts, and for English translations to be made of the sailing directions. King Charles II had asked to see the charts and it seems likely that he or his advisers brought some influence to bear on the High Court of Admiralty, which acquitted Sharp and his shipmates of piracy on 10 June. Sharp subsequently dedicated a handsome presentation copy of the charts to the King and was rewarded with a captain's commission in the Royal Navy. Instead of taking advantage of this he returned to the West Indies and resumed his old buccaneering life. When Admiral Benbow paid a visit to the island of St Thomas in 1699 during his search for the notorious Captain Kidd, he was informed by the Danish Governor that Captain Sharp, 'the noted pirate', was living there. Sharp would have been aged fifty-one at the time.

Basil Ringrose did not live to see his journals published. He joined the crew of the 16-gun privateer *Cygnet*, commanded by Captain Charles Swan, which sailed from England in October 1683. Swan's attempts to carry out legitimate trading with Spanish towns on the Pacific coast of South America were a total failure, so he joined several English and French buccaneer ships operating off the coast of Mexico. They had hoped to capture the Manila galleon but failed to sight the ship, which slipped past them and arrived safely in Acapulco. On 19 February 1686 Swan and his men captured the small town of Santa Pecaque, fifteen miles inland from the mouth of the Rio Grande de Santiago. A party of the buccaneers were returning from the town, leading horses laden with looted provisions, when they were ambushed by the Spaniards. When Captain Swan and the rest of his men arrived at the place of the ambush 'he saw all his men that went out in the morning lying dead. They were stripped, and so cut and mangled, that he scarce knew one man.'[19] Ringrose was among the dead. He was only thirty-three but he left a remarkable legacy of journals, sailing directions, maps and coastal profiles of the Pacific coast of South America.

Dampier, who survived his years among the buccaneers without injury, was among those members of Swan's crew who arrived shortly after the ambush had taken place. Since leaving Captain Sharp and the *Trinity* in April 1681 he had spent a year cruising the Caribbean, lived several months in Virginia and then joined a buccaneer ship commanded by Captain John Cook which was bound for the Pacific. During an extended voyage which took them across the Atlantic to the Cape Verde Islands and the coast of Africa, the buccaneers captured a Danish slave ship of 36 guns which they took over and renamed the *Batchelor's Delight*. They sailed her round Cape Horn and headed for the Juan Fernández islands. On 22 March 1684 they sighted the mountain peaks of the island and the next day dropped anchor close inshore in a bay at the southern end. Launching a canoe, they went ashore to look for Will the Miskito Indian.

Will had seen the *Batchelor's Delight* approaching under sail the previous day and, believing that she was an English vessel, he had killed three goats and dressed them with cabbage leaves 'to treat us when we came ashore'. He was waiting to greet them when they landed on the beach. Among the shoregoing party was another Miskito Indian, called Robin. He was the first to leap ashore, and 'running to his brother Mosquito man, threw himself flat on his face at his feet, who helping him up, and embracing him, fell flat with his face on the ground at Robin's feet, and was by him taken up also'.[20] There are echoes of this touching scene in *Robinson Crusoe*. It will be recalled that when Crusoe first met Man Friday and rescued him from being killed and eaten by a raiding party of 'savages', Friday prostrated himself at Crusoe's feet and laid his head upon the ground. Friday, like the Miskito Indians, was tall and well-built, with long black hair which was straight rather than curly, and his skin was a dun olive colour.

Dampier's description of how Will survived his three solitary years would have provided Daniel Defoe with some useful material:

> He had with him his gun and a knife, with a small horn of powder, and a few shot; which being spent, he contrived a way of notching his knife, to saw the barrel of his gun into small pieces, wherewith he made a harpoon, lances, hooks and a long knife, heating the pieces first in the fire, which he struck with his gunflint, and a piece of the barrel of his gun, which he had hardened; having learnt to do that among the English.[21]

With these home-made tools he had caught and killed seals and goats and fish. Half a mile from the sea he had built a small hut which he had lined with goat-skins, and in this he had constructed a bed out of branches which was raised two feet off the ground. The bedding for this was likewise made from goat-skins.

With Will back on board, the *Batchelor's Delight* headed north to the Galápagos Islands and then due east to Isla la Plata. It was there that they joined forces with Captain Swan and the *Cygnet*. For several months the two ships cruised together, making a number of raids on coastal towns and villages until 25 August 1685, when the ships parted company. Dampier elected to join the crew of the *Cygnet* because he knew Captain Swan intended to sail to the East Indies, 'which was a way very agreeable to my inclination'. It took them fifty-two days to cross the Pacific to the island of Guam, and from there they sailed on to the island of Mindaneo in the Philippines. The subsequent wanderings of the *Cygnet* were recorded by Dampier but are not relevant here. Dampier left the crew at the Nicobar Islands and made his way home via Cape Town and the island of St Helena. He returned to England in September 1691. He was aged forty and had been away for twelve and a half years.

While he wrote about earlier and later periods of his life, Dampier left no account of how he spent the next seven years. However, his more recent biographers have discovered that he left London for a few months to join an expedition which was planning to salvage Spanish treasure ships wrecked in the West Indies.[22] Before leaving Europe the expedition was hijacked by Henry Avery, who was second mate of one of the four ships which had assembled in the harbour of La Corunna in Spain. Avery led a mutiny of eighty-five sailors, seized one of the ships and sailed off to the Indian Ocean. He subsequently became a pirate legend by capturing a ship belonging to the Great Mogul of India which carried a fabulously rich cargo of gold and silver. Dampier did not join the mutiny but on his return to London in February 1695 he had some difficulty in convincing the High Court of Admiralty that he had not assisted the mutineers. He was acquitted but failed in his attempt to recover his unpaid wages.

During his travels with the buccaneers Dampier had managed to preserve his journals from rain and sea water by enclosing them in lengths of bamboo sealed at the ends with wax. Following advice from a number of eminent scholars and naturalists, he set about preparing his journals for publication. Early in 1697 he published the first of his books, *A New Voyage Round the World*. It was printed by James Knapton and dedicated to Charles Montague, Earl of Halifax and President of the Royal Society. The book was an immediate success; four editions were published within two years and it was translated into Dutch, French and German. In addition to its popular success the book made Dampier's reputation. The wandering West Country seaman with a dubious past became a much respected travel writer with an enviable record as a navigator and explorer. He was invited to address a meeting of the Royal Society and Robert Hooke produced a summary of his book for the Society's *Transactions*. On 6 August 1698 John Evelyn noted in his *Diary*, 'I dined with Mr Pepys, where was Captain Dampier, who had been a famous buccaneer . . . He was now going abroad again by the King's encouragement, who furnished a ship of 290 tons. He seemed a more modest man than one would imagine by relation of the crew he had assorted with.'[23]

Dampier's fame led to his appointment as the commander of a naval expedition of discovery to New Guinea and Australia. His ill-fated voyage in HMS *Roebuck*, and his equally disastrous voyage to the Pacific in command of the *St George* and the *Cinque Ports*, will be discussed later. Both voyages demonstrated all too clearly his failings as a leader but they did not undermine his standing as a navigator. On returning to England in 1707 he found that the Bristol backers of a new expedition to capture the Acapulco galleon wished to make use of his skills and his experience. This time he would not be the commander of the expedition but would be employed as pilot for the South Seas, a role for which he was uniquely well qualified.

2

The Sea Captain

The commander of the new expedition was Captain Woodes Rogers.
He was the son of a sea captain and was twenty-nine years old when
his two ships set sail from Bristol. He had many of the leadership
qualities which Dampier so lacked. The author of a book of voyages
published in 1767 described him as 'a bold, active, indefatigable
officer' and noted that his most singular talent was 'a peculiar art he
had of maintaining his authority over his seamen, and his readiness
in finding out expedients in the most difficult conjunctures'.[1] In his
journals and letters Rogers comes across as a frank and forthright
seafaring man who faced storms, mutinies, sea battles, personal
injuries and financial setbacks with admirable fortitude and resolution. However, recent research has revealed flaws in his character
which had been generally overlooked.[2] He seems to have had an
exceedingly hot temper and sometimes resorted to violent language,
threatening to cut people's throats and bloody their noses. On one
occasion he was so enraged by the behaviour of a naval officer
that he struck him on the head with a pistol. Another time he challenged a naval officer to a duel. His brave leadership in the taking
of Guayaquil was questioned in some quarters and he was described

by one embittered officer as 'a dead weight to all our undertakings'.[3] In his defence it should be pointed out that he often found himself in stressful situations which would have tested and provoked the calmest of men.

Rogers' family came originally from Poole, a small but prosperous seaport in Dorset, on the south coast of England. His father, who owned his own ship and had shares in a number of other ventures, was a successful operator in the triangular trade on which the prosperity of Poole was based. Situated at the head of the largest natural harbour in Europe, the port had established a flourishing trade with North America, and in particular with the Newfoundland cod fisheries. Ships sailed from Poole to Newfoundland with cargoes of salt and provisions; they exchanged these for dried and salted fish and sailed back across the Atlantic to Spanish and Portuguese ports where they sold the fish and returned to Poole with cargoes of wine, brandy and olive oil.

In addition to his voyages across the Atlantic Rogers' father may also have travelled around the coast of Africa, probably in connection with the slave trade. In his *Discourse of Winds*, published in 1699, Dampier acknowledged his debt to a Captain Rogers for his description of the coast from the Cape of Good Hope to the Red Sea. Elsewhere in the same book Dampier included an account of the bushmen of South Africa 'as I received it from my ingenious friend Capt Rogers who is lately gone to that place: and hath been there several times before'.[4]

Captain Woodes Rogers senior and his wife Frances had three children while they were living in Poole. Woodes Rogers was the eldest and was born in 1679. His sister Mary was born a year later and his younger brother John (who would later accompany Woodes on his voyage to the South Seas) was born in 1688. Nothing is known of the children's education and upbringing. Around 1696 the family moved to Bristol, where they had a house in the parish of St Mary Redcliffe. On 30 November 1697 the eighteen-year-old Woodes Rogers was apprenticed as a mariner to John Yeamans of Bristol and his wife Thomasina. His seafaring experience during the next few years has not been recorded but an examination of the most common destinations of Bristol ships of the period suggests that he would have made frequent sailings to Ireland and the Continent. He must have made at least one crossing of the Atlantic to the fishing grounds of the Newfoundland Banks because in *A Cruising Voyage Round the World* he noted the great variety of fish in the waters around the island of Juan Fernández, including crawfish and gropers 'and other good fish in so great plenty anywhere near the shore, that I never saw the like, but at the best fishing season in Newfoundland'.[5]

Meanwhile his father's shipping business continued to flourish. He was still making voyages to Newfoundland in 1700, and in 1702 he purchased the lease of a plot for a 'substantial mansion' on the south side of Bristol's newly created Queen Square. This very grand square marked a break with the city's medieval past and was a clear statement of its position as 'the greatest, the richest, and the best port of trade in Great Britain, London only excepted'.[6] Named in honour of the recently crowned Queen Anne, the square was surrounded on two sides by the River Avon and on the third side by the Quay (then known as the Key), where dozens of ships were moored, their masts towering over the nearby rooftops. The elegant brick houses of Queen Square with their handsome doorways and finely proportioned sash windows were conveniently situated for those concerned with the shipping and trade of Britain's second port. As John Macky observed in 1714, 'Behind the Key is a very noble Square, as large as that of Soho in London; in which is kept the Custom House; and most of the eminent merchants who keep their coaches reside here.'[7]

The house of Captain Rogers and his family was built on a double plot and was numbered 31–32. Two doors along at number 29 was the house of Admiral William Whetstone, who was soon to become the young Woodes Rogers' father-in-law. Captain Rogers would have known Whetstone before they became neighbours because the shipping community of Bristol centred around the harbour was relatively small and both men had made voyages to Newfoundland. Following a series of French attacks on the fishing stations servicing the rich cod fisheries on the Grand Banks, the fish merchants of Bristol and Poole had requested naval protection. In 1696 and 1697 the then Captain Whetstone, in command of the 60-gun *Dreadnought*, had been sent to convoy the fishing fleets across the Atlantic and provide protection for the fishing stations.[8] Whether they first met at sea or in Bristol is not known but the two men had much in common.

Before they could move into their new houses in Queen Square the country went to war with France and Spain – a war which would affect the lives of both families. Within weeks of the declaration of war Whetstone was promoted to Rear-Admiral and was despatched with a squadron to join Vice-Admiral Benbow in the West Indies. He would spend much of the next four years in the Caribbean. A by-product of the war was a surge in privateering on both sides of the English Channel. The losses suffered by Bristol shipowners at the hands of French privateers would provide the motivation for the young Woodes Rogers' expedition to the South Seas.

The War of the Spanish Succession was so called because it was sparked off by the death of the childless King Charles II of Spain. The major powers of western Europe had foreseen the likely problems of the Spanish succession and in a series of treaties had agreed on the peaceful division of the Spanish empire. The chief concern of the English and Dutch was improved access to the riches and markets of Spanish America and they were less concerned about the succession itself. Although rightly suspicious of the continuing ambitions of the French king, Louis XIV, they made no objection to Philip, duc d'Anjou, the grandson of Louis XIV, inheriting the Spanish throne and becoming Philip V of Spain. Instead of acting diplomatically at this critical time Louis XIV chose to ride rough-shod over the treaties. He encouraged French officials to take over the management of Spain's American empire. He sent French troops into the Spanish Netherlands, thus posing a direct threat to the Dutch in the United Provinces and indirectly threatening England. And when the exiled King James II died in France in September 1701 Louis infuriated Englishmen of all parties by publicly recog-nising the young son of James as James III of England. It had taken the Glorious Revolution of 1688 to oust the Roman Catholic James II and replace him with the Protestant monarchs William and Mary. The country had no intention of returning to Catholicism and when William died in March 1702 after a riding accident in Richmond Park he was succeeded on the throne of England by Queen Anne – the dull, ill-educated but staunchly Protestant daughter of James II. The French king had counted on divisions in England prevent-ing any serious reaction to his provocative act but he misjudged the mood of the country. The British ambassador was recalled from Paris and on 4 May 1702 England declared war on France. For the next eleven years England, Scotland, Austria, Prussia and the Netherlands would be ranged against the combined forces of France and Spain.

Events moved swiftly on the continent and at sea. The soldier and diplomat John Churchill, earl of Marlborough, was made commander-in-chief of the forces in the Netherlands. In July 1702 he crossed the Meuse and in October he took Liège from the French, the forerunner of a series of victories which would culminate two

years later in the crushing defeat of the French and Bavarian armies
at the Battle of Blenheim. In August 1702 Admiral Benbow with six
ships of the line intercepted a smaller French squadron commanded
by Rear-Admiral Jean-Baptiste du Casse on the coast of the Spanish
Main near Santa Marta. Over the course of four days a running
battle took place which was distinguished by the indomitable courage of Benbow and the incompetence of his captains. On the last
day Benbow had his right leg smashed by a chain-shot. He refused
to leave the quarterdeck but his ship was so badly damaged that he
was forced to break off the action. He died later of his wounds, his
heroism earning him posthumous celebrity and ensuring that his
name lived on as a popular name for seamen's taverns (including
the fictitious inn which provides the setting for the opening scenes
of *Treasure Island*). Four of Benbow's captains had to face a court
martial in Jamaica which was presided over by Woodes Rogers'
father-in-law, Admiral Whetstone.[9] Two captains were found guilty
of cowardice and were later executed by firing squad on the deck of
HMS *Bristol* at Plymouth.

The failure at Santa Marta was soon redeemed by the Battle of
Vigo Bay. In October 1702 the Spanish treasure fleet was heading
back across the Atlantic escorted by a powerful escort of French
warships. Warned that there were British fleets at Cadiz and at Brest,
the treasure fleet steered for Vigo on the north-west coast of Spain.
Once inside the long, narrow inlet at Vigo the French commander
protected the anchored fleet with a floating boom and began unloading the gold and silver. Heading north after a failed attempt to capture
Cadiz, Admiral Sir George Rooke, in command of a fleet of Dutch
and British warships, learnt of the whereabouts of the treasure fleet
and mounted an attack with fireships. The leading British warship
broke the boom and marines went ashore and captured the defending gun batteries. In the fierce battle which followed twelve French

ships were captured or burnt and all nineteen Spanish vessels were taken or destroyed. Although little known today compared with the battles of the Napoleonic era, the allied victory at Vigo was a devastating blow to enemy morale, comparable to Drake's fireship attack on Cadiz of 1587 or Nelson's victory at the Nile.

Another bad year for France and Spain was 1704. In July Sir George Rooke captured Gibraltar, which in itself was no great feat as the small fortress defending the exposed anchorage was manned by a garrison of only 150 soldiers. But the strategic value of a naval base commanding the entrance to the Mediterranean was obvious and the French despatched a fleet of fifty warships to recapture the fortress. They were met off Malaga on 13 August by an equally powerful Anglo-Dutch fleet commanded by Rooke. The ensuing action was a long, hard-fought duel with heavy casualties on both sides. Neither side could claim a victory but when the French fleet eventually withdrew Gibraltar remained in English hands.

These and other naval actions contributed to a change of direction in the war at sea. The French Government decided to abandon its navy and devote its resources to privateering. Unlike British privateering, which, from the days of Drake and Cavendish, had tended to be a matter of individual enterprise and was usually restricted to attacks on single ships, French privateering, or *guerre de course*, was on a large scale and was intended to cripple the enemy's trade. Squadrons of privateers, sometimes with naval warships chartered to private owners, were encouraged to attack rich convoys of merchant ships. It was a form of warfare at which the French excelled and produced a number of privateer commanders who became national heroes. Jean Bart of Dunkirk had shown the way in 1694 when he had captured an entire Dutch grain convoy in the North Sea. Prominent among his successors in the War of the Spanish Succession were the Comte Claude de Forbin, also from Dunkirk, and René Duguay-Trouin from St Malo. Forbin was a dashing Gascon nobleman who pulled off a major coup in May 1707 when his squadron captured two British 70-gun warships off Beachy Head, together with their convoy of twenty-two merchant ships. Duguay-Trouin was ennobled by Louis XIV for his exploits in 1709, by which date he was reckoned to have taken sixteen warships and some 300 English and Dutch merchantmen. An article published in a London newspaper in November 1707 complained that English ships were being taken like shoals of herrings: 'Our merchants are beggared; our commerce broke; our trade gone; our staple and manufacture ruined.'[10] This was an exaggeration but the privateering war conducted by France was certainly effective. Between 1702 and the end of the war in 1713 French privateers took nearly 7,000 prizes, compared with the 2,239 prizes taken by British privateers and warships in the same period.[11]

Captain Rogers junior (whose father had died in 1705) was among the Bristol shipowners who had suffered at the hands of French privateers, and this seems to have been the primary motivation for his voyage to the Pacific. In the book he wrote on his return, he observed, 'Most of us, the chief officers, embraced this trip of privateering round the world, to retrieve the losses we had sustained by the enemy.' He was inspired by the example of the French privateer Beauchesne-Gouin, who had sailed from La Rochelle to the Pacific with two ships in 1698 and initiated 'a vast trade in those seas'. Rogers had a copy of his journal and noted that in the first few years of trading with South America the French had carried home 'above 100 millions of dollars, which is near 25 millions sterling'. Another motivating force was an Act of Parliament passed in early 1708 which was designed to encourage British privateers by abolishing the ancient right of the Crown to have a share in the prize proceeds. This meant that after a captured enemy ship and her cargo had been assessed and valued by an Admiralty Court the captor would have 'the sole interest and property in such prize or prizes so taken' and the proceeds were to be divided among the officers, seamen and others 'according to their respective shares'.[12]

William Dampier must also have played a part in the setting up of Rogers' voyage. According to Edward Cooke, who was one of Rogers' chief officers, 'Captain Dampier never gave over the project, 'till he had prevailed with some able persons at Bristol to venture upon an undertaking which might turn to prodigious advantage.'[13] It seems more likely that it was Rogers who did most of the prevailing but Dampier's previous experience would have been of great assistance in the planning of the voyage.

Rogers had married Sarah, the daughter of Admiral, now Sir William, Whetstone, in January 1705, and by the time he sailed from Bristol in August 1708 they had three children: a girl named Sarah; a boy called William Whetstone after his grandfather; and a girl named Mary. Rogers had inherited his father's grand house in Queen Square and was now a Freeman of the City of Bristol because he had married the daughter of a Freeman. He had the status and the necessary connections to persuade a number of prosperous citizens to fund his ambitious expedition. Among his sponsors were three Mayors of Bristol, the Town Clerk, two Sheriffs of Bristol and Alderman John Batchelor, who had twice been Master of the Society of Merchant Venturers. The largest sum was contributed by Thomas Goldney, a prominent Quaker merchant who contributed £3,762. The total sum invested in the project was £13,188 12s., which in today's terms would be about £1 million.

Most British privateers confined their cruises to the English Channel and the Atlantic coast of France and Spain. Privateering cruises against Spanish targets in the Pacific were rare, and, apart from the raids of the buccaneers and the recent forays of the French privateers, the only voyages which were comparable to the one planned by Rogers were those of Drake, Cavendish and Dampier. Such voyages, which were likely to take three or four years, required careful planning; sturdy, seaworthy ships; reliable and experienced officers; and provisions and gear for many months at sea. Thanks to the combined experience of his sponsors and supporters, and the advice of William Dampier, the expedition was admirably prepared. In comparing it with other long-distance voyages John Callander considered that 'there was never any voyage of this nature so happily adjusted, so well provided for in all respects, or in which the accidents, that usually happen in privateers, were so effectually guarded against'.[14]

Two three-masted ships were purchased for the voyage: the *Duke* of around 350 tons and the *Dutchess* of about 300 tons (different sources give different figures). The *Duke* was armed with 30 guns, and in addition carried 200 small arms, 100 cutlasses, thirty barrels of powder, fifty rounds of shot for the carriage guns and 'about thirty hundreds of small shot'.[15] She had two suits of sails, six anchors, five anchor cables, twenty hundredweight of spars and cordage, and provisions for around sixteen months. The *Dutchess* was armed with 26 guns and had a similarly comprehensive list of small arms, ammunition, gear and provisions.

On 9 April 1708 the privateering commissions for the *Duke* and *Dutchess* were drawn up. The original documents are filed in a large cardboard box in the National Archives at Kew, along with dozens of commissions for other ships of around the same date. Issued by the Lord High Admiral, Prince George of Denmark (the consort of Queen Anne) and addressed to Sir Charles Hedges, Judge of the High Court of Admiralty, the commissioning document for the *Duke* required the Judge 'to cause a Commission or Letter of Marque or Reprisal to be issued out of the High Court of Admiralty unto Captain Woodes Rogers – Commander of the Duke Friggott [frigate] . . .' and authorised the said Woodes Rogers 'to Apprehend, Scize and take the Ships, Vessels and Goods belonging to France and other Her Majesty's Enemys'.[16] Rogers was required to keep an exact journal of his proceedings, to take note of all prizes taken and to record the time and place of capture and the value of each prize 'as near as he can judge'. He was also requested to obtain intelligence of the movements and strength of the enemy and to transmit this information to the Lord High Admiral whenever the opportunity arose. The same wording appears on the commission issued to Captain Courtney, commander of the *Dutchess*.

The National Archives also hold a great number of documents, leather-bound ledgers and loose papers concerning the organisation of the voyage, instructions on how the two ships were to keep in touch at sea, records of the wages paid to the crews of the ships, and details of the prizes captured. Among the most interesting of these documents is one giving instructions from the managers and owners of the ships to Woodes Rogers. This is dated 14 July 1708, two weeks before the ships sailed. He was required to sail with the first fair wind to Cork in Ireland, where he was to contact Messrs Robert and Noblett Rogers, who would supply the two ships with all necessary provisions for the voyage. During his stay in Cork he was to endeavour to get hold of 'what men you want, and can get' and then to depart in company with the *Hastings*, man-of-war. He was instructed on the procedure to follow on taking a prize or accepting a ransom for a prize. The owners then set out the main objective of the voyage:

> But our grand design being to seek out one or both ye ships belonging to Acapulco in South America, you are to consult your pilot Capt. William Dampier in Council on whose knowledge in those parts we do mainly

depend for satisfactory success. If you are so fortunate to come up with her, you are to attack her, and use all possible means to take her . . .'[17]

The document concludes by urging Rogers to prevent all animosities, quarrels and mischiefs at sea and 'to preserve a most agreeable concord and harmony during ye whole course of ye voyage'.[18]

A critical component for the success of the expedition would be the calibre of the officers and with one or two exceptions Rogers was well served by those selected. Captain Stephen Courtney, who was appointed commander of the *Dutchess*, was described as 'a man of birth, fortune, and of very amiable qualities'.[19] He had with him as his second-in-command Captain Edward Cooke, a merchant sea captain who had twice had his ship captured by the French. Like Rogers he would publish an account of the voyage. This is not as detailed or as well written as Rogers' book but is valuable because it gives us another viewpoint, and provides a first-hand account of life on board the *Dutchess*.

A key figure on the *Duke* was Dr Thomas Dover, a 46-year-old physician who had been an undergraduate at Oxford, gained his medical degree at Cambridge and would later make his name and fortune with his patent medicine, Dover's Powder. As a major investor in the voyage (he had contributed £3,312) he was appointed president of the council which the owners had insisted should meet at regular intervals to make key decisions on the running of the ships. In addition to his own expertise Dover brought with him a number of other medical men, including his brother-in-law, who was an apothecary, and James Wasse, a surgeon who had been trained in the medical school at Leiden. The downside of Dover's appointment was that he was quick-tempered and argumentative and would make life difficult for Rogers on several occasions. The other officers included Rogers' twenty-year-old brother John; and the owners' agents, Carleton Vanbrugh and William Bath, who were responsible for noting the details and value of all prizes and plunder.

Dampier, as we have already seen, was to be the pilot. So great was the respect he had acquired through his publications and his travels that the sponsors of the Bristol expedition were prepared to overlook the disastrous outcomes of his two most recent ventures. His voyage to New Guinea and Australia as a naval captain in command of HMS *Roebuck* had achieved little in the way of discoveries and had ended ignominiously with his ship sinking on the shores of Ascension Island. Dampier and his crew had been rescued six weeks later by a passing squadron of British ships but when he returned to England in 1701 he had to face a court martial for the loss of his ship, and then a second court martial for his treatment of his crew and in particular for his 'very hard and cruel usage towards Lieutenant Fisher'. He was fined all his pay for the voyage and the court concluded that he was not a fit person to be employed as commander of any of Her Majesty's ships.

Dampier's second voyage had been a privateering venture to the Pacific which had been backed by a group of London and Bristol investors. In September 1703 he had left the Irish port of Kinsale in command of the 200-ton *St George* of 26 guns, which was accompanied by the *Cinque Ports*, a vessel of ninety tons and 26 guns. According to Alexander Selkirk, who was on board the *Cinque Ports*, she was 'a good new ship in very good condition as to body, masts, sails'.[20] The *St George* he described as an old ship but a strong one 'and fitted out for the said voyage in all things and stores'. The voyage was dogged by mutinies and desertions and both ships eventually became so riddled with worm that they had to be abandoned. The first sign of serious trouble took place when they reached the island of Juan Fernández. Forty-two members of the crew of the *Cinque Ports* refused to serve under Captain Stradling, the young commander of the ship, and set up camp ashore. Dampier persuaded them to return to their ship and when a French merchantman of 36 guns hove in sight the two ships joined forces to attack her. The result was a humiliating failure. Dampier would later blame his crew for deserting their posts but he was accused of failing to consult Stradling on their tactics beforehand, and then of providing no effective leadership during the seven-hour action, and hiding behind a barricade of beds, rugs and blankets on the quarterdeck 'to defend himself from the small shot of the enemy'. Nine members of the crew of the *St George* were killed, and it was later learnt that the French ship had lost a great many more killed and wounded and had been about to surrender when Dampier called off the action.

From Juan Fernández they had sailed north to the Bay of Panama, where they made an abortive attack on the town of Santa Maria. In May 1704 Dampier and Stradling parted company after a series of disagreements. Stradling returned to Juan Fernández and it was there that Alexander Selkirk demanded to be put ashore. The only reliable account of the circumstances of his marooning comes from Woodes Rogers, who wrote, 'The reason of his being left here was a difference betwixt him and his captain; which, together with the ships being leaky, made him willing rather to stay here, than go along with them at first; and when at last willing, the captain would not receive him.' In his interview with Selkirk after his return to England the writer and journalist Richard Steele noted, 'He was put ashore from a leaky vessel, with the captain of which he had had an irreconcilable difference.' He too noted that Selkirk changed his mind when Stradling decided to take him at his word and abandon him on the island. He recorded that Selkirk had been looking forward to his new life 'till the instant in which he saw the vessel put off; at which moment his heart yearned within him, and melted at the parting with his comrades and all human society at once'.[21]

The *Cinque Ports* was indeed so leaky that she later sank off the coast of South America. Thirty-two members of the crew took to rafts but only eighteen, including Stradling, managed to reach the mainland. They were captured by the Spanish and taken to Lima and imprisoned. Dampier and his men fared little better. The hull of the *St George* was so badly eaten away by worm that 'in some places in the hold we could thrust our thumbs quite through with ease'. In spite of this, and the fact that mutiny, death and desertion had cut down the number of his crew to sixty-four, Dampier decided to make an attack on the Manila galleon as she neared the end of her six-month voyage across the Pacific.

They sighted the galleon on the morning of 6 December 1704 while they were cruising off a low-lying coastal plain with the volcano of Colima clearly visible in the distance. By ten o'clock the two ships were within gunshot distance. The galleon hoisted her Spanish ensign and fired a gun to leeward, a sign that she assumed the *St George* was a friend and not an enemy vessel. Among the prisoners on board the privateer was the Spanish captain of a local trading ship who had been brought up in London and once served as a gunner for an English buccaneer. He advised Dampier to head straight for the galleon and board her before her men had time to prepare for action. Perversely Dampier chose to hoist an English ensign and fired a shot directly at the galleon. The captain of the galleon immediately changed course, worked his way to windward of the privateer, cleared for action and ran out his guns. When the boatswain of the *St George* ordered the helmsman to steer alongside ready for boarding, Dampier told the helmsman he would shoot him in the head if he edged any nearer the galleon.

While Dampier and his officers argued about what to do next the galleon opened fire. Her guns were eighteen-pounders and twenty-four-pounders, against which the five-pounders of the privateer had no chance. Every direct shot from the galleon struck deeply into the decayed timbers of the privateer. Two feet of planking were stove in on each side of the stem and several shot hit the hull underwater, causing one of the crew to tell Dampier that they were sinking. According to John Welbe, a midshipman on the *St George*, Dampier's response was to cry out, 'Where is the canoe?' and he was for getting in the boat to save his life. The carpenter managed to stop the leaks but Dampier ordered them to stand off from the enemy, 'which accordingly we did: all the ship's company being exceedingly vexed at the captain's ill conduct'. As they drew away from the galleon Dampier announced that he was going below to sleep. When he woke the next morning the galleon was still in sight but he ordered the helmsman to steer directly away from her.

Within a few weeks half the crew of the *St George* had deserted and the privateering expedition was abandoned. Eighteen of the original crew were back in England by August 1706, including William Funnell, who wrote and published a detailed and critical account of the cruise. Dampier did not return to England until 1707. He issued an angry and confused response to Funnell's publication but this was contradicted by a broadsheet from midshipman Welbe which was entitled *An Answer to Captain Dampier's Vindication of His Voyage to the South Seas in the Ship St George*. The sponsors of the expedition, who had lost everything they had invested in the project, did not embark on legal proceedings against Dampier until 1712, when he returned from the expedition led by Rogers.

3

From Bristol to Cape Horn

The *Duke* and *Dutchess* had been moored alongside the Quay at
Bristol to receive the bulk of their stores and provisions. Situated
in the heart of the medieval city, the Quay was reckoned to be one
of the finest and busiest in the world. On either side of the long,
narrow waterway was a dense cluster of houses, shops, warehouses
and churches. Visitors arriving at the Quay were confronted by a
mass of people 'running up and down with cloudy looks and busy
faces, loading, carrying and unloading goods and merchandizes of
all sorts from place to place'.[1] The quayside was lined with wooden
cranes, and was full of barrels, bales, casks and teams of horses
drawing sledges loaded with heavy goods. The poet Alexander
Pope was astonished by the sight of what appeared to be a street full
of the masts of hundreds of ships: 'The street is fuller of them, than
the Thames from London Bridge to Deptford, and at certain times
only, the water rises to carry them out; so that at other times, a long
street full of ships in the middle and houses on both sides looks like
a dream.'[2]

In mid-June 1708 the *Duke* and *Dutchess* left the Quay and were
towed down the winding River Avon, through the Avon Gorge and

out to the anchorage at Kingroad in the great expanse of the Severn Estuary. Lighters and barges could still bring the remaining stores out to the ships but reluctant seamen were prevented from deserting. On Tuesday 2 August, at about four in the afternoon, the two ships weighed anchor and, in company with nine merchant ships, they crept downstream. The wind was so light that they continued to be towed until they dropped anchor in Bridgwater Bay, beyond the tiny island of Steep Holm. Around midnight the wind increased. They set sail and at six in the morning they ran past the village of Minehead, the ships heeling before a brisk south-easterly breeze.

With inexperienced crews and his ships 'out of trim, and everything in disorder', Rogers noted that the other merchant vessels sailed much better. This was a concern because a French warship of 46 guns was reported to be cruising in the vicinity and the two privateers were in no fit state to put up a fight. The ships were kept cleared for action but there was no sign of the warship and on 5 August they sighted the coast of Ireland. An incompetent Kinsale pilot nearly ran the *Duke* ashore in foggy, blowy weather but Rogers over-ruled him and on the afternoon of 7 August they rounded Cork Head and came to anchor in the Cove (Cobh in Irish), the outer harbour of the city of Cork. Here they stayed for the next three weeks. Noblett Rogers provided them with more seamen and the remaining provisions needed. They improved the trim of the ships and during a spell of fine weather they heeled them over and cleaned and tallowed them below the waterline. By the end of August they had a full complement of men and twice the number of officers usual on privateers, 'to prevent mutinies, which often happen in long voyages'.

They had set sail from Bristol with 117 men on the *Duke* and 108 on the *Dutchess*, but some forty of them deserted or were dismissed at Cork. The additional men recruited in the Irish port made up the numbers to 183 on the *Duke* and 151 on the *Dutchess*. Rogers noted that one-third of the seamen were foreigners and the British recruits included tinkers, tailors, hay-makers, pedlars, fiddlers, one Negro and about ten boys. He was, however, optimistic that this mixed bunch would prove to be adequate once they had got their sea legs and been taught the use of firearms.

At ten o'clock on the morning of 1 September the *Duke* and *Dutchess* and twenty outward-bound merchant ships set sail from Cork. They were escorted by HMS *Hastings*, which kept them company until they were clear of any French privateers cruising in the Atlantic approaches. Although deeply laden with stores the two ships now sailed as well as any others in the fleet. On the fourth day the warship's commander, Captain Paul, invited the senior officers of the two Bristol ships to join him for a meal aboard his ship, 'where we were very handsomely treated'. When they parted on 6 September they gave him a salute with their guns which he returned, and wished them a prosperous undertaking.

A week after leaving Cork the *Duke* and *Dutchess* were 184 miles due west of Cape Finisterre and on their own except for the *Crown-Galley*, a small vessel which was bound for Madeira. 'Now we begin to consider the length of our voyage,' Rogers wrote, 'and the many different climates we must pass, and the excessive cold which we cannot avoid, going about Cape Horn.'[3] It was agreed at a council meeting that they should get in a good stock of strong liquor at Madeira as the men would prefer that to warm clothing. And then, eleven days out from Cork, Rogers had the first serious test of his leadership. The cause was a ship flying a Swedish flag which they had intercepted and searched. Rogers could find no reason to take her as a prize and decided to let her go on her way. This caused a mutiny among his men which was led by Giles Cash, the boatswain of the *Duke*. Rogers' response was to whip one of the mutineers and put ten others in irons. They remained in irons for several days on a diet of bread and water, with sentries guarding them. Cash was sent aboard the *Crown-Galley* in irons to be put ashore at Madeira.

With light and contrary winds holding up their progress, they decided to miss Madeira and press on to the Canary Islands. On 18 September they saw the great mountain peak of Tenerife on the horizon to the south-west, and the next day, as they were passing the island of Grand Canary (Gran Canaria), they chased and captured their first prize. This was a small Spanish bark of twenty-five tons with forty-five passengers on board, including women and four friars from one of the neighbouring islands. The passengers were greatly relieved to find that their captors were English, and not Turkish corsairs, who would have sent them off to the slave markets of Morocco. At this date there were many more white Christian slaves confined in the Barbary states of North Africa than there were black African slaves labouring in the plantations of the New World.[4]

With fair weather and a stiff breeze the *Duke* and *Dutchess* headed for Tenerife to obtain a ransom for their prize and her cargo. Carleton Vanbrugh, the shipowners' agent, insisted on going ashore with the Spanish master of the bark in order to carry out the negotiations. Rogers, against his better judgement, let him go and was proved right when the next day a boat came out to them from the town of La Orotava with a flag of truce and a letter to say that unless the English privateers restored the bark and her cargo they would detain Vanbrugh. Rogers and Captain Courtney sent a firm but courteous letter back making it clear that Vanbrugh must be released and a ransom paid or they would sail away with the bark and the passengers, who were their prisoners. Failing to get a satisfactory answer to this, Rogers and Courtney warned the Vice-Consul of the island that at eight the next morning they 'would visit the town with their guns'. This had the desired effect and promptly at 8 a.m. a boat came out to the privateers with Vanbrugh on board, as well as an English merchant from the town and a ransom in the form of wine, grapes and hogs. The captured vessel was sold to the English merchant for 450 dollars, the passengers were released with their belongings and the four friars had their books, crucifixes and relics returned to them.

On 22 September the two privateers set sail for the Cape Verde Islands, some 900 miles south-west of Tenerife. The weather being fair and the seas calm, Rogers invited Captain Courtney and three of his officers to dine with him on the *Duke*. After their meal they held a council meeting to discuss the taking of the Spanish bark and the subsequent negotiations. It was concluded that 'we do all approve of all that was transacted'. However, while they were still gathered in the great cabin, Carleton Vanbrugh complained that Captain Rogers had not treated him as he ought to have done. Determined to avoid any future misunderstandings, Rogers immediately put his complaint to the council, who 'adjudged the said Mr Vanbrugh to be much in the wrong'. The unusually democratic regime on the two ships, with their frequent council meetings to determine and approve all major actions, sometimes made life difficult for Rogers, but this minor incident showed that he was often able to use the meetings to get his own way and impose his will on recalcitrant members of the crew.

It took them nine days to reach St Vincent (São Vicente), one of the smallest of the ten Cape Verde islands. Rogers' description of their arrival is typical of many passages in his book of the voyage, based as it is on his daily logbook or journal. Written in the language of a seaman, it contains useful information for mariners who may follow in his tracks:

At ten o'clock we anchored in the Bay of St Vincent in five fathom of water. 'Tis a fine bay: the northmost point bore north near a mile distant

and the westermost point bore west distant about two miles: Monks
Rock, which is like a sugar-loaf, high and round, and bold on every side,
lies almost in the entrance of this fine sandy bay. Sailors must be careful as they come in, not to run too near under the high land of the north
point, for fear of being becalmed, and sudden flaws coming every way
upon 'em.[5]

He noted that there was a constant trade wind blowing from the
north-east, except from October to January, when 'it sometimes
blows southerly with tornadoes and rain'.

While boats were sent ashore to fill up their empty water casks,
Joseph Alexander, who was a linguist, was despatched to the nearby
island of St Antonio (Santo Antão) with a letter to the local governor and a shopping list which included cattle, goats, pigs, chickens, melons, potatoes, limes, brandy and tobacco. Using the prize
goods from the Spanish bark as payment they succeeded in obtain-
ing everything they needed. The only problem was that Alexander
had disappeared – he had presumably decided that he preferred the
delights of a tropical island to facing the rigours of Cape Horn. As
always the matter was put to the vote of the council and it was unanimously agreed that it was better to leave him behind than to hold up
the voyage waiting for one man who had disobeyed orders.

On 8 October they put to sea, loaded with fresh provisions,
full water casks and wood for the galley fires. They had originally
intended to head for Trinidad but decided that it was such a small
island that they might miss it. Instead they set a course for the
Portuguese island of Grande in Brazil, which lies on the Tropic of
Capricorn sixty miles west of Rio de Janeiro. Dampier had called
there in 1703 while in command of the *St George* and knew there
was a safe anchorage where they could stock up with firewood and
fresh water.

For six weeks the two ships sailed south across the empty expanse of the Atlantic Ocean. There were days of calms with sudden showers of rain, and days of fresh gales and overcast skies. At last, on the afternoon of 18 November, they sighted land and rounding a headland which they took to be Cape Frio, they came to anchor in 22 fathoms. They were at the eastern end of a large island which lay across the entrance of a great bay. The high, upper slopes of the island were thickly wooded and an unbroken mass of trees came right down to the water's edge. The next day Dampier, with a boat full of seamen, went ashore to make enquiries and returned in the evening with confirmation that they had reached their objective and were lying off Grande. To have successfully made their intended landfall after a voyage of 3,000 miles was a considerable achievement and a testimony to Dampier's navigation skills. The charts at his disposal were rudimentary and navigation instruments at this period were limited to the compass for direction finding, the lead-line for measuring depths and the cross staff or back staff for finding latitude by measuring the angle of the sun at midday. Until the later decades of the eighteenth century and the introduction of the nautical almanac and the chronometer, longitude could be calculated only by dead reckoning (working out speed and distance and allowing for tides and currents) and this could lead to disastrous errors over long distances.[6]

The first task after the ocean voyage was to fill their water casks. Two boats went ahead of the ships, taking soundings as they went. With a light head wind the ships could make little progress under sail and had to be towed into a deep, sheltered cove where they could anchor close to the source of the fresh water. From the local Portuguese they learnt that French ships bound to and from the Pacific often used the same place to wood and water. The two weeks spent at Grande were filled with activity, interrupted at intervals by heavy tropical downpours and tempered in fine weather by the extreme heat. Repairs were carried out on the masts of the *Duke*, and both ships had to be heeled over and careened. The sailors spent a profitable time catching a variety of fish with nets and lines, and most mornings local villagers arrived with canoes full of fruit, chickens and corn 'to exchange for such things as we could spare'.

Edward Cooke went across the bay to the small town of Angra dos Reis with presents for the local Governor. 'At our first landing, the Portuguese fired several shot, taking us for French; but were afterwards sorry for it, and received us very kindly.' Cooke was told that some French ships had called in recently and plundered the town of plate and valuables. Although the town had two churches, a Franciscan monastery and a guard house with twenty soldiers, most of the inhabitants lived in low mud houses thatched with palm leaves. The Governor and the friars proved to be generous hosts and invited the privateers to attend a religious ceremony to mark the Conception of the Virgin Mary. Rogers, Courtney and some of their officers, accompanied by the ships' musicians, joined the local congregation for the church service. The musicians were installed in the gallery and enlivened the service with noisy sea shanties performed with trumpets, oboes and violins. Afterwards the musicians led a procession through the town: a statue of the Virgin Mary decked with flowers was carried on the shoulders of four men and this was followed by forty monks; next came the Governor with Rogers and Courtney, and they were followed by the rest of the privateer officers, and the chief inhabitants of the town, everyone carrying large, lighted candles. After the ceremony the privateers were lavishly entertained by the friars in the monastery and then by the Governor in the guard house. 'They unanimously told us, they expected nothing from us but our company, and they had no more but our music.'

The only blot on this pleasant interlude was caused by the impetuous Carleton Vanbrugh. A local canoe was spotted leaving the island one morning and it was suspected that two Irishmen, who had deserted the ship and fled into the woods, were using it to escape to the mainland. Vanbrugh took some men in a pinnace to intercept the canoe and gave the order to fire at the people in it. One of the Indians in the canoe was wounded by the shot and later died, in spite of the best efforts of the ships' surgeons. Once again the council met and formally reprimanded Vanbrugh for disobeying orders 'and acting contrary to what he was shipped for'. Several days later he was transferred from the *Duke* to the *Dutchess* 'for the good of our intended voyage'.

They sailed from Grande on 3 December with a strong northeasterly wind setting them on the way to Cape Horn. As the weather got steadily colder the six tailors on board the two ships were kept busy making warm clothes from blankets, and altering spare clothes from the officers for the use of those sailors who had made little or no provision for the conditions they were going to face.

Fresh gales alternated with light airs and thick fog. They sighted an albatross and a great number of seals and porpoises. On 23 December they passed close by the Falkland Islands and two days later saw a distant sail which they chased for a while, believing her to be a French ship homeward bound from the Pacific but they lost her when they had to beat into a fierce headwind. On 1 January 1709 the weather moderated, and with relatively smooth water they were able to drink in the New Year with the aid of a large tub of hot punch on the quarterdeck. While the musicians played, every man downed a pint and drank to friends back home, a good voyage and a safe return.

On 5 January the weather changed for the worst. As the wind increased to storm force the two ships found themselves in the midst of ominous great waves. Both ships were heavily reefed and Rogers noted that the *Duke* coped well with the heavy seas, but he was dismayed to see that the *Dutchess* was in serious trouble. While the crew were lowering her mainyard the sail fell to leeward into the sea, dragging the ship over so that she took in a great deal of water. In danger of sinking from the weight of water in her, the crew let loose the spritsail and managed to wear ship so that she could run downwind. For a while she scudded before the wind, followed by the *Duke*, but at around 9 p.m., just as the officers of the *Dutchess* were gathering for a meal in the great cabin, a breaking sea smashed through the stern windows, 'and hove the first lieutenant halfway between the decks, with several muskets and pistols that hung there, darting a sword that was against a bulkhead of the cabin through my man's hammock and rug, which hung against the bulkhead of the steerage, and had not the bulkhead of the great cabin given way, all we who were there must inevitably have drowned before the water could have been vented'.[7]

The ship's yawl was stove in on the deck and Cooke thought it a miracle that no one was killed by the shutters, bulkhead and weapons which were driven through the ship with prodigious force, 'but God in his mercy delivered us from this and many other dangers'. A few men suffered bruises and everything in the ship was soaked with icy water, including all their clothes, hammocks and bedding. While they tried to sort out the chaos below deck the *Dutchess* continued to run before the wind. Rogers was worried that if they continued their southerly course they would find themselves among ice because it was so bitterly cold. He was told by one of his lookouts that the *Dutchess* was flying an ensign in her maintopmast shrouds as a signal of distress. He continued to keep his ship in close contact with the *Dutchess* throughout the night and about three in the morning the weather began to moderate and he was able to get within hailing distance. He was greatly relieved to hear that they had not lost any men. The next day there was still a huge sea running but Rogers and Dampier were able to get across to the *Dutchess* in the yawl, 'where we found 'em in a very orderly pickle, with all their clothes drying, the ship and rigging covered with them from the deck to the maintop'.

Earlier in the voyage two men had been killed by falls from the rigging and now they suffered the first two losses from sickness. On 7 January John Veale, a landsman in the *Duke*, died after suffering swellings in his legs, and on 14 January the *Dutchess* buried a man who had died from scurvy. By this date they reckoned they were clear of Cape Horn. On the 10th they had obtained a latitude reading of 61 degrees 53 minutes, which they believed was the furthest anyone had yet been to the south. As they entered the Pacific and headed north an increasing number of men began to fall ill, a few showing the symptoms of scurvy and many suffering from the freezing cold.

Scurvy was the scourge of long-distance ocean passages and would continue to be so for many years to come. It had plagued the voyages of Vasco da Gama and Magellan, and it would take a terrible toll on the sailors of Anson's voyage of 1740–4, when nearly two-thirds of the men in the squadron died from the disease. The physical effects were graphically described by Pascoe Thomas, who was a teacher of mathematics on Anson's flagship, the *Centurion*. He described how hard nodes and black spots appeared on his limbs

> till almost my legs and thighs were as black as a negro; and this accompanied with such excessive pains in the joints of the knees, ankles and toes, as I thought before I experienced them, that human nature could never have supported. It next advanced to the mouth; all my teeth were

presently loose, and my gums, over-charged with extravasated blood, fell down almost quite over my teeth; this occasioned my breath to stink much.[8]

The physical breakdown of the body was accompanied by extreme lethargy. Particularly depressing was the reopening of old wounds and the fracturing of bones broken years before.

Although the cause of scurvy (a lack of vitamin C in the diet) was not established until the 1930s, experienced seafarers were aware of the link between scurvy and diet. Some ships of the East India Company were being supplied with lemon juice in the seventeenth century and although the Royal Navy did not make a regular practice of supplying ships bound on overseas voyages with lemons and lemon juice until the 1790s, most long-distance seafarers knew that fresh fruit and vegetables were an effective cure. Woodes Rogers was certainly aware of this. When he came to write his account of his voyage he recorded, 'The general distemper in such long runs is the scurvy; and the methods to prevent the ill effects of it are so well known, that they may easily be provided against.'[9] His journal entries make it clear that he and his fellow officers knew that the sooner they reached Juan Fernández and got the sick men ashore with access to fresh food, the better would be their chance of survival.

On 20 January they could see the distant mountain ranges of Patagonia to the east and a week later they identified the island of St Mary (Isla Santa Maria) off the coast of Chile, which was near the same latitude as Juan Fernández. Despite having Dampier on board they had some doubts about the exact position of the island, 'the books laying 'em down so differently, and not one chart agrees with another'. By now a lot of men in the *Dutchess* were ill from prolonged exposure to the cold and wet, and two more had died.

Turning away from the mainland of South America, the two ships headed west, aiming for the small island which lay 400 miles out across the heaving waters of the Pacific Ocean.

4

A Man Clothed in Goat-Skins

They sighted the island of Juan Fernández at 7 a.m. on 31 January 1709. The jagged outlines of the mountain peaks were clearly visible on the horizon twenty miles away to the south-west. At two in the afternoon, when the island was still some twelve miles away, Thomas Dover persuaded Rogers to let him take the pinnace ashore with a boat's crew to get fresh provisions and to look for a suitable anchorage. Later in the day, as it grew dark, the men on board the two ships were surprised to see what appeared to be a fire on the shore of the island. It was too bright to be the lights of the pinnace and they could only assume that there must be French ships at anchor nearby. Throughout the night Rogers and Courtney kept their ships ready for action. Guided by a gun, musket fire and lights in the rigging of the *Duke* and *Dutchess*, the pinnace returned in the early hours. The men in the pinnace had seen the fire when they were still some way from the shore and had decided to turn back, which was just as well because around midnight the wind had begun to blow.

At daybreak on 1 February they found that they had sailed past the island, so they tacked and headed back again, their progress hindered by sudden gusts of wind from the shore which were so fierce that they were forced to reef their topsails. Around midday they rounded a headland and saw before them a large bay, the only place on Juan Fernández which afforded any shelter for ships. The remaining coastline presented a forbidding wall of sheer black cliffs, broken here and there by dark inlets strewn with boulders against which the ocean swell surged and foamed. There was no sign of the French ships. Rogers sent the *Duke*'s yawl ashore with Captain Dover, Robert Fry (first lieutenant of the *Duke*) and six men, all armed as a precaution.

The wind now dropped and they had to hoist out the remaining boats and tow the ships into the bay — which in the days of Basil Ringrose and Bartholomew Sharp had been called Windy Bay, but in 1741 was renamed Cumberland Bay or Bahia Cumberland.[1] A mile from the shore they anchored in fifty fathoms. When the yawl failed to return Rogers despatched the pinnace with more armed men to see what had happened. He was concerned that the Spanish might have established a garrison on the island and seized the ship's boat. However, the pinnace soon returned, laden with crayfish and 'with a man clothed in goat-skins, who looked wilder than the first owners of them'. It was Alexander Selkirk, who had survived a solitary existence on the island for four years and four months, following his marooning by Captain Stradling of the *Cinque Ports* galley.

Selkirk had seen the ships approaching the day before and, believing them to be English, he had lit the fire on the beach. Next morning, when he saw the yawl heading for the shore, he waved a white flag and shouted to attract attention. Hearing him speak in English, the men in the yawl asked him to show them the best place for anchoring the ships and landing. He gave them directions and then ran along the shore with incredible swiftness. When the crew of the yawl stepped ashore on the shingle beach he greeted them joyfully. They invited him to come out to the ships but 'he first enquired whether a certain officer that he knew was aboard; and hearing that he was, would rather have chosen to remain in his solitude, than come away with him, 'till informed that he did not command'.[2] Dampier was clearly the officer he had in mind, even though it was Stradling who had been the cause of his extended stay on the island. Selkirk was aged twenty-eight when he had been left on the beach and was now thirty-two. His physical fitness, his practical skills as a sailor and his combative, independent nature had ensured his survival. He invited Dover and Fry to see his dwelling, but 'the way to it being hid and uncouth, only Capt. Fry bore him company; and having with much difficulty climbed up and crept down many rocks, came at last to a pleasant spot of ground full of grass and furnished with trees, where he saw two small huts, indifferently built, the one being the lodging room, the other the kitchen'.[3]

A recent archaeological excavation has almost certainly identified the spot where Selkirk lived and kept a lookout for approaching ships.[4] On a stretch of level ground high above Cumberland Bay and close to a freshwater stream, the archaeologists discovered post holes which correspond with the descriptions by Woodes Rogers and Edward Cooke of Selkirk's dwelling place. His two huts were constructed from the branches of pimento trees which were covered with long grass and lined with goat skins. In the larger hut he slept on a bed raised from the ground. 'In the lesser hut, at some distance from the other, he dressed his victuals.' The post holes, the nearby stream and the suitability of the location with its commanding views over the anchorage suggested that this was likely to be the right place, but the archaeologists also unearthed a fragment of a pair of navigational dividers which could only have been left by a seaman, and most likely by a sailor like Selkirk who was a ship's master or navigation officer. We know that when he was marooned he had with him 'his clothes and bedding; with a fire-lock, some powder, bullets, and tobacco, a hatchet, a knife, a kettle, a Bible, some practi cal pieces, and his mathematical instruments and books'.[5]

In their books of the voyage both Rogers and Cooke gave detailed accounts of how Selkirk had survived his solitary existence on the island.[6] Both accounts dealt with the practical details of Selkirk's existence but Rogers' more thoughtful version also described how he learnt to overcome his loneliness by reading, singing psalms and praying 'so that he said he was a better Christian while in this solitude than ever he was before, or than, he was afraid, he should ever be again'. Rogers noted that the castaway had so forgotten his language for lack of practice that he was difficult to understand, 'for he seemed to speak his words by halves'. In addition Rogers drew some moral lessons from Selkirk's experiences: in particular that 'a plain and temperate way of living conduces to the health of the body and the vigour of the mind, both of which we are apt to destroy by excess and plenty'. Characteristically Rogers decided he must put an end to such reflections which were more appropriate for a philosopher than a mariner.

The great advantage of Juan Fernández, as previous castaways and visiting buccaneers had discovered, was that it had an equable climate and abundance of food and fresh water. The brief winter only produced a light frost, occasional hail and much rain. The summers were not excessively hot, and the windy, changeable and often damp weather would have been nothing unusual for a Scotsman. The cabbage trees (*Juania australis*) produced bunched clusters of whit-ish leaves which looked and tasted like garden cabbages. Turnips seeded by previous visitors to the island now covered several acres. A variety of fish could be caught in the bay, though Selkirk could not eat them 'for want of salt because they occasioned a looseness', so instead he caught the crayfish (like a small lobster), which were plentiful and could be boiled or made into a broth. Above all there were the goats which roamed the mountainous island in thousands. These provided Selkirk with good meat, with bedding and with clothing when his own clothes wore out. He made a coat, breeches and a cap of goat-skin 'which he stitched together with little thongs of the same, that he cut with his knife. He had no other needle but a nail; and when his knife wore to the back, he made others as well as he could of some iron hoops that were left ashore, which he beat thin and ground upon stones.'[7]

There were no venomous or savage creatures on the island but Selkirk was initially plagued by the rats which had come ashore from ships and multiplied. They would gnaw his feet and clothes while he slept, until he tamed the equally numerous cats which lay in large numbers around his dwelling and kept the rats at bay. Apart from the loneliness and melancholy which afflicted him for the first eight months, his main fear was being discovered by the Spanish because he believed they would murder him or make a slave of him and send him to the silver mines. He had seen several Spanish ships pass by but only two had dropped anchor and sent men ashore. On one of these occasions the Spaniards had seen him, shot at him and chased him into the woods. He had outstripped them, climbed to the top of a tree and, although they urinated at the foot of the tree, they failed to see him, and after killing several goats they returned to their ship.

When Rogers consulted Dampier about Selkirk he was assured that he had been the best man in his ship, and on his recommendation he agreed to sign on Selkirk as a mate (we learn later that he was second mate on the *Duke*). In gratitude for his delivery Selkirk caught two goats which, when mixed with turnips and greens, provided an excellent broth for the men who were sick.

He also pointed out where they could find watercress, parsley and other antiscorbutic greens 'which mightily refreshed our men and cleansed them from the scurvy'. Of the twenty one men who came ashore sick with scurvy only two died.

Meanwhile the rest of the crew were hard at work, clearing the two ships in preparation for careening them. The topmasts came down, sails and stores were sent ashore and a tented camp was set up among the pimento trees. A smith's forge was sent ashore, the sailmakers began mending the worn and torn sails, the rigging was overhauled and the coopers supervised the cleaning and assembly of casks and barrels. A notable feature of Juan Fernández was the presence of fur seals and elephant seals which gathered in thousands along the shoreline, filling the air with a continuous clamour of moans and barks and hideous roars. They were easy to slaughter with muskets and axes and within ten days the sailors had produced eighty gallons of seal oil for use in lamps and for cooking.

By 12 February Rogers was able to note in his journal that the ships had been loaded with wood and water, the sails and rigging had been repaired, the men were all back on board and they were ready to depart. The next day a council meeting was held on the *Dutchess* at which it was agreed that they would head towards the mainland of Chile and then steer northwards, following the coast at a distance of six leagues (eighteen miles). The next objective was the island of Lobos, 2,000 miles from Juan Fernández and another staging post on the way to their main objective, the Manila galleon. A system of signals was worked out so that the ships could alert each other to the presence of a potential prize and could decide on the appropriate action to be taken. At three in the afternoon of 14 February they weighed anchor and sailed out of Cumberland Bay with a pleasant south-easterly wind setting them on their way.

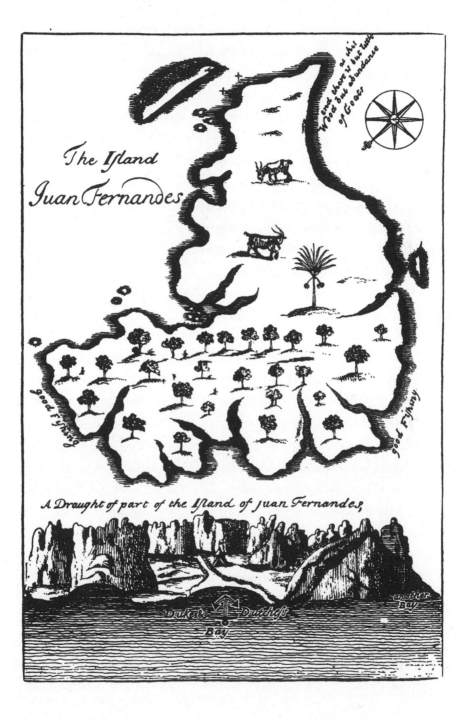

The Island
Juan Fernandes

and there is this
Wood but this with
abundance
of Goats

good Fishing

good Fishing

A Draught of part of the Island of juan Fernandes,

Duke &   Dutches
Bay

another
Bay

A month later, as they were approaching Lobos they captured the *Asunción*, a sixteen-ton sailing bark with a crew of nine men, mostly Indians. From them they learnt the welcome news that there were no longer any French ships on the Pacific coast of South America and no more were expected. They also learnt that Selkirk's former ship, the *Cinque Ports*, had foundered on the coast near the small town of Barbacoas (close to the equator in what is now Colombia). Only Captain Stradling and half a dozen of his crew had survived the wreck but they had been captured by the Spanish and sent to Lima, where they had been imprisoned in harsh conditions for the past four years. Selkirk's refusal to rejoin Stradling's 'leaky' ship had evidently been a wise move.

Lobos Island (Isla Lobos de Afuera) was a barren outcrop with no fresh water or vegetation and a pervading smell of rotten fish. The only inhabitants were seals, gulls, pelicans and vultures. Dampier, who had called there during his previous voyage, guided them into a sheltered cove where they dropped anchor. The captured bark was hauled ashore and converted into a small privateer by the ships' carpenters. She was fitted out with a new mainmast and mainsail, her deck was repaired and she was armed with four swivel guns. Renamed the *Beginning*, she was provided with a crew of thirty-two men under the command of Captain Edward Cooke. Three more prizes were taken during the eighteen days they spent in the vicinity of Lobos: the *Santa Josefa*, a fifty-ton merchant vessel from Guayaquil which they renamed the *Increase* and put under the command of Alexander Selkirk; a merchant ship of 450 tons called the *Ascensión* which was en route from Panama to Lima; and the *Jesús, Maria y José*, a vessel of thirty-five tons with a cargo of timber.

By 6 April the *Duke* and *Dutchess* and their flotilla of prizes were on their way, sailing north along the coast, past the saddle-shaped hills of Paita and past mile after mile of distant green shores lined with dense tropical forest. As they approached the equator the crews sweltered in the heat and there was some concern that they were running short of fresh water. On 12 May, at a council meeting held on board the *Duke*, it was decided that they would launch an attack on the town of Guayaquil, which lay at the head of a very large estuary some 200 miles ahead of them. This had never been one of their original objectives and although a surprise attack might prove almost as profitable as the capture of the Manila galleon, it was a risky enterprise.

Guayaquil was one of the largest ports on the Pacific coast of South America. It was a major shipbuilding centre and an important staging post for vessels trading between Lima and Panama. It had a population of some 2,000 and was graced by five churches, the largest of which faced a handsome square and had a lavish baroque interior with rich carvings and pictures. The town was not heavily fortified but its chief defence was its position. The hot and humid atmosphere drained the energy of those unused to it, while outbreaks of deadly fevers were commonplace. Before approaching the town an attacking force had to sail and row more than eighty miles up a river estuary lined with mangrove swamps and strewn with islands and mudbanks. They had to contend with tides so strong that it was impossible to make any progress against the ebb tide and while they anchored among the mangroves waiting for the tide to turn they would be tormented by swarms of mosquitoes which flourished in the equatorial heat. Nevertheless it was a tempting prize and had attracted a number of raids in the past. Thomas Cavendish had looted and set fire to the town in 1587, destroying four great ships which were being built on the stocks. Dutch privateers had carried out a raid in 1624; and in 1687 a combined force of English and French buccaneers had led a particularly savage attack on the town.

It may have been Dampier who convinced Rogers and his fellow officers that an attack would be worthwhile. In 1684, while serving in the buccaneer fleet led by Captain Eaton in the *Batchelor's Delight* and Captain Swan of the *Cygnet*, he had taken part in an abortive raid on Guayaquil. They had toiled up the estuary in boats, and got within sight of the town when their presence was betrayed by one of their Indian guides who had escaped and raised the alarm. 'Not a man after that had the heart to speak of going further.' For Dampier the taking of the town, like the capture of the Manila galleon, was a piece of unfinished business.

On 14 April 1709 the privateer fleet stood into the Gulf of Guayaquil. They sailed all night with a southerly wind and at daybreak they sighted a ship ahead of them. Not expecting any resistance, they sent two boats to intercept it. The men in the boats were lightly armed and among them was Rogers' younger brother John, who had insisted on joining the boat's crew led by Robert Fry. The other boat's crew was led by Edward Cooke. After rowing hard for nearly eighteen miles the boats drew near the ship, which fired a gun at them and hoisted a Spanish flag at her main masthead. As the two boats closed in they came under heavy fire from mounted guns and more than twenty muskets and pistols. The boats dropped astern with the loss of one man dead and three wounded and then made a second attempt to come alongside and board the ship. In the words of Rogers, 'At this attack my unfortunate brother was shot through the head and instantly died, to my unspeakable sorrow.' The boats abandoned the attack but in the afternoon the ship surrendered to the superior force of Rogers' fleet and the privateers found themselves in possession of the *Havre de Grâce*, a French-built ship of 250 tons bound for Lima with a crew of fifty Spaniards and 100 Indians and Negroes. Renamed the *Marquiss* [sic] she would become a useful addition to the privateer squadron.

At noon the following day, with flags at half-mast, Rogers presided over a short but harrowing ceremony. 'About twelve we read the prayers for the dead, and threw my dear brother overboard, with one of our sailors.' A volley of small arms was fired from the deck of the *Duke*, followed by the crackling of small-arms fire from the other vessels. 'All our officers expressed a great concern for the loss of my brother, he being a very hopeful active young man, a little above twenty years of age.' It is evident that Rogers was consumed by grief and by a sense of guilt that he had allowed his brother to take part in the attack but he was not going to allow this to deflect him from his objective: 'I began this voyage with a resolution to go through with it, and the greatest misfortune or obstacle shall not deter me, I'll as much as possible avoid being thoughtful and afflicting myself for what can't be recalled, but indefatigably pursue the concerns of the voyage.'[8]

It had been agreed at a council meeting that the force to attack Guayaquil would consist of 200 men divided into three parties led by Rogers, Courtney and Dover. They would make their way upstream in two barks and the ships' boats (two pinnaces, a large launch, a yawl and another boat). The *Duke*, the *Dutchess* and their prizes would remain in the vicinity of the island of Santa Clara, at the mouth of the estuary, with skeleton crews to guard the ships and their 300 prisoners. Around midnight on 18 April the raiding force left the ships and proceeded by stages up the river towards the large island of Puna, which lay across the centre of the estuary. They sailed with the incoming tide and then dropped anchor and hid among the mangrove swamps during the ebb tide. They made the final approach to Puna during the dark, rowing and towing each other with the flood tide 'that if seen in the night we might look like drift timber'. At daybreak they entered the small settlement on Puna. This consisted of around twenty houses which were raised on stilts and were entered by ladders. The Indian inhabitants were mostly fishermen who were frequently employed as river pilots. The privateers had no difficulty in capturing the Spanish lieutenant in charge, together with his family and other villagers. It was essential that no one on the island was able to send a warning to the town upstream.

After a difficult passage through the upper reaches of the estuary the raiding party arrived within sight of Guayaquil around midnight on 22 April and were perturbed to see a fire burning on a nearby hill and numerous lights in the town itself. As they drew nearer they heard a confused noise of church bells, small-arms fire and the boom of two guns. They later learnt that the lights and the hillside fire were part of a religious festival, but in the early hours of the morning a message had reached the town that Puna had been captured and an enemy was coming up the river. The bells and gunfire were to warn the town of their approach.

With the alarm having been given and the ebb tide flowing against them, the invading force retreated back down the river and anchored. Rogers, Courtney and Dover held an urgent meeting to decide what to do next. Rogers wanted to attack at dawn to prevent the townspeople sending away their valuables and strengthening their defences. Dover thought that to attack after the alarm had been given would waste lives and jeopardise the main objective of their voyage. When Dampier was consulted he told Rogers that the buccaneers never attacked a large place after it had been alarmed. In the end it was decided that two of their Spanish prisoners (the lieutenant in charge of Puna and the captain of the *Havre de Grâce*) should be sent to the town with a series of proposals. In the meantime the privateers took possession of two new ships which were moored off the town as well as several smaller craft. After some comings and goings the Governor of Guayaquil arrived to discuss terms with Rogers and his two fellow captains. The Governor was a young army officer from Tenerife named Ieronimo Bosa y Solis. Although he had been in his post at Guayaquil for only two years he proved to be a competent negotiator. The privateers demanded 50,000 pieces of eight as a ransom for the town and for the two new ships and other vessels captured; they insisted that the townspeople must agree to buy the two merchant ships they had recently taken, together with their cargoes of goods and black slaves; and the town must provide hostages as surety for the payment of the ransom, which must be delivered within nine days.

The Governor returned to the town and assembled a meeting of merchants and traders to discuss the demands. Not surprisingly the townspeople were angry and protested that they could find no more than half the sum demanded. A messenger returned to the privateers to say that they could raise only 30,000 pieces of eight. No mention was made of buying the captured ships. The negotiations dragged on, the privateers suspecting that the Spaniards were playing for time and were waiting for reinforcements. On 24 April the privateers hauled down their white flag of truce and attacked the town. The boats landed seventy men, who found themselves facing a formidable line of armed men, some on horseback. Rogers led the attack: 'We who landed kept loading and firing very fast, but the enemy made only one discharge, and retired behind their guns.' The Spanish had positioned four guns at the end of the main street and in front of the main church. As the privateers advanced the horses bolted. 'This encouraged me to call to our men to seize the guns, and I immediately hastened towards 'em with eight or ten of our men till within pistol shot of the guns.' As more privateers arrived to give support, the men behind the guns fled. In less than half an hour the privateers had routed the enemy and by sunset they were in possession of the town and the English flag was flying from the church tower.

To show the Spanish what would happen if the ransom was not paid, some of the houses fronting the main church were set on fire. The other churches and storehouses and cellars were searched, though little of value was found. Unlike the raids of the buccaneers of Henry Morgan's day, the sailors did not get riotously drunk and most behaved with considerable restraint. A much quoted incident concerned the discovery of some houses on the outskirts of the town which were full of women, 'and particularly at one place there were above a dozen handsome genteel young women, well dressed, where our men got several gold chains and ear-rings but were otherwise so civil to them, that the ladies offered to dress them victuals, and brought them a cask of good liquor. Some of their largest gold chains were concealed and wound about their middles, legs and thighs.'[9] The women were thinly clad in silk and fine linen and we learn that the sailors, under the command of Alexander Selkirk and a Mr Connelly, ran their hands 'on the outside of the lady's apparel' and discovered the chains, whereupon the interpreter politely asked the women to remove them.

Negotiations for the ransom of the town were resumed on 25 April and after a threat was made to set the whole town on fire, an agreement was concluded and signed the following day. The Spanish would pay a ransom of 30,000 pieces of eight, to be paid at Puna within six days. On the payment of this sum the privateers would release all hostages and prisoners. It was time to get back to the boats. The extreme heat and humidity were draining the energy of the sailors and Rogers admitted that 'this hot weather has weakened and disordered me very much'. The privateers marched out of the town with their colours flying, and returned to the barks, which were now heavily laden with bags of flour, beans, peas and rice; jars of oil and liquor; cordage and ironware; and more than £1,000 in gold plate and jewellery. The flotilla of barks and boats set off downstream and two days later Rogers and his men were back on board their ships, 'where I found all our people overjoyed at our meeting again'.

On 2 May, the last day on which payment of the ransom was due, a boat came out to the ships with 22,000 pieces of eight. The money was unloaded and the messenger was sent back with the threat that unless the rest of the agreed sum was brought by the following morning the privateers would sail away, taking all the hostages with them. There was no sign of the money the next day but it was decided to allow the Lieutenant of Puna to return to his island, together with four elderly Negroes who were sick and several of the prisoners they had taken at sea. Rogers noted that they parted very friendly with them, 'particularly an old padre that I had treated civilly at my own table, ever since we took him'.[10] Four more days passed with no sign of the rest of the agreed ransom, and the hostages were becoming very uneasy at the thought that they might have to end their days in Great Britain, a fate which they apparently regarded as worse than death. On 7 May the privateer fleet was off Point Arena when a bark came alongside which had on board Señor Morell (captain of the captured ship *Ascensión*) and a gentleman who was related to some of the hostages. They brought with them gold and silver plate valued at around 3,500 pieces of eight, as a contribution towards the ransom. Since many of the officers were impatient to leave behind them the heat and mosquitoes of Guayaquil and head for the Galápagos Islands it was agreed that all but three of the hostages should be released. In the early hours of the next morning the fleet set sail and by 6 a.m. the little island of Santa Clara was twelve miles astern.

It is evident from Rogers' account that the raid on Guayaquil was a disappointment for him. They had lost three men dead (only one of these from Spanish gunfire) and they had come away with 25,500 pieces of eight in cash and gold and silver plate. They also had some useful provisions and stores, but the rewards would have been much greater if they had been able to take the town by surprise. By the time they entered Guayaquil in force most of the church plate, cash and jewellery had been removed and hidden in the surrounding woods and villages. According to some of the hostages a surprise attack would have yielded 'above 200,000 pieces of eight in money, wrought and unwrought gold and silver, besides jewels'. The problem was the divided command and the fact that Rogers was bound by the democratic regime of the expedition to consult his fellow officers and bow to the majority decision. He had proved his resolution and personal bravery by leading the attack on the guns, but his decision to attack the town at dawn when they first arrived had been over-ruled by Thomas Dover.

The privateers' raid also had serious after-effects. A few months before their arrival at Guayaquil the town had been swept by an outbreak of a malignant and highly contagious fever which had caused the deaths of a dozen people a day for several weeks. When the usual burial places under the church floors had been filled the townspeople had to resort to burying the putrefying corpses in a mass grave close to the main church where Rogers and his men had made their headquarters. Within a week of leaving the Gulf of Guayaquil the *Duke* had fifty men seriously ill and the *Dutchess* more than seventy. The first death from fever occurred on 15 May and by the end of the month twelve more men had died. By 10 June Rogers was writing, 'Our men being very much fatigued, and many of them sick, and several of our good sailors dead, we are so weak, that should we meet an enemy in this condition, we could make but a mean defence.'

The Manila galleon was not expected to arrive off Mexico until November or December, so the privateers had six or seven months to wait before taking up an intercepting position between Acapulco and Cape San Lucas. It would prove a testing time for all of them but particularly for Rogers. He had to overcome a rash and ill-thought-out proposal from Thomas Dover and other officers who wanted to carry out a raid on the gold mines of Barbacoa; and he had to put down a mutiny from a group of sailors who were dissatisfied with the arrangements for dividing up the plunder from prizes. As he confided in his journal, 'If any sea officer thinks himself endowed with patience and industry, let him command a privateer and discharge his office well in a distant voyage.'[11]

From Guayaquil they sailed to the Galápagos Islands, intending to rest, refit and fill up with water a safe distance from any Spanish or French warships who might be on the look out for them. They spent two weeks cruising among the remote islands which would later be made famous by Charles Darwin. They noted the numerous giant tortoises and the sailors shot some of the iguana dragons and reckoned they were good to eat, but nowhere could they find any fresh water. Forced to sail back to the mainland they made for the island of Gorgona, which Dampier knew well from his previous travels. Situated some eighteen miles off the coast of modern Colombia, the island provided a temporary refuge. The anchorage was somewhat exposed but there was fresh water, and amid the dense woods were many tall trees suitable for making masts. There was also good fishing, and a variety of animals including monkeys, guinea pigs and hares. They anchored off the eastern shore on 7 June and for the next two months the island was their base. They careened the *Duke* and the *Dutchess*, and after careening the *Marquiss* they replaced some of her masts and spars. As at Juan Fernández, a village of tents was set up ashore to house the sick men and to provide shelter for the ships' carpenters, coopers, sailmakers and ropemakers while they carried out essential repairs.

The two ships sailed from Gorgona on 7 August and by the beginning of October they were off the coast of Mexico. Rogers noted in his journal that 'Captain Dampier, near this place, five years past, met the Manila Ship in the St George, and had a fight at a distance, but he says for want of men could not board her, and after a short dispute, was forced to let her alone'. No doubt Dampier put the best possible slant on an action which had failed miserably owing mainly to his poor leadership. Slowly they made their way towards the point where the Manila ship was likely to make her landfall after her journey across the Pacific. They sailed past Cape Corrientes and spent nearly three weeks among the Tres Marias islands, where, on 24 October, the council of officers drew up a resolution. It was agreed that, having examined the opinion of Captain Dampier and taken into account the information provided by prisoners, they would cruise off Cape San Lucas, the southernmost cape of California, and 'to wait here the coming of the Manila Ship belonging to the Spaniards, and bound for Acapulco; whose wealth on board her we hope will prompt every man to use his utmost conduct and bravery to conquer'.

5

The Manila Galleons

They sighted Cape San Lucas on 2 November 1709 and took up their stations. They spread out so that between them their lookouts could spot any vessel which appeared between the coast and a point some sixty miles out to sea. The *Marquiss* was stationed nearest the mainland, the *Dutchess* in the middle and the *Duke* on the outside, with the bark roving to and fro to carry messages from ship to ship. Rogers was keenly aware they were cruising close to the spot where Sir Thomas Cavendish had captured the Manila galleon on 4 November 1587. Cavendish had two relatively small ships, the 18-gun *Desire* of 120 tons and the 10-gun *Content* of sixty tons. The Manila galleon that year had been the *Santa Anna*, a much larger ship of 600 tons, but she had no carriage guns because the Spanish were not expecting a hostile attack. When Cavendish moved in to attack, her crew had to resort to hurling javelins and throwing rocks on to the heads of the English sailors. Thanks to the massive construction of the galleon her crew battled on for five hours but suffered such heavy casualties that her Spanish commander was forced to surrender. Many of his seamen were Filipinos and among his many passengers there were women and children. The total value of the galleon's cargo was reckoned to be around two million pesos.[1]

The annual voyage of the Manila and Acapulco galleons across the Pacific was the longest non-stop passage made by any ships in the world on a regular basis. The westbound voyage from Acapulco took between two and three months and was made easier by a call at the island of Guam towards the end of the voyage, but the eastbound voyage took a gruelling five or six months and sometimes as long as eight months. This put a considerable strain on food and water supplies and inevitably resulted in deaths from scurvy. The track of the galleons was determined by wind and weather patterns and by ocean currents. The shorter and quicker westbound voyage taken by the Acapulco galleon took advantage of the north-east trade winds and a westerly current in the region of latitude 13 degrees north, known as the North Equatorial Current. The eastbound Manila galleon had to follow a curving track some 2,000 miles to the north which took her past the islands of Japan with the help of the Kuro Siwo Current, then across the Pacific with the aid of the westerly winds and then south-east to Acapulco assisted by the California Current which flows along the coast of North America.

It took some years of trial and error before the winds and currents were worked out and the situation was complicated by the typhoons – the cyclonic storms which sweep across the Philippines with a destructive power similar to the hurricanes of the Caribbean region. To take advantage of prevailing winds and avoid the typhoons it was reckoned that the Manila galleon must set sail in May or June, which meant that she could be expected to arrive off the coast of California at any time between October and December unless delayed or blown off course by storms – and many of the galleons had to endure a succession of violent storms during the voyage. In 1600 the *Santa Margarita* was so disabled by months of heavy weather that she was driven south and wrecked on the Ladrones Islands (Islas Ladrones), off the coast of Panama. Only fifty of the 260 men on board survived the shipwreck and most of the survivors were then killed by the native islanders.[2]

The annual crossings of the Pacific had begun in 1565 and over the following 250 years more than thirty galleons were lost in storms or wrecked. Since no more than one or two galleons made the crossing each year this was a heavy toll in lives, ships and treasure. 'The voyage from the Philippine Islands to America may be called the longest and most dreadful of any in the world,' wrote Gemelli Careri, an experienced traveller, '. . . as for the terrible tempests that happen there, one upon the back of another, and for the desperate diseases that seize people, in 7 or 8 months, lying at sea sometimes near the line, sometimes cold, sometimes temperate, and sometimes hot, which is enough to destroy a man of steel, much more flesh and blood . . .'[3]

As far as Rogers and his men were concerned, the only thing that mattered was locating the Manila galleon, and they were experiencing troubles of their own. By 17 November they were running short of water. They sent the bark ashore, where they found a primitive settlement of local Indians. They were given a cautious welcome and allowed to fill up their water barrels from a nearby river. There was still no sign of the galleon on 14 December. They had now been at sea for seven weeks and the *Marquiss*, which was under the command of Edward Cooke, was in urgent need of repairs to her hull and rigging. She was sent to refit at a place which Rogers and Cooke refer to as Port or Puerto Seguro, on the basis that this was the name given to it by Thomas Cavendish. No such place exists today and it is evident from the description given by one of Cavendish's sailors, and by Rogers' detailed description, that the place they were referring to was the sheltered harbour now called Cape San Lucas or Cabo San Lucas. This is situated in the lee of the cape of the same name. Rogers described the entrance of the harbour as being marked by four high rocks which looked like the Needles at the Isle of Wight – and the promontory at the end of the cape certainly does bear a striking resemblance to the Needles.

Out at sea Rogers was increasingly doubtful about seeing the Manila galleon because it was nearly a month past the time when the ship was due. The chief concern now was the shortage of bread and provisions. There was no safe place on the American coast where they could obtain supplies and they had barely enough left to last them the fifty-day voyage across the Pacific to Guam, which was their next destination. On 19 December a council meeting was held on board the *Dutchess* at which the chief officers decided they would have to abandon their cruise for the Manila galleon. They were bitterly disappointed and as they put their signatures to the resolution 'all looked very melancholy and dispirited'.

Before heading west into the vastness of the Pacific all three ships needed to stock up with wood and water, so the *Duke* and *Dutchess* set a course for Cape San Lucas. They were hampered by calms and a contrary current and were still some way off the coast when, at nine o'clock on the morning of 21 December 1709, the lookout at the masthead of the *Duke* cried out that he could see a sail on the horizon. 'We immediately hoisted our ensign, and bore away after her, the Dutchess soon did the same.'

The calm weather continued all through the afternoon of 21 December. The *Duke* and *Dutchess* made little progress towards the distant sail and there was some speculation that the ship might be the *Marquiss* coming out of the harbour at Cape San Lucas. This led to some of the crew laying bets on whether it was the *Marquiss* or the Manila galleon. They watched the *Duke*'s pinnace make contact with the *Dutchess* and lie alongside her for a while before rowing on towards the strange ship. Robert Fry was despatched in the yawl to see whether the men on the *Dutchess* had managed to identify the ship, and while he was away the *Duke* hoisted a French ensign and fired a gun, which was answered by a gun from the ship. When Fry returned he brought the good news that 'it was the ship we had so impatiently waited for, and despaired of seeing her'.[4]

With dusk approaching it was agreed that the two pinnaces should keep close contact with the galleon during the night and at intervals show false fires (an early form of flare) so that the two privateers, which were hampered by the lack of wind, would know exactly where they were. The ships were cleared for action and everything was made ready for engaging and boarding the galleon in the morning. Throughout the hot night the pinnaces showed their lights, which were answered by lights on the privateers. At daybreak the crew of the *Duke* could see the galleon on their weather bow, about three miles away. The *Dutchess* was beyond and to leeward of her. At 6 a.m. the pinnace returned and her crew said that during the night the *Dutchess* had passed close to the galleon, which had fired two shots at her which she had not returned.

There was still no wind, so Rogers ordered his crew to get out eight of the ship's large oars or sweeps and for an hour they rowed until a light breeze sprang up. He then ordered a kettle of chocolate to be prepared for the ship's company, before arranging for prayers to be said. While these were in progress they were interrupted by the guns of the galleon, which was slowly bearing down on them with barrels of gunpowder hanging from her yardarms to discourage the privateers from attempting to board her. At 8 a.m. the *Duke* opened fire, first with her bow-chasers and then, as they came closer, with her full broadside. The thundering boom of the carriage guns was joined by the rattle of small-arms fire as the crews of the *Duke* and the galleon fired volleys of shot at each other with muskets and pistols. Rogers was the first and only serious casualty on his ship. 'I was shot through the left cheek, the bullet struck away great part of my upper jaw, and several of my teeth, part of which dropped down on the deck where I fell . . . I was forced to write what I would say, to prevent the loss of blood, and because of the pain I suffered by speaking.'[5]

The *Duke*'s gun crews had been well trained and were able to fire faster and more effectively than those of the galleon. They kept on firing as the *Duke* swung alongside the stout wooden hull of the galleon, causing so many casualties that the galleon's commander hauled down his ensign and surrendered. As there was still very little wind, the *Dutchess*, being to leeward, had difficulty in reaching the galleon. When she came within range she fired her guns and a volley of small shot, but the fight was over. As the clouds of acrid gunsmoke cleared and drifted away the three ships drifted on the calm waters of the Pacific. Edward Cooke, who watched the action from a hill overlooking the harbour where the *Marquiss* was anchored, reckoned the engagement lasted no more than half an hour.

Rogers sent a boat across to the galleon to bring her captain and officers over to the *Duke*. They learnt that the ship they had captured was called the *Nuestra Señora de la Incarnación Disenganio* and her commander was Monsieur Jean Pichberty, a French chevalier (in his report Rogers anglicised his name and rank to Sir John Pichberty). He was the brother-in-law of Admiral Jean-Baptiste du Casse, who had fought Admiral Benbow and Admiral Whetstone in the West Indies. On board his ship were 190 sailors and servants, ten passengers and eight black Africans. During the action they had lost nine killed, ten wounded 'and several blown up and burnt with powder'.

The vessel which the privateers had captured was not, strictly speaking, a galleon but a frigate-built merchant ship, armed with

20 carriage guns on a single gun deck and 20 swivel guns mounted on her rails. At 400 tons burden she was not much larger than the 350-ton *Duke* and her captain had little option but to surrender when faced with the 30-gun *Duke* and the 26-gun *Dutchess*. From her commander the privateers learnt that she had set sail from Manila in company with a much larger galleon, the *Nuestra Señora de Begoña*, a newly built vessel of 900 tons armed with 40 carriage guns on two decks and an equal number of swivel guns. The two galleons had lost touch with each other during the 7,000-mile voyage but had an agreement to meet off Cape San Lucas in order to present a combined front to the privateers – the captains of both ships had received information at Manila, via English trading posts in India, that two Bristol ships were planning to intercept and attack them.

For the rest of the day and during the night the three ships remained out at sea while their crews carried out repairs, and the privateers' surgeons dressed the wounds of the injured men on board the Spanish ship. The following day, 23 December, they headed towards Cape San Lucas and at 4 p.m. they rounded the distinctive rocky promontory at the end of the cape and dropped anchor in the sheltered waters of the bay beyond. The *Marquiss* was there to greet them 'and all the company much overjoyed at our unexpected good fortune'. That night Rogers felt something clog his throat. He swallowed with great pain and presumed the object was either part of his jawbone or the musket shot which had hit him. In his journal he made light of the injury but admitted that his head and throat were badly swollen and he had considerable difficulty in swallowing the liquids he needed for nourishment. In the morning a council meeting was held on the *Duke* but Rogers was unable to attend. The other chief officers agreed that the *Dutchess* and the *Marquiss* would set sail immediately and cruise for eight days with the objective of intercepting the other Manila galleon. They duly weighed anchor at eight in the evening and headed out to sea.

By dawn the next day they were six miles off Cape San Lucas. Edward Cooke, commanding the *Marquiss*, recorded in his journal, 'Sunday, December 25, being Christmas Day, at eight in the morning were two leagues of Cape St Luke, and saw a sail bearing S.W. distant about seven leagues, which we concluded to be the great Manila ship.'[6] Both ships gave chase but made little progress and by nightfall they were still several miles away. At around midnight the *Dutchess* came within gunshot of the galleon and opened fire. In the ensuing action the powerful guns of the galleon inflicted so much damage on the masts and rigging of the *Dutchess* that Captain Courtney was forced to break off the action in order to carry out repairs. The *Marquiss* was still some four miles from the scene at daybreak owing to the continuing lack of wind. And then, at 8 a.m., Cooke saw the *Duke* slowly emerging from Cape San Lucas and heading their way.

Rogers had wanted the *Duke* and *Dutchess* to go out together to intercept and attack the great galleon but he had been over-ruled. He had, however, arranged for two lookouts to be positioned on the hill above the harbour with orders to signal him if they saw another ship appear on the horizon. Meanwhile he had spent a productive Christmas Day negotiating terms with the commander of the captured Manila ship, who was clearly a man of influence. Jean Pichberty agreed to pay five bills of exchange, payable in London, for the sum of 6,000 dollars. This would cover the remaining ransom money due for the taking of Guayaquil and would enable the privateers to release the three Guayaquil hostages who were still being held as surety for the ransom.

During the afternoon of 25 December the lookouts on the hill above Cape San Lucas made the agreed signal with flags to indicate that a third ship had appeared in addition to the distant sails of the

Dutchess and the *Marquiss*. Rogers was determined to put to sea at once. Arrangements were hastily made to secure the large number of prisoners now in their hands, and at 7 p.m. the *Duke* set sail. His officers had tried to persuade him to remain on board the prize in the harbour but to no avail. He remained in command in spite of the injury he had sustained, but admitted, 'I was in so weak a condition, and my head and throat so much swelled, that I yet spoke in great pain, and not loud enough to be heard at any distance.'[7]

There was so little wind that the *Duke* was still nine miles to leeward of the galleon at noon the following day. Her crew watched helplessly as the diminutive *Marquiss* moved in to attack. She was dwarfed by the galleon but her sailors gave three cheers, fired a broadside and raked her massive sides with volleys of small-arms fire. She was joined by the *Dutchess*, which came up under the stern of the galleon and poured in a broadside before drifting away. For several hours the two privateer ships attempted to make some impression on the apparently impregnable galleon, moving in to attack and then falling away out of range of her guns. By nightfall the *Marquiss* had almost run out of ammunition. According to Cooke, they fired 'above 300 great shot, about 50 cross bars, and two great chests of steel bars, besides abundance of partridge small shot, and above nine barrels of powder'.[8] Not till the early hours of the next day was the *Duke* close enough to send a boat across to find out what sort of condition her two consorts were in. The boat returned with the news that the foremast of the *Dutchess* was seriously damaged and her crew had suffered many casualties. The *Marquiss* had escaped lightly but Rogers arranged for three barrels of gunpowder and a supply of shot to be rowed across to her.

At daybreak on 27 December the three privateers made a combined attack on the great galleon, later recorded in graphic seaman's language by Cooke:

Captain Courtney in the *Dutchess*, stood close up, gave his broadside and volleys and then ran ahead. The *Marquiss* coming up under her quarter, did the like, and the *Duke* next performed the same along her lee-side. We kept raking of her fore and aft, and then wore to get out of the way of the *Duke*'s shot, still firing, as did the other ships . . . The enemy fired at us all three at once, but slow, seldom missing our masts and rigging, and sometimes hulling us. After lying near half an hour along the chase's side, the *Dutchess* lay by to stop her leaks, and secure her foremast being much disabled, having 25 men killed and wounded and the sails and rigging much shattered.[9]

In addition to the damage caused by the guns of the galleon, the privateers were also subjected to a hail of hand-grenades (described as 'stink pots') which blew up several cases of powder on the quarterdeck of the *Duke* and started a fire on the *Marquiss* which the crew managed to extinguish before it spread. Around 11 a.m. the *Duke* broke off the action after her mainmast had received two direct shots. Rogers made the signal for the other captains and senior officers to come aboard his ship for a meeting. There was still a general determination to continue the action but the ships' carpenters warned that the foremast of the *Dutchess* and the mainmast of the *Duke* were likely to go by the board and take the other masts with them. The *Dutchess* had thirty men killed or wounded, and the *Duke* had eleven wounded, including Rogers, who had been hit in the ankle with a wood splinter which exposed his heel bone. He had lost a lot of blood and was unable to stand. It was evident that they had little chance of taking the great galleon. Between them they had fewer than 120 men fit for boarding the enemy, which, according to information they had obtained from the prisoners they had taken in the smaller galleon, had around 450 men on board, including a large number of Europeans, 'several of whom had been formerly pirates, and having now got all their wealth aboard, were resolved to defend it to the last'.

The problem was that the privateers' guns were making no impression on the powerful teak hull of the galleon, which towered above them and made it difficult to cause significant casualties among her crew. According to Cooke, 'we might as well have fought a castle', and Rogers noted that the ships built at Manila were much stronger and had thicker sides than ships built in Europe so that 'few of our shot entered her sides to any purpose, and our small arms availed less, there being not a man to be seen above board'.[10] It was agreed that it was better to secure the prize they had already taken than to resume the action and risk losing more men and further damage to their battered ships. As always the resolution was drawn up in writing and was signed by the captains commanding the three ships as well as eleven other officers, including William Dampier, Robert Fry and Alexander Selkirk.

On the evening of 28 December the ships limped slowly back towards Cape San Lucas. On the *Duke* it was necessary to take down the main topgallant mast and secure the mainmast with additional stays and runners, while the other ships also carried out running repairs. Contrary winds and currents slowed their progress and not till the evening of the following day did they reach the safe haven of the harbour in the lee of the cape. As they anchored alongside their Spanish prize a light shower of rain swept across the bay.

During the next two days negotiations were concluded with Jean Pichberty and the three Guayaquil hostages, all of whom signed a document to the effect that they had been well treated and that the financial transactions made for the payment of the ransom had been carried out voluntarily and with their full consent. On 1 January the hostages and the captain and crew of the Manila galleon sailed for Acapulco in the *Jesus, Maria y José*, the thirty-five-ton coasting vessel the privateers had captured off Lobos Island. The Spaniards were supplied with water and provisions for the voyage and the captain was allowed to retain all his books and instruments, 'So that they parted very friendly, and acknowledged we had been very civil to 'em.'

The captain took with him a letter from Rogers to Alderman Batchelor and the other sponsors of the expedition. The letter eventually reached Bristol and is preserved among the other documents relating to the voyage of the *Duke* and *Dutchess*. It is addressed from California, dated 31 December 1709, and provides a brief account of the taking of the smaller Manila galleon and the unsuccessful attack on the larger galleon: 'This ship was too strong for us, and has wounded all our masts . . .' Rogers mentioned the death of his brother and his own injuries, but, being aware that the letter must pass through enemy hands before it reached its destination, he gave no information about the value of the captured galleon's cargo, nor did he describe the raid on Guayaquil or the taking of other prizes. He ended, 'My endeavours shall not be wanting on all occasions when please God to restore me to my strength.'[11]

Before leaving Cape San Lucas and setting sail for home, Rogers had to face another mutiny. This time it was orchestrated by Thomas Dover and concerned the command of their valuable prize, which had been renamed the *Batchelor Frigate*, in honour of their chief sponsor. Rogers made it clear that he wanted an experienced sea officer to take command of the galleon on the homeward voyage. Dover wanted the command himself and persuaded a number of other officers, including Courtney, Cooke and Dampier, to support his claim. There followed a paper war in which both sides recorded their arguments at length. Rogers and his supporters made it clear that Dover, who was no seaman, was utterly incapable of acting as commander of a sailing ship, and Rogers further pointed out that 'his temper is so violent that capable men cannot well act under him'. In the end it was agreed that Dover be given nominal command but that Robert Fry and William Stretton would be responsible for navigating and sailing the ship 'and that the said Capt. Thomas Dover shall not molest, hinder or contradict them in their business'.[12] Alexander Selkirk was appointed to the key post of master of the ship.

They spent less than two weeks at anchor in the harbour of Cape San Lucas, repairing their damaged ships and stocking up with wood and water. Rogers was still suffering from his injuries (it would be many months before he was fully recovered) but for most of the men it was a pleasant interlude. The weather was calm and the air was fresh and healthy, in marked contrast to the tropical heat of Guayaquil. They had little rain but there were heavy dews during the nights. The surrounding countryside was mountainous, with barren, sandy wastes relieved by a scattering of shrubs and bushes. The local Indians became increasingly friendly. They much admired the privateers' ships and paddled out to them on bark logs and climbed aboard. Rogers described them as tall and straight with much darker complexions than other native people they had seen on the Pacific coast. They had long black hair which hung down to their thighs. 'The men stark naked, and the women had a covering of leaves over their privities . . . The language of the native was as unpleasant to us as their aspect, for it was very harsh and broad . . .' The Indians' huts were so badly constructed of branches and reeds that they appeared to be temporary dwellings, and they did not have any pots, utensils or furniture of any kind. They lived chiefly on fish but had no nets or hooks and caught the fish by diving underwater and striking them with sharpened sticks. Although he was critical of the Indians' appearance and primitive way of life, Rogers was impressed by their honesty: 'They coveted nothing we had but knives and other cutting instruments, and were so honest that they did not meddle with our coopers or carpenters tools, so that whatever was left ashore at night, we found it untouched in the morning.'[13]

On 10 January 1710 the *Duke*, the *Dutchess*, the *Marquiss* and the Manila galleon (now the *Batchelor Frigate*) weighed anchor, rounded the end of the cape and sailed out into the Pacific. Their destination was the island of Guam, which lay more than 6,000 miles away on the far side of the great ocean.

On the advice of the Spanish pilot of the Manila galleon they followed the route taken by the west-going Acapulco galleons. From Cape San Lucas they headed west-south-west until they reached the latitude of 13 degrees north. From there they sailed due west along the line of latitude to Guam. The crossing of the Pacific took them two months and it proved to be an arduous and difficult voyage. The *Duke* had sprung a leak, so one of the pumps had to be manned continuously. To conserve food and water the crews were strictly rationed. Each mess of five men was restricted to one small piece of meat and a pound and a half of flour per day. When some of the *Duke*'s crew were caught stealing pieces of pork Rogers ordered the ringleader to be flogged by every member of the watch and his companions were put in irons. The black slaves were allowed even less food and water than everyone else and three of them died during the passage. Three other people were buried at sea: an Englishman who had joined the privateers at Guayaquil; the Spanish pilot who had been wounded during the capture of the galleon; and a Welsh tailor on the *Duke* who had been shot in the leg during the same action and 'being of a weak constitution, fell into a dysentery which killed him'.

Apart from catching two dolphins they rarely landed any fish but the strict rationing and favourable winds enabled them to reach

Guam with fourteen days of provisions left. On the morning of 11 March they sighted the distant hills of the island and by midday they were sailing along a green and verdant shore lined with coconut palms. They were greeted by sailing craft with outriggers which flew past them at astonishing speeds. During the afternoon of the same day they dropped anchor opposite a small village and sent ashore two interpreters with a letter for the Governor of Guam. As Guam was a remote outpost of the Spanish empire and a key staging post for the Acapulco galleons, the privateers were not sure what sort of welcome to expect. To their considerable relief they received a reply from the Governor to the effect that they would be given all the hospitality the island afforded. Within two days of their arrival they were being presented with bullocks, limes, oranges and coconuts, and on 16 March the chief officers were invited to the Governor's house for a magnificent meal of sixty dishes. By the time of their departure on 21 March they had taken on board more bullocks, sixty hogs, rice, corn, baskets of yams and some 800 coconuts.

The next destination was the Dutch trading port of Batavia (Jakarta), which was more than 3,200 miles away. They headed south-west for Ternate, one of the Moluccas. On 15 April they encountered three waterspouts, 'one of which had like to have broke on the *Marquiss*, but the *Dutchess* by firing two shot, broke it before it reached her'. They survived several storms but the *Duke* was taking in more water than ever, so that it took four men half an hour to pump her free of water and the pumping had to continue night and day. They threaded their way past innumerable islands, never quite certain where they were until on 29 May they reached Butan on the south-east corner of the Celebes. Here they were courteously received by the King of Butan. Presents were exchanged and they replenished their wood and water, but they had to pay extravagant prices for the provisions brought out to them by the local inhabitants. They set sail on 8 June and two days later intercepted a small vessel whose Malayan captain agreed to pilot them through the shoals and islands that lay between them and Batavia. By 14 June they were passing the island of Madura, off the north coast of Java, and on the afternoon of 20 June they saw thirty or forty ships lying in the roadstead of the great Dutch port. They dropped anchor just after sunset 'at the long desired port of Batavia'.

The sailors were so delighted to find themselves in a civilised place where alcohol was cheap and plentiful that some of them were seen hugging one another with glee. Rogers himself was astonished to see such a noble city in this part of the world and the Europeans so well established. Batavia was the centre for the flourishing Dutch empire in the East Indies. Much of it looked like Amsterdam: there were fifteen canals which were crossed by numerous stone bridges and lined with handsome brick houses; there were elegant churches and an impressive town hall overlooking a square in the centre of the city; there were hospitals and schools and printing houses. On the outskirts were fine country houses with gardens shaded by fruit trees and decorated with statues and fountains, 'so that this city is one of the pleasantest in the world. I don't think it so large as Bristol, but 'tis more populous.'

Batavia was ruled by Abraham van Riebeck, the Governor-General, who lived like a prince with a personal escort of guards bearing halberds, and a garrison of more than 1,000 soldiers. His residence was a palace within a heavily fortified citadel and when the privateers sent a deputation to meet him they were greeted in a great hall decorated with armour and hung with flags. He examined and approved their commissions as private men-of-war and agreed to their using the port facilities to careen their ships. However, the chief administrator of the port proved obstructive and more than four weeks passed before they were able to take the *Marquiss* across to Hoorn Island and heave her on her side. When they did so the carpenters discovered that her bottom planks had been eaten to a honeycomb by teredo worms. They had no option but to sell her at a knockdown price of 575 Dutch dollars and transfer her prize goods to the other three ships.

During their prolonged stay in the Dutch port Rogers wrote a second letter to Alderman Batchelor in Bristol. He gave no more information about the value of the Manila galleon's cargo and explained, 'I don't write fuller here nor to any one else, because of the distance and uncertainty of going safe.'[14] He did mention that they had lost seventy men by death or desertion, and he did admit that he was much thinner and weaker than usual and had been so ill as a result of his wounds that he had not been able to conduct his normal business. His journal entry for 30 June records in more detail the extent of his wounds, and indicates the extreme discomfort he must have been under:

8 days ago the Doctor cut a large musket shot out of my mouth, which had been there near 6 months, ever since I was first wounded; we reckoned it a piece of my jaw-bone, the upper and lower jaw being much broken, and almost closed together, so that the Doctor had much ado to come at the shot, to get it out. I had also several pieces of my foot and heel-bone taken out, and God be thanked, am now in a fair way to have the use of my foot, and to recover my health. The hole the shot made in my face is now scarcely discernible.[15]

For all its amenities Batavia could be a deadly place for visiting seamen, and during the eighteen weeks the privateers spent in the vicinity four of them fell ill with 'fevers and fluxes' and died. Sixty years later Captain James Cook called in at the port during his first great voyage of exploration in the *Endeavour*. He had not lost a single man from sickness in a voyage which had taken him from England around Cape Horn to Tahiti and then on to New Zealand and Australia, but in Batavia his men went down with fevers (probably malaria and typhoid) and within a few weeks thirty-one were dead.

Before leaving Batavia the privateers recruited seventeen more men, mostly Dutchmen, to replace those who had died and those who had deserted. On 24 October they weighed anchor and set sail for the Indian Ocean and the Cape of Good Hope. They sighted Table Mountain on 27 December and the following day they entered the harbour of Cape Town. They saluted the Dutch fort with nine guns and dropped anchor a mile offshore. The anchorage was exposed to fierce gusts of wind from the mountains and to winter storms from the sea, but the town, which Edward Cooke reckoned to be about the size of Falmouth, enjoyed a fresh and healthy climate. Some 250 houses and a church were surrounded by small vineyards and plantations of oak trees. The dockyard and naval storehouses had everything needed to refit and service the ships of the Dutch East India Company, while a fine hospital 'furnished with physicians and surgeons as regularly as any in Europe' was able to look after 600 to 700 sick men from the ships returning from the Far East.

Although Rogers spent much of his time ashore during the three months they stayed at Cape Town, he remained thin and in poor health but he was able to write a long and optimistic letter to Alderman Batchelor. 'I heartily congratulate your good fortune,' he began, and for the first time he revealed the riches of the Manila galleon. 'Her cargo consists of most sorts of goods India affords proper for Acapulco and New Spain, the chief of which are silks, brocades, Bengale goods of several sorts, raw silk, musks, spices, steel ware and china ware.'[16] He reckoned that the likely value of the cargo was one million Spanish dollars. In addition to this the possessions of the ship's officers, men and passengers amounted to not less than 2,000 to 3,000 pieces of eight. In terms of English money he estimated that the prize, after allowing for damage to some of the goods, was worth around £200,000 (£15.5 million today). He was already aware that they were likely to face all sorts of problems when they returned home with their prize goods and he asked Batchelor and his fellow owners to be ready to act for them 'and to hasten to us as soon as you hear of our arrival in any part of Great Britain'.

With no sign of an end of the war in Europe, and the consequent danger from French warships and privateers, it was agreed that the *Duke*, the *Dutchess* and the *Batchelor* should join a Dutch convoy of East Indiamen for the voyage home. The convoy was under the command of Admiral Pieter de Vos and consisted of sixteeen Dutch ships and nine British ships, including the Bristol privateers and their prize. They sailed from Cape Town on 5 April and headed out into the heavy swell of the South Atlantic. On 30 April they made the island of St Helena, which Cooke noted was 'garrisoned by the English, for the refreshment of India Ships', and early on the morning of 7 May they passed Ascension Island, then uninhabited and no more than a tiny speck in the great expanse of the ocean.

As they approached the waters off Europe the Dutch admiral hoisted a broad pennant and all the other Indiamen hoisted long naval pennants from their mastheads so that they would look like a squadron of men-of-war rather than peaceful merchantmen. And to avoid French ships lying in wait in the English Channel and the Irish Channel the convoy made a long detour. They sailed west of Ireland and around the coast of Scotland, pausing briefly off the Shetland Isles to pick up provisions and to join a squadron of ten Dutch warships which had been sent to escort the convoy down the East Coast of England to the Netherlands. On the morning of

23 July 1711 the leading ships in the convoy sighted the Dutch coast and pilot boats came out to meet them. The guns of all the British ships fired a thunderous salute to the Admiral, while the Dutch ships 'fired all their guns for joy at their safe arrival in their own country'. The Bristol ships waited for the flood tide to take them over the harbour bar into the River Texel. At eight in the evening they finally dropped anchor in Texel Road about two miles offshore. Cooke noted that the voyage from the Cape of Good Hope had taken them three months and seventeen days.

The day after their arrival Rogers made his way to Amsterdam, where there was a letter from the Bristol owners. This advised them to remain at their current moorings until some of the owners came over to see them. There were a number of problems to be sorted out, the most critical being the hostile reaction of the directors of the English East India Company, who 'were incensed against us, though we knew not for what'. The company had a monopoly of trade between Britain and the East which included everywhere from the Cape of Good Hope to the Straits of Magellan. The company's agents had kept the directors informed of the movements of the Bristol privateers and the directors were determined to seize and confiscate the Manila galleon.[17] When Squire Holledge and a small group of the shipowners arrived on 5 August they were welcomed by a salute from the guns of the three ships. After a brief visit to each ship they travelled to Amsterdam with the ships' officers to see the Chief Magistrate of the city. They presented him with a brief account of the voyage and swore that their only trading in the Indies had been for provisions and basic necessities.

Some of the crew were now becoming mutinous not only because they wanted their share of the prize goods but also because they wanted to get home. The ships' council agreed to make an immediate payout of twenty Dutch guilders to each sailor, ten guilders to each landsman 'and to every officer in proportion as his occasion required'. Meanwhile the shipowners had persuaded the Admiralty to provide an armed escort to accompany the ships back to England. Among the surviving correspondence of the expedition is a letter to John Batchelor from Sir Thomas Hardy, Rear-Admiral of the Blue. Writing from his flagship HMS *Monk* on 9 September, the admiral assured Batchelor and his colleagues that warships would be sent to bring the ships across from the Netherlands and a fourth-rate ship would take them up the Thames to the Nore. He ended, 'I wish you success over the East India Company.'[18]

6

The Voyagers Return

On 19 September 1711 a squadron of four British warships led by the 70-gun *Essex*, under the command of Commodore Kerrill Roffey, arrived in the estuary of the River Texel. Their first attempt to escort the privateers back across the Channel to England was foiled by the weather. As they left the Dutch coast they were hit by a south-westerly gale which proved too much for the Manila galleon. In his logbook Commodore Roffey noted that 'at eight took ye prize in tow it blowed very fresh and ye prize had split her masts and had no other'.[1] They retreated back to the Texel. The stormy weather continued for a week but on 1 October they were at last able to set sail and, with the galleon once again under tow, they crossed the Channel and dropped anchor in the Downs, the anchorage which lies between the Goodwin Sands and the town of Deal. Their arrival off the shores of Kent was noted briefly by several London newspapers. The entry in the *Daily Courant* read, 'Deal, Octob.2. This morning came in Her Majesty's ships Essex, Canterbury, Medway, and Dunwich, and under their convoy the Aquapulco Ship, and 2 Privateers of Bristol, from Holland.'[2]

At Sheerness two of the shipowners' representatives, Giles Batchelor and Edward Acton, were hoping to board the privateers as soon as they entered the Thames. So bad was the weather that their boat had been nearly swamped on their way downstream to Sheerness, but they had survived and were able to report to John Batchelor that they had met an agent of the East India Company who had acknowledged that it was the company's intention to seize the Bristol ships and their prize. However, 'as the wind is still fresh and the tide far spent they cannot stir till morning'.[3]

On 4 October a favourable wind shift enabled the *Essex* and her charges to round the North Foreland. The *Duke* and *Dutchess* stood into Margate Road while the *Essex* and the galleon continued threading their way through the channels and mudbanks of the Thames Estuary, anchoring when the tide turned against them and sailing on the incoming flood tide. The weather continued changeable, with fresh gales and squally showers sweeping across the turbulent, grey waters of the estuary. On 8 October the *Essex* and the galleon anchored at the Nore, off the mouth of the River Medway, and the next day the galleon parted from her escort and headed upstream. She was joined by the *Duke* and *Dutchess* and at last, on 14 October 1711, they reached their final destination – the small riverside village of Erith. At this date Erith was no more than a single street of houses leading down to the waterfront. There was an ancient church with a spire and beyond was a wooded hill – the remnant of what had once been a dense forest of oaks and yew. Situated on the south side of a bend in the river and twenty-eight miles downstream from the congested quays of the Pool of London, Erith was used by those shipowners who wanted a quiet anchorage where they could unload their cargoes. What the sailors on board the *Duke* and *Dutchess* made of such a remote spot is not recorded. Rogers simply concluded his account of the circumnavigation of the world with the words, 'This day at 11 of the clock, we and our consort and prize got up to Eriff, where we came to an anchor, which ends our long and fatiguing voyage.' Edward Cooke, in the closing paragraph of his description of the voyage, noted that it was three years and two months since they had set off from Bristol in August 1708.

Erith might lack the taverns and brothels and port facilities to be found upstream at Wapping and Rotherhithe but it was not too remote for the sharp-eyed representatives of the East India Company. The day following the arrival of the privateers a man called Daniel Hilman, with several assistants appointed by the company, rowed out and thrust on board each ship a piece of paper on which was written: 'I seize this ship and on all goods aboard for the use and on behalf of the United Company of Merchants of England to the East Indies.'4

The legal right of the East India Company to carry out this action was questionable. The shipowners had already sent a petition to Queen Anne and the Attorney-General explaining their situation but had been informed that it was Her Majesty's wish that an accommodation be reached by the two parties and recommending that a conference be arranged to settle matters. Batchelor and two of his fellow shipowners had met representatives of the company on 17 August and had protested their innocence of breaking the company's monopoly of trade with the East. They had pointed out that their ships and their captains had commissions and letters of marque signed by the Lord High Admiral; they had been encouraged in their venture by the Act of Parliament of 1708 which had been intended to promote privateering. They explained that the goods they had on board their ships had all been captured from Spanish ships; they had not taken a single vessel in the Indian Ocean or in waters over which the East India Company claimed exclusive rights; and although they had sold some of their captured goods at the Dutch settlement at Batavia this had been necessary for the purchase of stores and equipment to enable them to complete their voyage.

The Court of the East India Company had informed Batchelor and his colleagues that it had a different opinion regarding their innocence. It had instructed the Company's agents in the Netherlands to 'have an eye upon ye proceedings of the Duke and Dutchess of Bristol and their prize' and to note whether they unloaded all or part of their cargoes there.[5] Faced with such intransigence the shipowners eventually decided they had no option but to buy off the company. They agreed to pay the considerable sum of £6,000, to which was added a bribe of £161. 5s. 0d. to an unknown individual who would ensure that the governors of the company made no further claim on the ships and their cargo. One of the Bristol owners, Thomas Goldney, later complained bitterly about the weakness of his colleagues but the others may have been persuaded by the advantages of having the company on their side. It did result in their being lent the services of a senior manager of the Leadenhall Warehouse in the Port of London to oversee the unloading and sorting of the huge variety of riches stowed in the ships' holds – riches which included bales of brocaded silk, sewing silk and silk ribbons; chests of china ware and steel ware; boxes and crates of indigo, musk, cinnamon, pepper and cloves; and a certain amount of gold, silver and pearls.

The unloading and sale of the goods took many months and when all the sales were completed the total value of the captured goods was reckoned to be just under £148,000 (today about £11.3 million).[6] This was modest by comparison with the riches brought back by Francis Drake in the *Golden Hind*, or with the later expedition led by Commodore Anson which captured the Acapulco galleon in 1743 with treasure estimated at £400,000. Nevertheless the Bristol shipowners achieved a handsome return on their investment. It had been agreed that two-thirds of the total sum would go to the owners and one-third to the crew. Thomas Goldney had invested £3,726 in the venture and was rewarded with £6,826. Dr Thomas Dover had invested £3,312 and received £6,067.[7]

The crew were not so fortunate. A man of dubious character called Stephen Creagh (an acquaintance later said he 'knew nothing good of him') had gone to the Netherlands and persuaded 209 crew members to take him on as their agent. In due course he instituted a case in the Court of Chancery in which he not only accused the ships' owners and captains of being guilty of irregular practices, but also charged Woodes Rogers with fraud against the owners. The case came to nothing and served only to delay the warehousing of the cargoes. Some members of the crews had still not received the full pay due to them three years later and in June 1714 they sent a petition to the House of Lords. In a second petition they complained that thousands of pounds were lying idle while they and their poor families were 'perishing from want of bread, and daily thrown into gaols or in danger of being so'.[8]

William Dampier, who had now completed his third global circumnavigation, did not live to receive his share of the profits. His extraordinary powers of endurance had enabled him to survive tropical hurricanes and the rigours of life with the log-cutters of the Bay of Campeche. During the course of twelve years with roving bands of buccaneers he had endured forced marches through the dense jungle of the Isthmus of Panama, and he had lived through storms, shipwrecks and ruthless attacks on Spanish towns and ships. He had led an abortive expedition to Australia and been reprimanded by a naval court martial. And during the course of a second circumnavigation in command of the privateer *St George* he had attacked but failed to capture the Manila galleon. Finally, in his late fifties, he had joined Rogers' privateering expedition, where his navigational skills and his knowledge of barely charted islands and places of refuge had contributed significantly to the success of the venture. He was now aged sixty and showed no inclination to write or publish any observations on his recent experiences. He retired to a house in Coleman Street in the City of London where he lived with his maternal cousin Grace Mercer, who acted as his housekeeper. The street was on the outer edge of the area destroyed by the Fire of London in 1666 and was a mix of old and new buildings. It was near the medieval Guildhall and close to the Bethlem Royal Hospital for the mentally ill. Usually referred to as Bedlam, the hospital had been moved to a new building in Moorfields in 1675, but was still notorious for the brutal treatment of its inmates.

It seems possible that Dampier was given a small advance on the money owed to him for his role as pilot for the Bristol privateers while the legal proceedings in Chancery dragged on but he was chiefly dependent on the Customs House sinecure which he had been awarded following the publication in 1697 of his much acclaimed book *A New Voyage Round the World*. He died early in 1715, leaving debts of £677 17s. 1d. In his last will, which he signed on 29 November 1714, he was recorded as being of sound and perfect mind but 'weak and diseased'. The will was proved on 23 March 1715 and in it Dampier left one-tenth of his estate to his brother George and the remainder to Grace Mercer, who eventually received Dampier's share of the prize money from the Master in Chancery, which amounted to £1,050 17s. 10d.[9]

Alexander Selkirk seems to have done better than most of the crew financially and certainly deserved to do so. Unlike the other privateers, who had been away for just over three years, he had been away for more than eight years, half of that time spent surviving alone on a Pacific island. Rescued by Rogers' expedition, he had proved an extremely capable seaman. He had been made master of the *Increase*, the ship they had captured off the island of Lobos, and had later been appointed master of the captured Manila galleon, the renamed *Batchelor*, under the nominal command of Thomas Dover. As master and navigator he was entitled to ten shares of that part of the prize money allotted to the crew, which would have amounted to £450, and he was also entitled to a certain amount of Storm money and Plunder money. When interviewed by Richard Steele for an article which appeared in *The Englishman* in December 1713 he said, 'I am now worth eight hundred pounds, but shall never be so happy as when I was not worth a farthing.'

In addition to his share of the prize money, we learn from the will which Selkirk drew up in 1717 that he owned a house as well as gardens, yards and orchards in his native village of Largo in Scotland. When his will was disputed by his second wife (of which more later) she maintained that he had left in the hands of his first wife some money, plate, bonds and securities 'to the value of five hundred pounds and upwards, particularly four gold rings, one silver tobacco box, one gold head of a cane, one pair of gold candlesticks, one silver-hilted sword, a considerable parcel of linen cloth and divers sea books and instruments'.[10] Some of these items, notably the gold rings, candlesticks and sword, were probably acquired during the looting of Guayaquil or were plundered from ships they had captured off the coast of South America.

Rogers, who had carried the chief burden of command throughout the voyage, had the most difficult homecoming of them all. Not only was he the principal target of the legal action instituted in the courts by Stephen Creagh, but his share of the profits failed to cover his debts. Some of the crew had expected the value of the plunder to be in the region of £3 million and accused Rogers of stealing a portion of it and hiding it at Batavia. This may have been a wild and baseless accusation but more serious was a letter written to the owners by Thomas Dover and signed by Dampier and others. The letter was sent soon after their arrival in the Netherlands and complained that Rogers 'is disposing of what he thinks fit out of this ship . . . We called a Council and would have had the chest out of him of pearl, jewels and gold but he swore by God we should not upon which I proposed to the Council to confine him . . . and was threatened with death.'[11]

Rogers was entitled as captain to twenty-four shares, which came to £1,015 4s. 0d.[12] With the addition of Storm money and other allowances granted to him, the total amounted to little more than £1,530. Before the proceedings in Chancery were concluded he was declared bankrupt. On 10 January 1712 readers of the *London Gazette* were informed that 'a Commission of Bankrupt is awarded against Woods Rogers of the City of Bristol'. He was required to report to the White Lion in Broad Street, Bristol, and then to the Trumpet in Shire Lane in the City of London, where 'the creditors are to come prepared to prove debts, pay Contribution-money, and chuse an Assignee or Assignees'.[13] The most likely reason for Rogers' financial problems was his wife Sarah's debts because she had had no source of income while he was away. She had left their gracious house in Queen Square, Bristol, and taken their three children to live with her father, Admiral Whetstone. When Whetstone died in April 1711 she continued to live with her mother-in-law, Lady Whetstone, but she must have run up considerable debts during the three years of Rogers' absence.

Rogers may have been aware of the problems he faced on his return. He had been in great pain for many months and was frequently unable to perform his duties as captain. In an earlier letter, written to the shipowners from Cape Town, Thomas Dover had complained that Rogers was 'a dead weight' whose behaviour was marked by violent threats to the crew. Embittered as Rogers was by the knowledge that he stood to gain very little from the voyage in spite of his steadfast leadership during storms, mutinies, the raid on Guayaquil and the attack on the Manila galleon, we can see why he might have been driven to the desperate measures described by Dover in his letter from the Netherlands.

Whether Rogers was reunited with his wife and family in London or Bristol is not known but, ten months after his return, his wife gave birth to their fourth child, a boy who was christened at St Michael's Church in the city. Sadly the child lived for only eight months and was buried in the same church in April 1712. It may have been soon after this that the couple separated. Sarah continued to live in Bristol and Rogers spent most of his time in London. His priority now was to publish his sea journal in book form. This may have been prompted by the knowledge that Edward Cooke was intending to publish his own account of the voyage, and no doubt the financial rewards of publication were a significant motive. But Rogers makes it clear in the introduction to his book that his primary objective was to tell his side of the story: 'I was not fond to appear in print; but the solicitations of my friends who had read my journal, and the mistaken reports that were spread abroad of our voyage, prevailed with me at last to publish it.'

While Rogers was involved with legal disputes and family concerns, Edward Cooke was free to concentrate on the preparation of his book. As second captain of the *Dutchess* he had been involved in most of the key decisions and actions during the circumnavigation and he had a good story to tell. Five months after the privateers' ships dropped anchor in the Thames his book was in print. On 27 March 1712 an advertisement appeared in a London newspaper which began, 'This day is published A Voyage to the South Sea, and round the World by the Bristol ships the Duke and Duchess, in the years 1708, 1709 and 1711 . . . by Capt Edw. Cooke.'[14] It was illustrated with a fold-out map, coastal profiles, charts of a number of islands and woodcuts of some of the fish, birds and animals encountered during the voyage. Cooke shrewdly dedicated his book to

Robert Harley, who had recently become the leading politician of the day and had a particular interest in the South Seas.

Three months later, on 26 June, an advertisement appeared in the same newspaper for Rogers' book. It was entitled *A Cruising Voyage Round the World* and was priced at six shillings. It lacked the numerous illustrations of Cooke's volume but it did include a detailed account of how Alexander Selkirk had endured his years as a castaway. Cooke had dismissed Selkirk's adventures in a few sentences but 'that short hint raised the curiosity of some persons to expect a more particular relation of his living in that tedious solitude'. His printers hastily brought out a second volume in which he did full justice to Selkirk's ordeal.

Neither Rogers' nor Cooke's account showed the intense curiosity about the natural world or the keen observation and powers of description which distinguished Dampier's publications. Indeed Rogers made it clear that he had chosen to keep to the language of the sea, 'which is more genuine and natural for a mariner'. He knew that people expected books about distant voyages to be concerned with new and wonderful discoveries, but he explained that he had restricted his descriptions to those places which would be useful for future trade. His lengthy introduction drew attention to the vast wealth of Spain's empire in South and Central America, and he pointed out that in recent years the French had proved remarkably successful at trading in the South Seas and had 'carried home above 100 millions of dollars, which is near 25 millions sterling'. Rogers encouraged his countrymen to establish a trading settlement in Chile, where the climate was so wholesome. His taking of Guayaquil with a handful of undisciplined men showed that the Spanish would offer little opposition, and the natives of Chile, who were a brave people, had such an aversion to the Spanish that they would readily side with the English in order to be free from the cruelty and oppression they had suffered for so long.

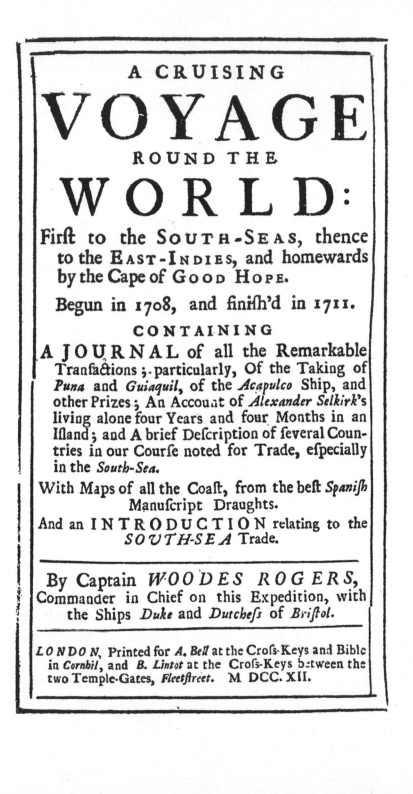

A CRUISING
VOYAGE
ROUND THE
WORLD:

Firſt to the SOUTH-SEAS, thence
to the EAST-INDIES, and homewards
by the Cape of GOOD HOPE.

Begun in 1708, and finiſh'd in 1711.

CONTAINING

A JOURNAL of all the Remarkable
Tranſactions; particularly, Of the Taking of
Puna and *Guiaquil*, of the *Acapulco* Ship, and
other Prizes; An Accouпt of *Alexander Selkirk*'s
living alone four Years and four Months in an
Iſland; and A brief Deſcription of ſeveral Coun-
tries in our Courſe noted for Trade, eſpecially
in the *South-Sea*.

With Maps of all the Coaſt, from the beſt *Spaniſh*
Manuſcript Draughts.
And an INTRODUCTION relating to the
SOUTH-SEA Trade.

By Captain *WOODES ROGERS*,
Commander in Chief on this Expedition, with
the Ships *Duke* and *Dutcheſs* of *Briſtol.*

LONDON, Printed for *A. Bell* at the Croſs-Keys and Bible
in *Cornhil*, and *B. Lintot* at the Croſs-Keys bｅtween the
two Temple-Gates, *Fleetſtreet.* M DCC. XII.

Rogers' arguments were very much in tune with the times. Daniel Defoe had been writing pamphlets encouraging the South Sea trade for several years.[15] The cause had been taken up by Robert Harley, former speaker of the House of Commons and now Lord Treasurer and head of the Tory administration which had enjoyed a landslide win in the general election of 1710. Although he was a notoriously poor speaker Harley was a master of behind-the-scenes diplomacy. He was largely responsible for setting up the South Sea Company. This was an ambitious scheme to take over a large proportion of the national debt incurred during the war with France and Spain, and at the same time to profit from trading with Spain's colonies in South America. A bill was introduced in May 1711 which was intended to give 'the Company of Merchants of Great Britain Trading to the South Seas and other parts of America' a monopoly similar to that enjoyed by the East India Company in the Far East. The bill received the royal assent on 12 June, a few months before Rogers' expedition arrived in the Thames with a captured galleon as visible proof of the riches of the South Seas. During the winter months following their return both Rogers and Cooke were consulted by the company. Cooke submitted a list of the principal harbours on the Pacific coast of South America, and Rogers provided some practical advice on a scheme for sending a major expedition from Britain to the Pacific.[16] The high hopes of the promoters of the South Sea Company were never realised. All depended on securing peace with Spain and not till 1713 did the company gain limited access to Spanish markets in America. The much-sought-after *asiento de negros* allowed the company to ship 4,800 African slaves every year across the Atlantic, but Spain would agree to only one ship a year being allowed to trade with South America. The company did survive the South Sea Bubble of 1720 when thousands of people were ruined by the crash of its stock but the venture became an object lesson on the folly of wild and unrealistic speculation.

When the *Duke* and *Dutchess* had set out on their privateering voyage in the summer of 1708 England had been at war with France and Spain for six years. Marlborough had followed his famous victory at Blenheim with another victory over the French at Malplaquet but it was at a heavy cost in lives. He told his wife that it had been a very bloody battle but 'it is now in our powers to have what peace we please'. However, neither Britain nor her enemies were in the mood for peace and it would be another five years before representatives of the warring nations finally gathered in the Dutch city of Utrecht to end the War of the Spanish Succession. Robert Harley, who in 1711 had been elevated to the peerage as Baron Harley, Earl of Oxford and Mortimer, was one of the leading advocates for peace. In addition to his diplomatic efforts he enlisted the help of Daniel Defoe and Jonathan Swift to influence public opinion in Britain. Defoe, who had been working for Harley for several years, wrote a series of articles setting out the benefits of peace in the *Review*, the periodical he founded in 1709. Jonathan Swift, recently appointed editor of the *Examiner*, published a pamphlet entitled 'The Conduct of Allies' in which he both attacked the Whigs for prolonging a war which had proved ruinously expensive for the nation and blamed the Dutch for their failure to share the financial burden. The pamphlet went into six editions and sold 11,000 copies in two months. Harley also persuaded the Queen to create eleven new peers in order to overcome the Whig opposition to peace in the House of Lords. A series of unofficial negotiations finally paved the way for the Treaty of Utrecht, which was signed on 11 April 1713 by representatives of Britain, France, Spain, Savoy and the United Provinces of the Netherlands.

A key clause of the treaty stipulated that Philip V of Spain must renounce for himself and his descendants any right to the French throne, thus removing the great fear of Britain and her allies that there might be a union of the French and Spanish crowns. Britain gained the North American territories of Newfoundland, Nova Scotia and Hudson's Bay; and in the Mediterranean she acquired Gibraltar and Minorca, both of strategic importance for naval operations. Austria gained the Spanish Netherlands, Sardinia and the Kingdom of Naples. France agreed to dismantle the harbour fortifications of Dunkirk, which had sheltered an extremely effective flotilla of French privateers. During the war these corsairs had prowled up and down the English Channel and captured or ransomed 1,685 merchant ships.[17]

News of the peace treaty was greeted in England by the ringing of church bells and by the lighting of bonfires in the streets. Handel composed the *Utrecht Te Deum*, which was performed at a thanksgiving service in Wren's recently completed St Paul's Cathedral on 7 July 1713. Across the Atlantic the *Boston News-Letter* reported that the proclamation of the peace was greeted 'with all demonstrations of joy, and followed by firing the guns of the town, and at the forts, both of Salem and Marblehead'.[18]

Meanwhile some interesting developments had been taking place in the social life of London. Throughout the City and the West End coffee houses had become meeting places where men from many walks of life met to gossip, transact business and exchange news. The first coffee house had opened in London in 1652 but it was during the reign of Queen Anne that coffee houses proliferated and by the time of her death in 1714 there were reckoned to be 497 in the capital. Certain premises tended to attract men with similar interests: St James's Coffee House in St James's Street became a meeting place for Whigs while Tories made for the Cocoa Tree in

Pall Mall; literary men tended to gather in Button's Coffee House in Russell Street, Covent Garden; merchants and shipowners met to discuss shipping news in Edward Lloyd's premises in Lombard Street.

The coffee houses became the breeding ground for the newspapers. At first these were no more than single sheets which were distributed to those using the coffee houses but so great was the demand that they were soon being printed and circulated on a commercial scale. 'What attracts enormously to these coffee houses,' wrote a Swiss visitor, 'are the gazettes and other public papers. All Englishmen are great newsmongers.'[19] Defoe's thrice-weekly *Review* and Swift's weekly *Examiner* have already been noted but there were several others, notably the *Daily Courant*, which had the distinction of being the first daily newspaper in the world when it appeared on the scene in 1702. One of the most influential of all the papers was the *Spectator*, first issued in 1711. This was the creation of Joseph Addison and his friend Richard Steele. They had been contemporaries at Oxford and both entered politics but it was through their journalism that they made their mark. What distinguished the *Spectator* from other newspapers and periodicals was that it provided an intelligent commentary on events and included witty observations on the manners, morals and literature of the day.

It was Richard Steele who interviewed Alexander Selkirk and provided another view of the circumstances of his marooning and the practical measures he took to ensure his survival.[20] 'I had the pleasure frequently to converse with the man soon after his arrival in England in the year 1711,' he wrote. 'It was a matter of great curiosity to hear him, as he is a man of good sense . . .' Steele underlined the fact that Selkirk chose to be put ashore at Juan Fernández because of his irreconcilable difference with his disagreeable

commander but noted that his resolution changed when he saw the
vessel put off from the shore and he realised he was parting from his
comrades and all human society at once. He recounted how Selkirk
overcame his initial depression by frequent reading of the scriptures
so that he learnt to enjoy his solitary existence. 'It was his manner
to use stated hours and places for exercises of devotion which he
performed aloud, in order to keep up the faculties of speech . . .'
Steele also noted how Selkirk's manner and appearance changed as
he became accustomed to the busy life of London:

> When I first saw him I thought if I had not been let into his character
> and story I could have discerned that he had been much separated from
> company from his aspect and gesture; there was a strong but cheerful
> seriousness in his look, and a certain disregard to the ordinary things
> about him, as if he had been sunk in thought . . . Though I had frequently
> conversed with him, after a few months' absence he met me in the street,
> and though he spoke to me, I could not recollect that I had seen him;
> familiar discourse in this town had taken off the loneliness of his aspect,
> and quite altered the air of his face.

Selkirk seems to have relapsed into the restless and irresponsi-
ble behaviour which was not uncommon among sailors ashore.
After spending a year or so in London as a lodger with Katherine
Mason, the wife of a Covent Garden tailor, he evidently moved
to Bristol because in September 1713 the records of the Queen's
Bench show that Alexander Selkirk 'of the parish of St Stephens in
Bristol, Nauta' was arraigned for committing an assault on Richard
Nettle, a shipwright.[21] He then decided to return to Largo. There
he fell in love with a local girl, Sophia Bruce, and persuaded her
to move down to London with him. In the first of his two wills he
appointed his 'loveing and well beloved friend Sophia Bruce of Pell

Mell London Spinster' as his heir.[22] This will was signed at Wapping on 13 January 1717. According to sworn evidence given by Sophia six years later he married her on or about 4 March 1717 and then 'went on board his Majesties Ship the Enterprize without altering the said will or making any other will and did not return to Great Brittain till about Eight Months after', when he took up with Sophia again and stayed with her in London for the next eight months.[23] HMS *Enterprise* was a 40-gun ship commanded by Captain Mungo Herdman and her logbooks indicate that she spent this period on a series of cruises which took her around the west coast of the British Isles as far north as Stornaway and then south to Lisbon and Vigo Bay. She was back in Plymouth by the autumn of 1720.[24] Her muster books for this time are missing, so we do not know exactly when Selkirk signed on to her books or whether Sophia was correct in saying that he left the ship after eight months and returned to her in London. It seems more likely that he remained a member of the crew of the *Enterprise* until 20 October 1720, when Captain Herdman was given command of HMS *Weymouth*, and the entire crew of the *Enterprise* were 'turned over' to the *Weymouth*, a new ship of 50 guns which was moored at Plymouth.

It is well documented that Selkirk was first mate on the *Weymouth* and, unfortunately for Sophia, it is also well documented that he went through a second marriage in Plymouth. In the registers of St Andrew's parish church there is an entry which records that Alexander Selkirk and Frances Candish were granted a licence by Mr Forster on 12 December 1720.[25] Frances Candish appears to have been an attractive widow who was the proprietor of a public house at Oreston in the parish of Plymstock, which was close to the waterfront of Plymouth Sound. On the same day as the marriage, no doubt prompted by his new wife, Selkirk made a second will in which he gave and bequeathed all his wages, sums of money, lands, tenements, goods and chattels 'unto my well-beloved wife Frances Silkirk of Oarston'. He made her his sole executor of this, his last will and testament, 'hereby revoking all former and other wills'.[26]

In 1723, following the death of Selkirk, the two women would meet in the Court of Chancery to determine which of them had the stronger claim to receive his wages, his lands and possessions. The legal battle was acrimonious and poor Sophia found herself described as 'a person of very indifferent character and reputation' and that Selkirk had been 'a boarder or lodger with her for about the space of five or six months'. By this time Frances had married a third time, and she and her new husband, Francis Hall, were determined to get their hands on all Selkirk's money and estate as well as the gold candlesticks, gold rings and silver-hilted sword he had acquired during his privateering voyages. Frances evidently had the stronger case in law because Sophia lost everything. It is not known whether Sophia remained in London or returned to her native Largo but an undated letter from her survives which was written to Mr Say, a dissenting minister of Westminster, in which she appealed for help. It begins:

Reverend Sir,

I being a person much reduced to want, by reason of this hard season, makes me presume to trouble you, which I hope your goodness will not resist to relieve, I being the widow of Mr Selchrig who was left four years and four months on the island of John Ferinanda [sic], and besides I had three uncles in Scotland, all ministers . . .[27]

It has to be said that it was not uncommon for sailors like Selkirk to live up to their traditional image of having a wife in every port. Usually these were casual affairs but on occasion a sailor made it official. Rogers noted in *A Cruising Voyage Round the World* that during the weeks the *Duke* and *Dutchess* were stocking up in Ireland, 'Our crew were continually marrying, tho they expected to sail immediately. Among others there was a Dane coupled by a Romish Priest to an Irish Woman, without understanding a word of each other's language, so that they were forced to use an interpreter . . .' In 1732 a special court was set up for the relief of poor widows of commissioned officers and warrant officers of the Royal Navy. An examination of the records shows that between 1750 and 1800 there were twenty-two cases in which two wives applied for the pension of the same man.[28] The usual practice of the charity's commissioners was to award the pension to the first wife provided that she could supply proof of the date of her marriage. Sophia Bruce was unable to provide this proof and so lost her case.

HMS *Weymouth*, with Selkirk on board, left Plymouth on 21 December 1720 and headed for Portsmouth. She remained in the anchorage at Spithead for the next six weeks while a convoy of merchant ships bound for Africa was assembled. On 5 February she set sail in the company of HMS *Swallow*, under the command of Captain Chaloner Ogle. The two ships had orders to escort the merchant ships to the Guinea Coast and then to track down the pirates who were operating in that area. It would prove to be the last of Selkirk's ocean voyages.

The remaining years of Rogers' life would also be much concerned with the pirates. Following the publication of *A Cruising Voyage Round the World* in 1712 he embarked on a curious project which began as a commercial venture to make money from slave trading. It involved a voyage to Madagascar, where he made contact with the remnants of a pirate colony, and developed into a scheme to establish an English settlement on the island. During the voyage of the *Duke* and *Dutchess* Rogers had been much impressed by the success of the Dutch settlements at Batavia and in South Africa and had noted that the Dutch at Cape Town 'generally send a ship every year from hence to Madagascar for slaves, to supply their plantations'. Having found the backing of enough sponsors to purchase the 460-ton merchant ship *Delicia*, he approached the East India Company and in October 1713 obtained their approval to buy slaves in Madagascar for sale in the East Indies.[29]

Rogers arrived in Cape Town in the early part of 1714, and then spent two months on the coast of Madagascar. Once a flourishing rendezvous for pirates who preyed on shipping in the Indian Ocean and the haunt of such celebrated pirates as Henry Avery, Captain Kidd and Thomas Tew, the island was now home to a miserable collection of pirates who had married native women and were accompanied by a motley collection of children and grandchildren. According to one description of Rogers' visit, 'they had nothing to cover them but the skins of beasts . . . and being overgrown with beard, and hair upon their bodies, they appeared the most savage figures that a man's imagination can frame'.[30] It seems that Rogers did manage to get hold of enough slaves to make it worth his while to head for the East India Company's trading post at Benkoelen in Sumatra, where he sold them and made contact with the Governor, Joseph Collett.[31]

By 1715 Rogers was back in England. The records of the Society for the Promotion of Christian Knowledge show that in April 1716 he was negotiating with the society to send books to Madagascar. On 7 May he wrote to Sir Hans Sloane, the celebrated physician, naturalist and collector: 'I being ambitious to promote a settlement on Madagascar beg [you will be] pleased to send me what accounts you have of that island . . .'[32] There is no record of Sloane providing him with any information and within a year of this request Rogers had abandoned his plans for Madagascar and become involved in a much more ambitious scheme. This would lead to his appointment as Governor of the Bahamas and would bring him into direct conflict with some of the most notorious pirates of the day.

7

Sugar, Slaves and Sunken Treasure

The Caribbean was in many ways an ideal location for pirates and it is not at all surprising that it should have been the setting for an explosion of piracy in the early eighteenth century. The string of large and small islands stretching in an arc from the Florida Keys to Trinidad and Tobago enjoyed a sunny climate which was in stark contrast to the grey skies and cold winters of the lands bordering the North Atlantic, or the energy-draining humidity of the jungles of Panama and the Spanish Main. The heat of the sun was tempered by offshore and onshore breezes, while plentiful rain ensured the luxuriant growth of plants, trees and shrubs. Sailors dropping anchor in one of the thousands of bays and lagoons of the Caribbean usually had little difficulty in finding fresh water and food. Coconut groves lined the beaches, turtles and turtles' eggs were abundant and a variety of fish lived among the coral reefs. There were sheltered coves in hundreds of deserted islands where a pirate ship could hide for weeks undetected, and shelving white sands where the ship could be run ashore so that she could be repaired and cleaned of weed and barnacles.

These attractions were offset by some serious drawbacks: the annual hurricane season sometimes caused widespread destruction

of houses, crops and shipping; mosquitoes and sandflies were rife,
particularly among the mangroves and swamps which were a feature
of many islands; and most deadly of all were the diseases. Malaria
and yellow fever were the chief killers but there were also many
deaths from dysentery, dropsy and some of the diseases brought
over from Africa such as guineaworm and leprosy. It is unlikely that
the pirates were too worried about these hazards because most of
them were of the same mind as Bartholomew Roberts, who is cred-
ited with saying, 'A merry life and a short one shall be my motto.'
As far as the pirates were concerned the overwhelming attraction
of the West Indies was the ever-increasing procession of merchant
ships of all sizes waiting to be plundered as they made their way on
predictable trade routes to and from the ports of North America,
Europe and West Africa.

The Spanish, following in the wake of Columbus, had been the
first to establish settlements on the larger islands of Cuba, Hispaniola,
Puerto Rico and Jamaica in the years between 1496 and 1515. The
British were next on the scene and during the 1620s and 1630s laid
claim to Antigua, Barbados, Montserrat, Nevis and St Kitts. The
islands were at first valued for the production and export of tobacco,
cotton, ginger and indigo, but it was the introduction of sugar plantations in the 1640s which transformed the economy of many of the
West Indian islands. Like oil in the twentieth century, sugar was in
huge demand in Europe. It made those who controlled its production
wealthy and caused islands to be fought over and change hands. In
1655 the British ousted the Spanish from Jamaica and by the end of the
century had added Grenada and St Lucia to their Caribbean empire.
The French meanwhile had laid claim to Guadeloupe, Martinique
and St Barts and had taken over the western part of Hispaniola, Haiti.

The native populations of Arawak and Carib Indians had no
defence against the invaders. Columbus had been impressed by

the peaceable nature of the Arawaks and had noted, 'They would make fine servants . . . With fifty men we could subjugate them all and make them do whatever we want.' The harsh treatment of the Spanish who enslaved them, and European diseases from which they had no immunity, led to their rapid decline. Within a few decades of the arrival of the white men, the Arawaks and Caribs had been wiped out, apart from a few isolated groups on some islands. As slave labour was needed to work on the sugar plantations the Spanish began shipping black Africans across the Atlantic. A report presented to King Ferdinand of Spain as early as 1511 declared that the work of one black slave was equal to that of four Indian slaves – the Indians, in common with most Europeans, lacked the physical stamina to work in the cane fields in the heat of the day.[1] In due course the British and French participated in the slave trade and the numbers of black Africans shipped across the Atlantic increased dramatically. Between 1650 and 1675 nearly 370,000 slaves were exported from trading stations on the coast of West Africa. Between 1675 and 1700 the total number of slaves exported rose to 600,000, an annual average of over 24,000 and most of these went to the islands of the Caribbean.[2]

The slave trade proved to be even more profitable than the sugar plantations. A cargo of slaves from the African coast was worth at least twice as much as the barrels of sugar which occupied the same space – provided that the majority of the slaves survived the voyage.[3] The mortality rate on slave ships was around 10 per cent, because the slaves went down with dysentery or smallpox, or were so traumatised by the horrific conditions that they committed suicide.[4] The so-called triangular trade operating between Europe, Africa and the West Indies enriched generations of white plantation owners, merchants and shipowners. Many of England's noble families were involved and were able to build splendid houses on their country estates in the English counties, as well as fine houses on their plantations in the Caribbean. Sugar was a labour-intensive industry and by 1667 the small island of Barbados had 50,100 black slaves and a white population of 15,400.[5]

The ports serving the sugar-producing islands grew as rapidly as the plantations. By 1692 the population of Port Royal, Jamaica, was around 6,500. The wharves were lined with storehouses, ships' chandlers and sail lofts. There was an Anglican church, a Roman Catholic chapel, a court house, two prisons, several markets, dozens of shops and taverns and a great number of brothels. Lists of trades and professions at this date show the town had one baker, two barbers, four blacksmiths, eleven coopers, four masons and ten tailors. Not surprisingly for a busy port there were fifty-three mariners, four sailmakers, three shipwrights and four fishermen, but there were also forty-four tavern keepers and 125 merchants. An examination of the ships and cargoes coming in and out of Port Royal in the 1680s gives some idea of the plunder available for privateers and pirates cruising in the vicinity of the Windward Passage. Two hundred and forty ships arrived in the port from England and Africa, and 363 from the North American colonies, in the years between 1686 and 1691. The incoming cargoes included black slaves, wines and beers, muskets and pistols, ploughs and cartwheels, and naval stores such as canvas, tar and cordage. Outgoing cargoes included sugar, tobacco, tortoise shells, hides, cotton, indigo, ginger and pimento. In 1686 no fewer than 225 ships arrived in the Port of London from the West Indies, and when we take into account the ships travelling to and from other ports, such as Bristol, Liverpool, Boston, Charleston and the Atlantic ports of France, Spain and Portugal, we can see why the pirates had no shortage of victims.

Most of the merchant ships travelling to the West Indies from London between 1650 and 1750 ranged from 150 to 200 tons, while those travelling from the smaller ports were mostly of 100 tons or less.[6] The crews were relatively small compared with those of privateers and pirate ships. A typical merchantman of eighty to 100 tons would have a crew of eleven or twelve, consisting of the master, the first mate, second mate, a carpenter, cook, half a dozen able seamen and a boy. A larger merchantman of 150–200 tons would have a crew of fifteen to twenty men and this would usually include a gunner and a boatswain in addition to those already mentioned.[7] Most ships would be equipped with a few carriage guns and a supply of small arms, but since the crew were unlikely to have had much practice in gunnery or hand-to-hand combat they stood no chance against a privateer or pirate ship armed with anything from ten to forty guns and a crew of between fifty and 150 men armed with muskets, pistols and cutlasses.

In the early years of the eighteenth century it was the privateers rather than the pirates who were the major threat to merchantmen in the Caribbean. During the War of the Spanish Succession the governors of the West Indian islands were generous in issuing privateering commissions, which allowed an enterprising merchant sea captain with a letter of marque and a well-armed ship to make a small fortune from captured prizes, while former pirates who managed to obtain commissions could become patriots and legitimately plunder enemy merchantmen. The Spanish coast-guards (*guardacostas*) who operated around the coasts of Cuba, Hispaniola and Puerto Rico joined in the privateering bonanza. Instead of restricting their operations to the protection of Spanish shipping many of them launched indiscriminate attacks on vulnerable merchant ships. One commentator observed that the governors of Spanish settlements 'grant commissions to great numbers of vessels of war, on pretence of preventing interloping trade, with orders to seize all ships or vessels whatsoever, within five leagues of their coasts, which our English ships cannot well avoid coming, in their voyage to Jamaica'.[8]

The Council of Trade and Plantations in London was besieged by complaints from colonial governors and merchants. 'We have been sadly pestered by our enemy privateers, who have taken several ships and vessels in sight of the island,' wrote the Governor of Jamaica in 1710, and he pointed out that French privateers 'are in swarms around us'.[9] Lieutenant Governor Hodges of Montserrat reported that seven privateers from neighbouring French islands 'having on board between 6 and 700 men made an attack on us about 10 in the morning . . .'.[10] The privateers took forty-five 'very fine slaves' from one English family in Montserrat and twenty-five slaves from another family.[11] Lieutenant General Hamilton of Antigua complained of 'the daily insults committed by the enemys privateers' and pointed out that it was impossible for one man-of-war to adequately guard the islands because the privateers 'narrowly watch the motion of the man of war, that when she is to windward they are commonly to leeward and appear even at the mouths of our very harbours'.[12] A merchant from the same island wrote, 'The Caribee Isles are so much troubled with the French privateers from Martinico, that no vessels can pass in or out of them.'[13]

Edmund Dummer, the founder of the mail service to the West Indies, received increasingly alarming reports from the captains of his packet boats and passed the information on to Mr Popple, the Secretary of the Council of Trade and Plantations. In 1709 he said he had been receiving great complaints from Jamaica and the Bahamas about the recent Act of Parliament for the encouragement of privateers, 'which tends to the ruin of all trade with the Spanish West Indies, disabling the men of war and merchant ships of seamen . . .'.[14] A year later he had received news of 'the multitude of privateers upon and about the Leeward Islands, by whom they fear every day to be plundered as St Eustatius has been. And from Jamaica they say their trade with the Spaniards is nearly ruined by our own privateers, for under that licence all nations, French, Dutch, Spanish and English consort together . . .'[15] He was in no doubt that privateers posed a serious threat for the future and issued a gloomy warning: 'It is the opinion of everyone, this cursed trade will breed so many pirates that when peace comes we shall be in more danger from them than we are now from the enemy . . .'[16]

Dummer's warning would prove to be justified but the signing of the Treaty of Utrecht in 1713 did not result in a sudden and dramatic rise in piracy. For two years there was an ominous lull in pirate attacks. The Royal Navy laid off thousands of sailors, and privateering commissions against enemy merchant ships ceased to be valid, but the former privateers and the unemployed sailors thronging the seaports on both sides of the Atlantic did not immediately turn to piracy. The newspapers and the correspondence of colonial governors were surprisingly free of reports of pirates during 1713–14. There was a rumour passed on from Jamaica that hundreds of pirates were gathering in the Gulf of Darien, and an ominous report from the Governor of Bermuda that three sets of pirates using open boats had been operating among the Bahamas and warning that these islands might become 'a nest of pirates'. But there was very little else.

Two separate events appear to have sparked off the surge in piracy which began to gather way in 1716 and was in full swing by 1717–18. The first was the wrecking of the Spanish treasure fleet on the coast of Florida in 1715, and the second was the expulsion by the Spanish of the logwood cutters from the Bay of Campeche and the Bay of Honduras. Both these events led a considerable number of tough and potentially dangerous men to head for the island of New Providence in the Bahamas. The sheltered harbour at Nassau became the meeting place for a miscellaneous group of treasure hunters, logwood cutters, privateers and unemployed seamen. This group spawned a generation of pirates who would be made famous by Captain Charles Johnson's book of 1724, *A General History of the Robberies and Murders of the Most Notorious Pyrates*. Their exploits would lead to Captain Woodes Rogers being despatched to the Bahamas with a squadron of naval ships and orders to drive the pirates from the islands.

The wrecking of the Spanish treasure fleet was one of a series of maritime disasters which took place during the early years of the eighteenth century. In November 1703 southern England and the English Channel were swept by the Great Storm which wrecked three warships on the Goodwin Sands, destroyed the Eddystone Lighthouse, sank or wrecked numerous coastal vessels and fishing boats, flooded much of the east coast and caused a loss of life which was estimated at anything between 8,000 and 15,000. Then in 1707 Admiral Sir Cloudesley Shovell was returning with a fleet of warships from the Mediterranean when three of his ships foundered on the rocks of the Scilly Isles with the loss of 1,315 men, including the admiral himself. This disaster was the result of navigational error and would lead to the Longitude Act of 1714, which offered a generous financial reward to anyone who could solve the problem of accurately determining longitude at sea. In 1712 Jamaica was devastated by a hurricane which sank or drove ashore fifty-four vessels in Port Royal harbour, including a naval sloop.[17] Two slave ships were among those sunk: half the crew and 100 slaves on the *Ann Galley* were drowned and the *Joseph Galley* lost all her crew and 107 slaves who were chained below deck. And then in the summer of 1715 came the news that all ten ships of the Spanish treasure fleet which had set out from Havana on 24 July had been driven ashore on the reefs off the coast of Florida. It was one of the worst shipwreck disasters in Spanish history.

The war had held up the annual sailings of the treasure fleet from the New World for three years and so the fleet which sailed in 1715 carried an unusually rich cargo. There were chests of gold and silver coins, gold bars and gold dust; there were pearls, Colombian emeralds and gold jewellery from Peru; and from the Manila galleons there were silks, spices and precious K'ang-Hsi Chinese porcelain. In overall command of the fleet was Captain-General Don Juan Esteban de Ubilla and on his ship alone were 1,000 chests of silver coins, each chest containing some 3,000 coins. The total value of the cargo carried by the entire fleet is estimated to have been seven million pieces of eight, which in today's terms would be worth more than £135 million.

Making use of the Gulf Stream, the fleet sailed north in calm weather until the morning of 30 July, when the sun disappeared 'as though behind a muslin cloud' and the ships began to roll in an increasingly heavy swell. By noon it was so dark that the ships were ordered to light their stern lanterns. By evening the wind had increased to storm force and the ships were labouring in mountainous waves. A survivor would later recall: 'It was so violent that the water flew in the air like arrows, doing injury to all those it hit, and seamen who had ventured much said they had never seen the like before.'[18] During the night the fleet was scattered before the full force of the hurricane and driven towards the lines of breakers along the Florida coast. The first ship to hit the reefs was the former British warship *Hampton Court* of 70 guns. She had been captured by Dunkirk privateers in 1707 and sold to Spain. Dismasted and rudderless, she was broken on the rocks and 223 of her officers and men lost their lives.[19] By the morning of 31 July all ten ships had been driven ashore or sunk. More than 1,000 men died in the storm and the survivors were scattered along an inhospitable shore between St Augustin and Palmar de Ayes (near present-day Sebastián).

The senior officer to survive the storm was Admiral Don Francisco Salmon and he sent the flagship's pilot and eighteen men in a boat to Cuba to inform the Governor of the disaster. It took ten days for the boat to reach Havana and the response was immediate. Ships with government officials and soldiers were despatched, and divers were rounded up to dive on the wrecks. By late October over five million pieces of eight and considerable quantities of gold and silver had been recovered. News of the loss of the treasure fleet spread rapidly across the Caribbean and along the east coast of North America. Casual looters and more organised expeditions set out to find and plunder the wrecks.

In Port Royal the captain of HMS *Diamond* reported that sailors were deserting his ship at the rate of five a day. He was concerned that if he stayed a week longer in harbour he would not have enough crew to sail the ship home. In a report to the Admiralty he observed that the mariners in the vicinity were 'all mad to go a wrecking, as they term it, for the generality of the island think they have [the] right to fish upon the wrecks, though the Spaniards have not quitted them'.[20] Lord Hamilton, the Governor of Jamaica, was determined to benefit from the gold rush and, after failing to persuade the commanders of the naval ships at Port Royal to head for Florida, he decided to send privateers to loot the wrecks. He had for some time been assembling a small fleet of armed merchantmen as a defence against raids by Spanish privateers and pirates, and he had no difficulty in persuading the captains of two of these local vessels to 'go a wrecking'. Their privateering commissions officially directed them 'by force of arms to seize, take and apprehend all pyratical ships and vessels' but this was used as a cover for what amounted to an unofficial treasure-hunting expedition.

The leader of this expedition was Henry Jennings, 'a man of good understanding, and a good estate', who was the commander of the forty-ton ship *Barsheba*, which was armed with 8 carriage guns and carried a crew of eighty men. He was accompanied by the thirty-five-ton sloop *Eagle*, with 12 guns and eighty men under the command of John Wills.[21]

Near the entrance of the Florida Straits the privateers intercepted a Spanish mail boat. Her commander, Pedro de la Vega, not only knew where the main camp for the Spanish salvage operations was situated but he was persuaded to lead them to the spot. As the three ships sailed north along the coast they passed the remnants of two of the ships wrecked in the storm as well as the remains of camp fires and wooden crosses marking the graves of victims of the disaster. By the evening of 26 December 1715 they were in the vicinity of the Spanish camp, a fortified enclosure guarded by some sixty soldiers.

Jennings treated the raid like a military operation. He anchored the ships offshore and waited till the early hours of the morning to make his attack. One hundred and fifty armed men were selected for the raid and were divided into three companies. Armed with muskets and cutlasses, they rowed ashore in three boats and landed at daybreak. With a drummer and a flag bearer at the head of each company they marched towards the camp, causing such panic that many of the Spaniards fled. Admiral Don Francisco de Salmon realised he stood no chance against such a force and surrendered. He asked Jennings whether war had been declared but was told that the privateers had simply come to fish on the wrecks and claim the mountain of wealth. The Spanish admiral declared that the treasure belonged to His Catholic Majesty the King of Spain. He offered them 25,000 pieces of eight if they would leave peacefully but the offer was refused. He had no alternative but to reveal the whereabouts of the chests of silver which had been buried within his camp.

The privateers sailed away with treasure valued at 120,000 pieces of eight as well as four bronze swivel guns.

The *Barsheba* and *Eagle* headed first for the Bahamas, the nearest islands under nominal British control. After a brief stay in the harbour of Nassau they sailed on to Jamaica and arrived at Port Royal on 26 January 1716. It was evident to Lord Hamilton that the very large amount of treasure brought back in such a short time could not have been salvaged by fishing on the wrecks but must have been stolen from the Spanish ashore. He would later declare that he took no share of the treasure himself 'for that I heard it was taken from the shore', but he made no move to arrest Jennings and White for exceeding their commission and committing piracy.

Two months later Jennings headed off on another cruise to the Spanish treasure wrecks, this time accompanied by the fifty-ton sloop *Mary*, and the smaller sloops *Discovery* and *Coco Nut*. Off the north-eastern coast of Cuba he encountered Sam Bellamy and Paul Williams, two pirates in command of a band of men who had been attacking small merchant ships using piraguas. The privateers and the pirates joined forces to capture a handsome French merchant ship, the *St Marie*, which was commanded and part-owned by Captain D'Escoubet of La Rochelle.[22] The ship was cut out from her anchorage in naval fashion by Bellamy's pirates, who came alongside in their native canoes and let loose a fusillade of musket shot. Most of the crew of the *St Marie* were ashore and D'Escoubet surrendered without firing a shot. The pirates found themselves in possession of a ship of 16 guns, which they later increased to 32 guns, as well as a valuable cargo and 30,000 pieces of eight. To maintain the now shaky pretence that he was still a legitimate privateer Jennings forced D'Escoubet to write a letter to Lord Hamilton which assured him that 'those gentlemen treated me very civilly' and explaining that the privateers 'took my vessel because she was fit for the expedition they were going on'.[23]

Before returning to Jamaica with his prize, Jennings again called in at Nassau to stock up on water and provisions and divide up the loot. The harbour and the town which stretched along the water-front had become home to an ever-increasing number of pirates and was rapidly gaining a reputation as a den of iniquity. While Jennings was ashore his crew ransacked the cargo of his French prize. By the time he returned and managed to restore order much of the loose coin and some of the cargo was missing. He decided to cut his losses and headed back to the Spanish treasure wrecks. His arrival in the *Barsheba* with the *St Marie* and another Jamaica privateer appar-ently frightened off the Spanish guardships because an observer later reported that twenty-four English vessels, some from Jamaica and some from Bermuda, were fishing on the wrecks, presided over by the *St Marie*, which would 'not permit either French or Spaniards to come here'. When Jennings eventually returned to Jamaica he received a hostile reception. The Spanish Governor of Havana had learnt that Lord Hamilton was part-owner of the ships which had raided the treasure camp on the Florida coast. He demanded the return of the treasure and the punishment of the perpetrators. And the French Governor of Hispaniola had sent a delegation to Jamaica which included Captain D'Escoubet, demanding that the *St Marie* and her cargo, and another stolen French vessel, be restored to their rightful owners.

In addition to his involvement in the looting of the treasure wrecks Lord Hamilton was suspected, with good reason, of supporting the Jacobite plot of 1715 to dethrone King George I and replace him with James Stuart, the son of the deposed King James II. Hamilton was related to many of the Scottish leaders of the rebellion and his enemies believed that he had intended to use his flotilla of privateers to further the Jacobite cause in Jamaica and other West Indian colonies. In July 1716 the British warship *Adventure* sailed into Port Royal bearing an arrest warrant for Hamilton. He was to be sent back to England and replaced as Governor of Jamaica by Peter Heywood. A few weeks later another ship brought a proclamation which declared that Henry Jennings and his associates were henceforth to be regarded as pirates. By this time the former privateers were back in the Bahamas, their ships and their crews swelling the numbers of vessels and disaffected men who would pose a serious threat to the trade of the West Indies.

Meanwhile the Spanish had decided to seek revenge for the attacks on the treasure wrecks by sending a force to root out the mainly English logwood cutters from the coastal jungles of the Bay of Campeche and the Bay of Honduras. Dampier had spent a year as a young man working alongside these men who toiled in the most difficult conditions imaginable. On the banks of creeks infested with alligators and mosquitoes they were subject to intense heat and tropical storms. 'During the wet season, the land where the logwood grows is so overflowed, that they step from their beds into the water perhaps two feet deep, and continue standing in the wet all day, till they go to bed again.' Dampier described the logwood cutters as strong and sturdy and able to carry burdens of three or four hundredweight. Most of them were former sailors and when they were not earning a hard living from felling trees they would spend days on end getting blind drunk on rum. Unable to continue this work, not surprisingly they turned to piracy. In the words of Captain Johnson, 'being made desperate by their misfortunes, and meeting with the Pyrates, they took on with them'. And Johnson neatly summed up the circumstances which created the pirate community at Nassau: 'The rovers being now pretty strong, they consulted together about getting some place of retreat, where they might lodge their wealth, clean and repair their ships, and make themselves a kind of abode. They were not long in resolving, but fixed upon the Island of Providence, the most considerable of the Bahama Islands . . .'[24]

8

Governor of the Bahamas

On 5 September 1716 an alarming sheaf of documents arrived on the desk of Mr Burchett at the Admiralty Office in Whitehall. Unlike the tedious complaints which were regularly received from governors and merchants in the Caribbean, these documents contained detailed information which could not be ignored. The documents came from Alexander Spotswood, the Lieutenant Governor of Virginia, and were characteristic of the man who would acquire a formidable reputation as the bane of the pirates and the nemesis of Blackbeard. He enclosed the sworn deposition of John Vickers, a former resident of the Bahamas who had fled to Virginia. Vickers described the recent raids of Jennings on the Spanish wrecks and shipping, and gave a disturbing account of the violent men who were terrorising the inhabitants of New Providence.[1] Spotswood also enclosed his letter of instructions to Captain Beverley, commander of the sloop *Virgin*, which commissioned him to investigate the current situation in the Bahamas (the number of inhabitants and the state of the forts) and ordered him to see whether any of the wrecked treasure ships were near any coasts or islands belonging to Britain and, if they were, to recover and save as much as he could and 'to assert the claim of His Majesty to the said wrecks by the Law of Nations as being within the jurisdiction of the Admiralty of Great Britain'.[2]

In his covering letter Spotswood provided a masterly account of recent events in the Bahamas. He described the settlement of the pirates on New Providence, the robberies they had inflicted on the French and Spanish, and the likely consequences of allowing such a crew of robbers to establish themselves on the island. He mentioned the capture of a ship of 32 guns by the pirates: 'What a vessel of this force, manned by a company of such desperadoes, may be able to attempt, is easy to imagine.' He considered that all these matters should be brought to the attention of His Majesty and his ministers and concluded that it was in the interest of Great Britain 'that some Government be speedily established in the Island of Providence and the place made defensible against the sudden attempt of pirates or the neighbouring Spaniards, who have so often obstructed the settlement thereof'.[3]

Spotswood had also ordered Captain Howard, the commander of HMS *Shoreham* on the Virginia station, to sail down to St Augustin on the Florida coast. He was to deliver various letters and investigate and report on the Spanish wrecks. Captain Howard's report was received by Mr Burchett at the Admiralty a few weeks after he had received Spotswood's documents. Captain Howard described how a number of sloops, with commissions from the Governor of Jamaica, were fishing on the wrecks and had gone ashore and taken 20,000 pieces of eight from the Spaniards. He said that the crews of three of these sloops had subsequently become pirates. 'One Hornigold, Jennings and Fernando who got two hundred men and are joined by a French man . . . they harbour at Providence where they re-victual and clean.'[4] In his view two small frigates or sloops would be able to rout them out before they acquired more strength.

The Lords of the Admiralty were so concerned about the letters from Governor Spotswood and Captain Howard that Mr Burchett was instructed to pass them on to the Council of Trade and Plantations and to George, Prince of Wales, who was acting as regent while his father, King George I, was paying an extended visit to Hanover. His Royal Highness ordered the Council of Trade and Plantations to consider what course the Government should take 'to dislodge those profligate fellows or pirates that may have possessed themselves of the Island of Providence'.[5]

Exactly how Woodes Rogers got to hear of these developments is not known, nor can we be sure whether it was his idea to put his name forward as Governor of the Bahamas or whether he was approached by some of the influential merchants of London and Bristol who traded with the West Indies. What we do know is that a key figure in the subsequent proposals for dealing with the problems of the Bahamas was a wealthy London merchant and shipowner called Samuel Buck. He had sent two of his ships, the *Samuel* and the *Sarah*, to New Providence in April 1716. They carried cargoes for trading but their captains were also instructed 'to view the state of that place to consider what improvement could be made, and how the pirates might best be dislodged, and a trade settled'.[6] The *Sarah* had been captured by pirates but when the *Samuel* returned Buck decided to set up a partnership with the aim of establishing a new settlement on Providence. He and five copartners would raise the money to send out ships, workmen and soldiers, and restore government to the islands, which had been sorely neglected in recent years.[7] In 1670 King Charles II had handed responsibility for the Bahamas to six aristocrats, including the Duke of Albemarle, Lord Craven and Lord Berkeley. As 'absolute Lords and Proprietors' they were given authority to enact laws and to appoint governors or deputy governors of the islands.[8] The governors whom they had appointed had failed to establish their authority or improve the defences, with the result that the islands had four times been attacked and plundered by the Spanish and were now without any form of government.

It may have been Samuel Buck who suggested that Rogers apply for the post of governor, or it may be that Rogers heard about the problems of the Bahamas and saw his opportunity. What is certain is that he abandoned his Madagascar project and by July 1717 was lobbying for the Bahamas post. He entered into partnership with the other sponsors and addressed a letter to the Lords Proprietors explaining that he and his partners had raised funds for an armed merchant ship and were proposing to take her to the Bahamas 'with such smaller vessels as shall be necessary to carry all things fit for a new settlement'.[9] The merchant ship would act as guardship to the settlement while fortifications were improved and barracks built for the garrison. He asked their lordships to grant him and his partners a twenty-one-year lease, on certain conditions – for instance, for the first seven years they would pay only a peppercorn rent.

Rogers also approached King George. He sent a paper which set out the current problems of the Bahamas and his offer to proceed to New Providence with a ship and a garrison to restore order. He also sent the King a petition in which he pointed out that he was 'conversant with remote undertakings' and was therefore emboldened to request that His Majesty might be graciously pleased to appoint him governor of the islands.[10] His proposals were accompanied by a petition signed by fifty-six merchants who traded with different parts of the King's dominions in America and had suffered severe losses at the hands of the pirates. They stressed the need to restore order in the Bahamas, which had been so often plundered by the enemy during the late war and were now at the mercy of loose people and pirates 'to the utter ruin of the industrious inhabitants and to the great prejudice of trade in general . . .'.[11]

In July 1717 another group of merchants sent a memorial to Joseph Addison, the poet and essayist who had co-founded the *Spectator*. In addition to his work as a writer and journalist Addison was also a Member of Parliament and had recently been appointed as one of the commissioners of the Council of Trade and Plantations. The merchants informed Addison of the strategic importance of the Bahamas, 'the key to the Gulf of Florida', and of the danger from the French and Spanish as well as the pirates. They expressed their support for Rogers' proposals for settling and securing the islands, and pointed out that he was a person of integrity and capacity. They recommended him 'as a person every way qualified for such an undertaking'.[12]

On 3 September Addison was able to report to the Council of Trade and Plantations that the King had agreed to a number of measures to deal with the situation in the West Indies. The Admiralty would be sending one fourth-rate and two fifth-rate men-of-war 'to suppress the pirates and protect the trade'. A proclamation was to be prepared to announce the royal pardon to those pirates who surrendered themselves within a certain time. And, being very well satisfied with the character given of Captain Woodes Rogers 'by the most considerable merchants of London and Bristol', the King was pleased to appoint Captain Rogers to be Governor of the Bahama Islands 'to drive the pirates from their lodgement at Harbour Island and Providence'.[13]

The newspapers duly reported that some men-of-war were to be sent to the West Indies and gave details of the royal pardon being promised to the pirates who surrendered, but they made no mention at this stage of Rogers' appointment. There had been a rash of robberies by highwaymen and others during that year and the details of these and the subsequent executions dominated the London news. The savage response of the authorities to these domestic crimes is worth noting because it puts in context the massed hangings of pirates which would take place in the colonies between 1718 and 1726.[14] In January 1717 three highwaymen had robbed the Bristol Mail coach at Brentford. They were caught two days later and were sentenced to death following their trial at the Old Bailey. They were hanged at Tyburn on 20 May. Eight people were hanged for burglary three weeks later. In August four people were hanged at Maidstone and a week later seven were executed at Kingston-upon-Thames, including a husband and wife found guilty of coining. The woman was burnt to death. Fourteen men and a woman were sentenced to death and were executed on 17 October. On 18 October the Irish Mail coach was held up by five highwaymen on Finchley Common, north of London. They robbed all the passengers, including a lady 'whom they stripped of her gold watch, rings, clothes, smock and all, leaving her naked, the coachman being obliged to wrap her in his greatcoat, and the lady forced to go home in that condition'.[15] Four of the five highwaymen were caught and later hanged. Lesser punishments recorded by the London newspapers included burning malefactors in the hand, public whippings, the pillory, fines and imprisonment in Newgate or Marshalsea prisons.

Six weeks after the decision to appoint him as Governor of the Bahamas a report appeared in the *Post Boy* newspaper. Readers were informed that 'Captain Rogers, who took the Acapulco Ship in the South-Seas' had kissed His Majesty's hand at Hampton Court Palace on being made Governor. A brief report a few days later declared that 'Captain Rogers sets out in a few days for his government of the Island of Providence', but this announcement was premature as it would be seven months before Rogers set sail from Spithead. In addition to preparing and provisioning his ship he and his copartners had to raise an independent company of soldiers and find people who would be prepared to settle on New Providence and help with the restoration of the fort, build houses and clear the land for planting crops. Not till the end of April 1718 would the squadron of warships and armed merchantmen be ready to embark on their mission.

Meanwhile the situation in the Caribbean was rapidly deteriorating. It is evident from many other reports received by the Council of Trade and Plantations around this time that the pirates were now operating right across the Caribbean and along the Eastern seaboard of North America, and had acquired some powerful vessels.[16] The seriousness of the situation was summed up by Peter Heywood, who had succeeded Archibald Hamilton as Governor of Jamaica. 'I think the pyrates daily increase, taking and plundering most ships and vessels bound to this island,' he wrote on 21 December. The pirates had landed on the leeward side of the island and robbed the local inhabitants and the situation was now so bad 'that no ships that are bound for Great Britain dare stir without a convoy . . .'.[17]

During the autumn and winter of 1717 and into the spring of 1718 Rogers, Buck and their partners made preparations for the expedition to the Bahamas. Four merchant ships were fitted out, loaded with cargoes suitable for trading in the West Indies, and supplied with seamen. The biggest of the ships was the 460-ton *Delicia* of 30 guns, which had a crew of ninety. She was accompanied by the 300-ton *Willing Mind*, 20 guns and twenty-two men; the 135-ton *Samuel*, of 6 guns and twenty-six men; and the seventy-five-ton sloop *Buck*, of 6 guns and twelve men.[18] The partners managed to assemble more than 100 men to form a company of soldiers, and some 200 civilians, some of whom were accompanied by women and children. Among the civilians were men with useful trades such as carpenters, coopers and builders. Enough basic provisions were bought to last for fourteen months, as well as tools and equipment for building houses, repairing fortifications and clearing the land. The intention was to plant enough crops of sugar, tobacco, ginger, indigo and cotton to enable the settlers to earn a living and the copartners to recover the costs of setting up the expedition. It was later estimated that the total cost of the ships, the wages of the sailors and soldiers and the cost of rebuilding the fort at Nassau amounted to more than £90,000.[19]

To accompany the merchantmen the Admiralty provided three warships: the fifth-rate ship *Milford*, 32 guns, commanded by Captain Chamberlain (promoted commodore in recognition of his role in charge of the squadron); the sixth-rate *Rose*, 20 guns, Captain Whitney; and the sloop *Shark*, 10 guns, Captain Pomeroy. All three ships were fitted out at the royal dockyards on the Thames. In mid-January 1718 the *Milford* was lying on moorings at Woolwich, the *Rose* and the *Shark* were at Deptford. Captain Whitney arrived at Deptford dockyard on 18 January and noted in his logbook that the *Rose* was in the wet dock, 'there being orders from the Lords Commissioners of the Admiralty to fit her for a foreign voyage to the southward'. During the next six weeks the ships were overhauled, their masts taken out and replaced, new rigging set up and stores and provisions taken on board. By 18 March they had left the dockyards and were anchored in Galleons Reach, the stretch of the Thames between Woolwich and Barking. There they were joined by the *Delicia*. In light winds and fair weather they made their way downstream, out of the Thames Estuary and round the North Foreland to the anchorage at the Downs, where they paused briefly so that Commodore Chamberlain could send letters ashore. Strong winds and squally weather greeted them as they entered the Solent on 25 April. After five days at anchor among the warships and smaller craft at Spithead, the *Milford* signalled to the squadron to weigh anchor. At 2 p.m. on 1 May they set sail for the West Indies. As they proceeded down the Channel they were joined by the *Samuel* and then by the transport ship *Willing Mind* and the sloop *Buck*.

It took them three weeks to reach Madeira, and at this point Chamberlain ordered the *Rose* to leave the squadron and press ahead to Barbados. He gave Captain Whitney instructions to find pilots to assist their arrival at New Providence. The rest of the squadron followed on more slowly towards the Bahamas. The *Rose* reached Barbados on 4 July and anchored in Carlisle Bay. Four days later, with a pilot on board, she headed north and made her way past Montserrat and Anguilla until 23 July, when her lookouts sighted the long, low-lying island of Eleuthera. At 3 p.m. the next day five ships were seen on the horizon. Whitney cleared his ship for action and headed south towards the distant sails. When he hailed the nearest ship he found it was the *Delicia* carrying Governor Rogers. As he drew closer to the three merchant vessels and their naval escort Whitney saluted the *Milford* with seven guns and received a seven-gun salute in reply. All the ships heaved to so that Whitney could be briefed by Commodore Chamberlain. It was agreed that they would wait till early next morning and then the *Rose* would go ahead and lead the way along the coast of Eleuthera, towards New Providence. They sighted their destination on the afternoon of 25 July and headed for the harbour entrance of Nassau, unaware of the hostile reception that awaited them.

Woodes Rogers had overcome many obstacles and faced many setbacks during his privateering voyage round the world but even for a man of his experience the situation in the Bahamas was daunting. He had been briefed on what to expect by merchants trading in the West Indies, and by the reports of colonial governors, but the reality of the situation on New Providence was worse than any of the reports.

Unlike Jamaica with its fine natural harbour and its mountains, valleys and pastures, the Bahamas consisted of more than 700 low-lying islands, many of them barren outcrops scattered with scrub and mangroves or sandy islets surrounded by coral reefs. Only a few of the islands were inhabited, notably Eleuthera, the nearby Harbour Island and New Providence. When Columbus crossed the Atlantic in 1492 his first landfall had been on one of the outer islands of the Bahamas. It was inhabited by Arawak Indians called Lucayans who had migrated there from South America. Columbus had named the island San Salvador and claimed it in the names of the Spanish monarchs King Ferdinand of Aragon and Queen Isabella of Castile. Failing to find any gold or silver in the Bahamas, the Spanish who followed Columbus more or less abandoned the islands. In 1629 England put in a formal claim to the Bahamas but no settlement took place until the 1640s and 1650s. When King Charles II handed responsibility for the Bahamas to the Lords Proprietors in 1670, there were a few people eking out a living on Eleuthera, and on New Providence some plantations of cotton and tobacco had been established and a small town had grown up along the waterfront of the harbour. Originally called Charles Town, this was renamed Nassau in 1695 in honour of King William III, who was from the Dutch house of Orange-Nassau. The harbour was relatively shallow and the approaches were not easy but the anchorage was protected by a low offshore island called Hog Island and provided a convenient base for merchant vessels and privateers.

The Spanish on the great islands of Cuba and Hispaniola resented the presence of the English interlopers in an area which they regarded as theirs by right of discovery and conquest. Relations varied between neutrality and outright hostility. Some of the inhabitants of New Providence made a useful income by recovering goods and treasure from the many ships wrecked on the reefs of the Bahamas. Most of the wrecked ships were Spanish, which provoked a savage retaliation against the islanders. We learn that 'their vessels were many times seized, their persons imprisoned and not seldom murdered and inhumanely treated by the Spaniards'.[20] In 1682 the Spanish made a concerted attack on New Providence from Cuba, destroying the plantations, demolishing houses, plundering the inhabitants and, according to one report, roasting alive the Governor, Colonel Clarke. Two years later the Spanish launched a second attack, destroying the new improvements, committing further barbarities and 'leaving those that escaped in a miserable condition dispersed in the holes and woods amongst the islands'.[21]

The various governors who followed Colonel Clarke conspicuously failed to exert their authority. Colonel Cadwalader Jones, who arrived in 1690, was regarded as such a useless and 'whimsical' man that he was twice imprisoned and once confined on a ship in the harbour under armed guard. His successor, Nicholas Trott, arrived in 1694 and was present when the notorious pirate Henry Avery sailed into the harbour in a ship laden with loot from the capture of a fabulous treasure ship in the Indian Ocean. Trott permitted Avery and his crew to share out their plunder and trade with the inhabitants. When Colonel Haskett arrived in 1701 his attempts to impose order were met by open rebellion. He was confined in irons for six weeks and then put on a boat and sent back to England. In 1703 the Spaniards landed again. They demolished the fort which the inhabitants had built, burnt down houses and took the Deputy Governor off to Havana as a prisoner. French privateers attacked the islands of Eleuthera and Exuma in 1708 and, according to the deposition of Elizabeth Stroude of the Bahamas, they beat and tortured the women to find out where they had hidden their wealth.[22]

By 1713 New Providence had become a regular meeting place for pirates. In that year the Governor of Bermuda warned the Council of Trade and Plantations that 'till the Bahamas are settled in some form they will still be a nest for pyrates; and we are now informed they are gathering together again, having riotously and quickly spent what they wickedly got'.²³ We have already seen the arrival in New Providence of the logwood cutters and former privateers like Henry Jennings, but in the years immediately preceding Rogers' arrival there had been further developments. By 1715 an unofficial leader had emerged from among the disparate crews and groupings of pirates based at Nassau. His name was Benjamin Hornigold. He had served aboard Jamaican privateers during the recent war and, after the Peace of Utrecht, turned to piracy. Unlike many of his fellow pirates he continued to regard himself as an English patriot and restricted his attacks to Spanish and French ships. He had begun his piratical career by using open boats to attack small merchant vessels and by the end of 1713 had brought back to Nassau plundered slaves, silks, rum, sugar and silver coins worth an estimated £13,175.²⁴ By 1715 he was attacking bigger ships off the coast of Cuba and in December of that year he captured a large Spanish sloop which he renamed the *Benjamin*. He armed her with ten carriage guns and sailed her back to Cuba with a crew of 200. Off the Cuban coast he joined forces with Sam Bellamy and the French pirate Olivier La Buse to form a formidable squadron of three pirate ships: the *Benjamin*, the *Marianne* (commanded by Bellamy) and La Buse's *Postillon*. Against Hornigold's wishes they captured an English ship in the Yucatan Channel and then two Spanish brigantines. By May 1716 Hornigold was back in Nassau, which was now gaining a reputation as a lawless and dangerous place.

A vivid picture of the state of things at this time is contained in the formal deposition of John Vickers which Alexander Spotswood had sent to London together with his own assessment of the situation. Like several other law-abiding citizens of New Providence,

Vickers had fled to Virginia. He described how Henry Jennings had arrived at the island on 22 April 1716 with a captured French ship which he had taken in the Bay of Hounds. Vickers claimed that 'there are at Providence about 50 men who have deserted the sloops which were upon the wrecks, & commit great disorders in that island, plundering the inhabitants, burning their houses, and ravishing their wives'. He mentioned that earlier in the year a pirate called Benjamin Hornigold had sailed out of Nassau in the sloop *Mary* with a crew of 140 men and had captured a Spanish sloop on the coast of Florida, and he went on to say that 'it is common for the sailors now at Providence (who call themselves the Flying Gang) to extort money from the inhabitants . . . many of the inhabitants of that island had deserted their habitations for fear of being murdered'.[25]

The leading member of Hornigold's crew was an impressive figure who would later be described by one of his victims as 'a tall spare man with a very black beard which he wore very long'.[26] This was a former privateer from Bristol whose name was variously recorded as Edward Teach, Thatch, Titche, Tatch and Tach, but who would become better known as Blackbeard. In the autumn of 1716 he was given command of a sloop which he had captured with Hornigold and for the next year he continued to cruise in company with Hornigold. Captain Johnson published a dramatic account of Blackbeard's life in his *General History of the Pyrates* of 1724, but the first mention in print of the man who would become the most notorious of all the Caribbean pirates was a report from Captain Matthew Munte. Sent to the Deputy Governor of South Carolina in March 1717, the merchant sea captain noted: 'Five pirates made ye harbour of Providence their place of rendezvous, viz. Hornigold, a sloop with 10 guns and about 80 men; Jennings, a sloop with 10 guns and 100 men; Burgiss, a sloop with 8 guns and about 80 men;

The English Ship Hampton Court in a Gale, by Willem van de Velde the Younger, *c.* 1680.
Captured in 1707, this ship later became the flagship of the Spanish treasure fleet which was
wrecked on the coast of Florida in 1715. *(Birmingham Museums & Art Gallery)*

A Spanish gold doubloon, minted in Mexico in 1714, and subsequently looted by pirates. The doubloon was a two-*escudo* coin and was worth the same as four pieces of eight. *(Private collection / Peter Newark Pictures / The Bridgeman Art Library)*

The 8-*reales* coin or 'piece of eight' was the most commonly used coin throughout Spain's empire in the New World. Also called a *peso* or Spanish dollar, it was a silver coin and usually had a design representing the pillars of Hercules on the reverse. *(Private collection)*

A pre-Columbian gold pendant in the form of a stylised human figure, from Popayan, Colombia. The gold found in the lands of the Aztec and the Inca empires was the driving force behind the exploits of the Spanish conquistadors. *(British Museum, London, UK / The Bridgeman Art Library)*

Queen Square, Bristol, Looking South-east, by T. L. Rowbotham. Captain Woodes Rogers' father bought a house in this elegant square and it later became the home of Rogers and his family. *(Bristol's Museums, Galleries & Archives)*

Merchant Ships off Dover, by Charles Brooking. The ship in the centre is similar in size and rig to the ships commanded by Woodes Rogers in his privateering voyage round the world. *(National Maritime Museum, Greenwich, London)*

An English Ship at Sea Driven Before a Gale, by Willem van de Velde the Younger, *c.* 1680. Woodes Rogers' ships had to contend with conditions even worse than this when rounding Cape Horn in January 1709. *(Rijksmuseum, Amsterdam)*

Engraving after Peircy Brett of the encampment set up by the men of Anson's expedition on the island of Juan Fernández in 1741. Woodes Rogers' crews had set up camp on the same spot in 1709 following their encounter with the marooned sailor Alexander Selkirk. *(By permission of the British Library)*

A Merchant Vessel Being Careened on a Tropical Shore, by Samuel Atkins. The brig has been beached and heeled on one side so that her carpenters can carry out repairs while the weed and barnacles are being burnt off the bottom. *(Private collection)*

An engraving from Edward Cooke's *A Voyage to the South Sea* showing the local Indians and the birds and fish from the Bay of Puerto Seguro (Cabo San Lucas) on the coast of California where Woodes Rogers' expedition spent several weeks. *(By permission of the British Library)*

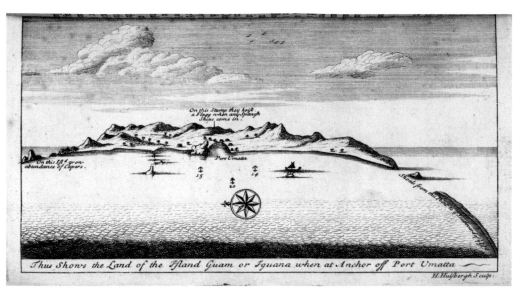

The island of Guam in the Pacific, which was used as a staging post by the westbound Spanish treasure galleons. Woodes Rogers called there on his homeward journey in 1710. The engraving is from Edward Cooke's *A Voyage to the South Sea. (By permission of the British Library)*

An Action Between English and French Privateers, by Samuel Scott. The privateer ship *Duke*, commanded by Woodes Rogers, would have looked very similar to the ship on the right when she went into action against the Manila galleon. *(National Maritime Museum, Greenwich, London)*

Portrait by Thomas Murray of William Dampier, the former buccaneer and explorer who sailed with Woodes Rogers' expedition as pilot for the South Seas. *(National Portrait Gallery, London)*

A painting from the school of Sir Godfrey Kneller of Daniel Defoe, novelist, journalist, political commentator, and the author of *Robinson Crusoe. (National Maritime Museum, Greenwich, London)*

Captain Woodes Rogers and His Family, by William Hogarth. The Governor of the Bahamas is shown seated beside the fort at Nassau along with his son, his daughter and a maidservant. *(National Maritime Museum, Greenwich, London)*

The female pirate Anne Bonny, who left her sailor husband for Calico Jack Rackam. She proved fiercer in action than her fellow pirates and told Rackam that 'if he had fought like a man, he need not have been hanged like a dog'. *(National Maritime Museum, Greenwich, London)*

Mary Read, who spent some years as a soldier in Flanders before joining the pirates led by Calico Jack. Following their capture in 1720 Mary Read and Anne Bonny were tried for piracy in Jamaica but were reprieved when they were found to be pregnant. *(National Maritime Museum, Greenwich, London)*

The execution of Major Stede Bonnet on the waterfront at Charleston, South Carolina. The pirate, who is holding a posy of flowers, has just been pushed off the back of a horse-drawn cart while the priest, who has heard his confession, looks on. *(Private collection)*

An engraving from Captain Johnson's *History of the Pyrates* depicting the formidable figure of Blackbeard the pirate. He is shown on a tropical shore, armed with a musket, a sword, several pairs of pistols, and with smoking matches stuffed under his hat. *(National Maritime Museum, Greenwich, London)*

Shipping anchored off the British settlement at Dix Cove near Cape Coast Castle on the west African coast where fifty-two of the pirates led by Bartholomew Roberts were hanged on the beach. *(National Maritime Museum, Greenwich, London)*

Captain Bartholomew Roberts and his ships on the coast of Guinea. Roberts captured more ships than any other pirate of his day but was tracked down by a naval expedition and killed in a battle off Cape Lopez in 1722. *(National Maritime Museum, Greenwich, London)*

Crusoe Sees a Footprint in the Sand, an illustration from an edition of *Robinson Crusoe* published in the 1860s. It was Woodes Rogers' description of Alexander Selkirk's life as a castaway which provided Daniel Defoe with the idea for his most famous book. *(Private collection)*

White, in a small vessel with 30 men and small arms; Thatch, a sloop 6 guns and about 70 men.'[27]

During the summer of 1717 Blackbeard was cruising off the coasts of Virginia and Delaware, where he made a series of attacks on merchant vessels which were duly reported in the *Boston News-Letter* and recorded in depositions from the captains of the ships captured. At some point in the autumn of the same year Blackbeard teamed up with Major Stede Bonnet, the most improbable of pirates. Bonnet was the son of a sugar planter on Barbados and had inherited the family estates. He had married a neighbour's daughter but, owing to 'a disorder of his mind' or 'some discomforts he found in a married state', he decided to abandon his wife and estates and take up piracy. He acquired a fine sloop of 10 guns which he named the *Revenge* and embarked on a series of raids. Exactly where and when he first met Blackbeard is not clear, but it is evident that Bonnet knew nothing about ships and lacked any ability to manage a pirate crew. Blackbeard offered to take over command of his ship, 'telling him that as he had not been used to the fatigues and care of such a post, it would be better for him to decline it and live easy, at his pleasure in such a ship as his . . .'.[28] It was later reported in the newspapers that Bonnet had been observed on board Blackbeard's ship and 'he had no command, he walks about in his morning gown, and then to his books of which he has a good library aboard'.[29]

Blackbeard made good use of the *Revenge*. On 28 November he was cruising in company with his smaller sloop *Adventure* some sixty miles west of Martinique when his lookouts spotted a large ship on the horizon. She was *La Concorde*, a French slave ship of 200 tons armed with 14 guns.[30] She had taken on board 516 African slaves at the coastal trading post of Whydah (now Ouidah in Benin). She had a crew of forty but during the voyage across the Atlantic half of the men had gone down with scurvy or dysentery. Confronted by two armed sloops, their decks lined with 250 pirates, the French captain, Pierre Dosset, decided against resistance and surrendered. A prize crew was put aboard her and the three ships sailed to the tiny island of Bequia, near St Vincent in the Grenadines. There the slaves were taken off and the ship was converted from a French Guineaman to a powerful pirate ship of 40 guns. She was renamed the *Queen Anne's Revenge* and became Blackbeard's flagship.

Recent research, and the discovery of the remains of the ship in the waters off Beaufort, North Carolina, have revealed a lot of information about her.[31] She had been built at Nantes in 1710 and was owned by the slave merchant René Montaudouin. After spending three years as a privateer in the Caribbean preying on English merchant vessels she had been adapted for the slave trade in 1713. Her first slaving voyage had taken her from Benin to Martinique and her second was from the River Congo to Saint Domingue (which became Haiti), both voyages proving highly profitable for her owner. The French report on the capture of *La Concorde* 'by Edouard Titche, English' indicates that only 455 of the 519 slaves survived her third slaving voyage.

Within weeks of the acquisition of his new command Blackbeard and his flotilla embarked on a piratical cruise among the Windward Islands. At the end of November it was reported that 'a great ship from Boston was taken at or near St Lucia or St Vincent by Captain Teach the pirate in a French ship of 32 guns'.[32] The captured ship was the *Great Allen*, commanded by Captain Taylor. Having whipped the captain to find out where he had hidden his money, the pirates plundered his cargo, put the crew ashore and set fire to his ship.

On 5 December the pirates intercepted the sloop *Margaret* a few miles west of Crab Island near Puerto Rico. Her master, Henry Bostock, later provided a detailed description of the incident.[33] He said that the pirates had stopped the *Margaret* with small-arms fire and ordered him to come on board the French Guineaman, where he met Blackbeard on the quarterdeck. He was asked what he had on board and when he said he had a cargo of cattle and hogs Blackbeard sent a boat across to the *Margaret* and took from her hold four beef cattle, thirty-five hogs, a barrel of gunpowder, five small arms, two cutlasses, the captain's books and instruments and some linen. Bostock was detained on board the pirate ship for eight hours. He was not abused in any way and was able to find out some useful information. He learnt that the pirate ship, which had been captured six or seven weeks before, had 36 mounted guns and a crew of around 300. As well as a ship well stocked with provisions Bostock saw 'a great deal of plate on board of them, tankards, cups, &c, particularly one of his men took notice of a very fine cup which they told him they had taken out of one Captain Taylor'.[34] In addition to setting fire to Taylor's ship the pirates, Bostock learnt, had burnt several other vessels, including 'a sloop belonging to Antigua one McGill owner'. Their current plans were to sail to Samana Bay in Hispaniola to careen and then lie in wait for the Spanish squadron due to sail from Havana to Puerto Rico with money for the garrisons.

By the time Rogers' expedition reached the Bahamas in July 1718 Blackbeard had moved on to the coast of North America and was terrorising the inhabitants of Charleston, South Carolina. Of more immediate concern to Rogers and his approaching squadron was the presence in Nassau harbour of Charles Vane, the most aggressive and brutal of the local pirate captains. As with most pirates, little is known of his background and early life. He seems to have been associated with Henry Jennings and may have joined him in plundering the Spanish wrecks, but he first came to prominence when news of the King's pardon for pirates reached New Providence. Copies of the royal proclamation were brought to Nassau by the son of Governor Bennett of Bermuda in December 1717 and caused conflict and divisions among the pirates. Most of them, notably Jennings and Hornigold, were prepared to accept the pardon but a hard-line group including Charles Vane, Paulsgrave Williams, Edward England and John Rackam refused to submit to the crown.

In February 1718 Captain Pearce, commander of HMS *Phoenix*, 26 guns, arrived at Nassau hoping to persuade more pirates to accept the royal pardon.[35] He found fourteen vessels lying at anchor. Some were flying English, Dutch, French or Spanish flags but several were flying black or red pirate flags. When he learnt that Vane, the leader of the rebellious pirates, had taken his sloop *Lark* to a nearby island, Captain Pearce tracked him down, forced Vane to surrender and escorted the *Lark* back to Nassau. The naval officer's resolute action had an adverse effect on those pirates who had already accepted the royal pardon. Alarmed that Vane and his crew would be executed, they told Pearce that more of the local inhabitants would surrender if Vane, England and the other fourteen men on the *Lark* were released. Pearce agreed to do so, and during the next two days he was gratified to receive the surrender of many more pirates. He had soon accumulated 209 signatures or marks on the necessary documents.

Vane had no intention of giving up piracy and he persuaded forty other men to sneak out of the harbour in two boats and capture a small Jamaican sloop that was sailing by. In defiance of the anchored British warship they brought the sloop into the harbour with a pirate flag flying at her masthead and proceeded to plunder her. An attempt by Pearce to board the Jamaica sloop was repulsed, and he later wrote, 'I several times summoned the inhabitants together in His Majesty's name and used all the arguments possible to prevail with them to assist me in suppressing the said pirate. But they always rejected all methods I proposed.'[36] His authority was constantly flouted during the following weeks. Three of his sailors deserted his ship and joined the pirates, and Vane's company was now more than seventy-five strong. With his ship increasingly vulnerable to attack, Pearce made preparations to depart. On 8 April the *Phoenix* sailed from Nassau in company with five merchant vessels and headed for New York.

Vane now embarked on a series of vicious attacks on passing merchant ships, three of them being documented in detail by some of the victims. On 14 April Vane intercepted the Bermuda sloop *Diamond* near Rum Key. Vane was sailing the sloop *Ranger* of 6 guns and had a crew of seventy. The pirates boarded the *Diamond*, stole 300 pieces of eight and a Negro slave, beat up the captain John Tibby and his crew and then hanged one of the seamen by his neck until he was almost dead. The seaman, Nathaniel Catling, would later testify that after they let him down on the deck, 'one of them perceiving he began to revive cut him with a cutlass over his collar bone and would have continued the same till he had murdered this deponent had not one of their own gang contradicted it, being, as he said, too great a cruelty'.[37] The captain was then forced to cut away his mast and bowsprit before the pirates set fire to the sloop.

The same day Vane and his men attacked another sloop, the *William and Martha* of Bermuda, under the command of Captain Edward North. They took everything of value on the vessel, and assaulted the captain and crew 'by beating them and using other cruelties, particularly to one, who they bound, hands and feet and tied (upon his back) down to the bowsprit with matches to his eyes burning and a pistol loaded (as he supposes) with the muzzle into his mouth, thereby to oblige him to confess what money was on board'.[38] North observed that while he was on board the pirate sloop he heard such expressions as 'Curse the king and all the higher powers' and 'Damn the Governor' and that the usual toast when drinking was 'Damnation to King George'.

On 19 April the Bermuda sloop *Samuel*, captained by Joseph Bossa, was attacked near Crooked Island by the *Ranger*.[39] The pirates stripped her of her cargo of dry goods, and again beat up the captain and the crew. From the various depositions given by the victims when they returned to Bermuda we learn that during this cruise Vane plundered at least twelve vessels, in each case subjecting the crew to beatings and other cruelties in revenge for the fact that the Bermuda authorities had imprisoned a man called Thomas Brown on suspicion of piracy. No records have come to light of Vane's activities in the subsequent weeks but, according to Captain Johnson, he was back in Nassau by 4 July with a number of prizes, including a French ship of 20 guns and a French brigantine laden with sugar, indigo, brandy, claret and white wine. He apparently stormed ashore with a sword in his hand and threatened to burn down the principal houses of the town, 'and tho he committed no murders, his behaviour was extremely insolent to all who were not as great villains as himself'.[40] For twenty days Vane ruled Nassau, stopping all vessels entering the harbour and preventing any ships from leaving. When he was informed that a governor had been appointed and was on his way from England, 'he swore, while he was in the harbour, he would suffer no other Governor than himself'.[41]

9

Welcome to Nassau

At 4 p.m. on 25 July 1718 the lookouts on HMS *Rose* sighted the eastern end of the island of New Providence. Captain Whitney had been ordered by Commodore Chamberlain to go ahead of the squadron and lead the way from the outer island of Eleuthera, past Harbour Island and the off-lying reefs, to Nassau. The 20-gun warship made good progress in a strong breeze and by 6 p.m. she was approaching the harbour entrance. The pilot guided her through the channel until she was able to drop anchor in three to four fathoms. Ahead was a long, narrow stretch of water with Hog Island on one side and the derelict waterfront of Nassau on the other side, the only prominent landmark being the crumbling walls and bastions of the fort. Thirty or forty merchant vessels of various nationalities were at anchor in the channel or were lying half-submerged in the shallows, their scorched black timbers indicating that they had been set on fire before sinking.[1] Several of the vessels at anchor were stripped of their fittings and some were missing masts, bowsprits and rigging. There were a few visiting trading ships and brigs but most in evidence were the pirate sloops – powerful-looking vessels in good order and well armed with carriage guns and swivel guns.

The largest vessel in the anchorage was a French-built merchant-man of 22 or 24 guns which was flying the St George's flag of England at her maintopmast head. To the surprise of Captain Whitney and his crew she fired three shots at the *Rose*. Whitney lowered a boat and sent his first lieutenant across to know the reason for this hostile action. The lieutenant discovered that the captain of the ship was the pirate Charles Vane. Most of his crew appeared to be drunk and when Vane was asked why he had opened fire 'his answer was, he would use his utmost endeavour to burn us, and all the vessels in the harbour that night'.[2]

At around 7 p.m. the *Shark*, the *Buck* and the transport ship *Willing Mind* negotiated the harbour entrance and anchored near the *Rose*. The larger ships *Delicia* and HMS *Milford* remained outside until they could get a pilot to guide them in. That evening Charles Vane made his preparations. He shifted his men and valuables into two shallow-draft vessels and loaded the guns of his French prize with double shot and partridge shot. At midnight he set the ship on fire and towed her towards the new arrivals. All wooden ships were extremely vulnerable to attack by fireships. Naval ships with their magazines loaded with barrels of gunpowder were particu-larly vulnerable, but what made the situation at Nassau even more dangerous was the narrowness of the channel and the shallows on either side. Fortunately the British sailors were alert. As the flaming ship bore down on them, they hacked through their anchor cables, set their topsails and managed to escape out of the harbour without running aground.

The next morning the ships made their way back into the harbour, all except the *Milford* and *Delicia*. A local pilot had come aboard the *Milford* at 6 a.m. but he mistook the height of the tide and as they approached the entrance both ships ran aground on the harbour bar, where they remained for the next two hours. By the time they got into the harbour Vane had set sail with all his men in a schooner and a sloop of 10 guns. With their shallow draft they were able to escape out of the confined channel at the eastern end of the harbour. By the time the sloop *Buck* and another sloop had been despatched to track him down, Vane was on his way. 'When he perceived our sloops, he took down his St George's flag, and hoisted a black flag, which is their signal to intimate that they will neither give or take quarter.'[3] The sloops followed Vane out to sea but they had to abandon the chase, 'finding he out-sailed them two foot to their one'.

During the afternoon the *Milford* and the *Delicia* were anchored in the deeper part of the channel not far from the fort. Officers were sent ashore to meet the local inhabitants and assess the situation. The captain of the *Shark* sent a boat with some men to locate and recover the anchor, which they had cut loose during the night.

The next day, Sunday 27 July, was cloudy with rain early in the morning and a fresh breeze tugging at the flags and rattling the rigging of the anchored ships. At 10 a.m. Captain Woodes Rogers, now His Excellency Woodes Rogers, Esquire, Governor, Captain-General and Vice-Admiral of the Bahama Islands, prepared to go ashore. Accompanied by Commodore Chamberlain and the men he had brought with him to assist him in governing the islands, he was rowed across the harbour in the longboat of the *Delicia*. As the boat passed each of the warships he was greeted with an eleven-gun salute. By the time he stepped ashore a large crowd had gathered at the water's edge to greet him. The descriptions of his reception vary. Rogers himself simply wrote, 'I landed and took possession of the Fort, where I read out his Majesty's Commission in the presence of my officers, soldiers and about three hundred of the people here, who received me under arms and readily surrendered shewing then many tokens of joy for the re-introduction of government.' Captain Pomeroy in a letter to the Admiralty confirmed that the

Governor was received 'with a great deal of seeming joy by those that stile themselves marooners' and reckoned there were no fewer than 400 to 500 people on the island. The most picturesque description of the scene comes from an additional chapter which Captain Johnson added to his *General History of the Pyrates*. According to his version, Rogers was greeted by Thomas Walker, the chief justice, and by Thomas Taylor, the president of the council, and by the pirate captains Hornigold, Davis, Carter, Burgess, Courant and Clark. The pirates 'drew up their crews in two lines reaching from the water-side to the Fort, the Governor and other officers marching between them; in the meantime, they being under arms, made a running fire over his head'.[4]

There are very few references to the appearance of Nassau at this time. Before the Spanish raids there appears to have been a small but thriving community with some farms and plantations, but we have seen that on at least three occasions the Spanish landed on New Providence, burnt down and demolished the houses and plundered the inhabitants so that they fled to the surrounding woods for shelter. The arrival of the pirates and logwood cutters must have led to the construction of some buildings on the waterfront for shipwrights and carpenters and for shops and taverns, but it seems likely that it was little more than a shanty town. We know that the fort was in ruins and that soon after Rogers' arrival one of the bastions facing the sea fell down, 'having only a crazy cracked wall in its foundation'. There were certainly a few houses in reasonable condition, including one which would become the Governor's house, but there was no accommodation for the soldiers, so sails had to be brought ashore from the ships and makeshift shelters constructed within the walls of the fort. The roads and pathways were overgrown with bushes and undergrowth. What would have struck the newcomers more than the derelict condition of the town was the foul stench which came from a vast pile of cow hides. This was blamed on the pirates 'having sometime before the Governor's arrival, having brought in great quantities of raw hides which putrefied and infected the air so much that it killed all ye cattle that were on the island, and afterwards infected the inhabitants so that many of the people carried from England died of the same contagion'.[5]

At this time it was still believed that many diseases were spread by poisonous vapours or miasmas in the air. It was not known that mosquitoes were responsible for spreading malaria and yellow fever or that cholera was a waterborne disease which was transmitted to humans through eating food or drinking water contaminated with the cholera bacteria. The rotting and foul-smelling cow hides were unlikely to have been directly responsible for the sickness which overwhelmed the community but were indicative of dangerously unhygienic conditions which could have led to cholera, the most likely killer in this case. A later report on Rogers noted 'that he was in danger of intestine commotions, and weakened by contagious diseases soon after his landing, that destroyed above half the best people he brought with him'.[6] The logbook of HMS *Milford* records the death of the surgeon, the master and two crew members within a week of their arrival at Nassau.[7] Rogers' first report to London lists the names of eighty-six soldiers, sailors and passengers who had died after his arrival. It would be the first and most devastating blow to his plans for the reconstruction of the community.

Rogers' first task was to appoint a Council and officers to help him rule the islands. After making enquiries about the characters of those inhabitants who were not pirates, he held an Assembly on 1 August. Twelve men were appointed to the Council. Six of these were drawn from the people he had brought with him. These included Robert Beauchamp, who was made Secretary General and First Lieutenant of the Independent Company of Soldiers; and Christopher Gale, who was made Chief Justice because he had proved 'an honest and genteel character' during his thirteen years as Chief Justice in North Carolina. Six of the councillors were local inhabitants. The next task was to offer the royal pardon to the pirates. Two hundred of these came forward and took the oath of allegiance to King George.

On 5 August a formal council was held at the Governor's house and a number of practical measures were drawn up and agreed. The first of these was to repair the fort, to mount as many guns as possible and to clear the brushwood and shrubs within gunshot of the fort. Among the other resolutions passed at this and subsequent assemblies were the following: each inhabitant was to be responsible for clearing the ground of the lot they possessed; where there were vacant lots a person could apply to the Secretary's Office, enter his or her name in a book, and could then 'build a habitable house according to the present manner of building in this island'; a palisade was to be constructed around the fort and every male aged between eighteen and sixty was to bring along to the fort ten sticks of straight wood nine foot in length for this purpose; every man who understood stone-laying was to assist in the building works; and all male Negroes were to report to the fort at six o'clock every morning for ten days to assist in the speedy repair of the structure.[8]

A list drawn up on 31 October indicated the items that were urgently needed and not available on the island. At the head of the list were guns: eight twenty-four-pounders and eight eighteen-pounders; 150 small arms with bayonets and 100 pistols. Tools were next on the list: sixty pickaxes, sixty iron spades and 'a large smiths bellows, anvil and all manner of tools to furnish a shop'.[9] And finally a number of workmen were needed: six house carpenters, eight bricklayers and masons with tools, three blacksmiths and twenty able-bodied labourers.

In spite of the sickness decimating the new arrivals, some good work was carried out in the first month or so. Urgent repairs were carried out on the fort, and a smaller fort of eight guns was erected to guard the eastern entrance of the harbour. The inhabitants were formed into three companies of militia and were organised to keep a regular watch at night. Rogers noted, 'The people did for fourteen days work vigorously, seldom less than two hundred men a day.'[10] And on hearing news that Charles Vane had been seen in the vicinity of Green Turtle Key, about 120 miles north of New Providence, with some captured vessels, Rogers commissioned the reformed pirates Captain Hornigold and Captain Cockram to become pirate hunters. They set off in a sloop to track down Vane and report on his movements.

It was perhaps inevitable that the initial enthusiasm which greeted the arrival of Rogers' expedition would not last. By the end of October Rogers was reporting that 100 of the pirates who had accepted the royal pardon had taken up piracy again. He reckoned they were 'weary of living under restraint and are either gone to several parts of North America, or engaged themselves on services at sea'.[11] The local inhabitants soon returned to their old ways, preferring an idle life to serious labouring. And in spite of Rogers' entreaties and his warnings about possible attack from the Spanish, the commanders of the naval ships which had acted as his escort abandoned the settlement to its fate. The *Milford* and the *Shark* left Nassau on 16 August and headed for New York. The *Rose* left four weeks later also bound for New York. Rogers and his people were left with the armed merchantman *Delicia* to defend the harbour and act as a guardship.

Charles Vane continued to pose a threat. Following his hasty departure from Nassau he had roved around the Bahamas. He had captured two sloops and a brigantine and then headed for South

Carolina. According to the *Boston News-Letter* he had taken eight vessels off the Carolina coast while in command of a brigantine of 12 guns and ninety men.[12] He was accompanied by Charles Yeats, who was in a large sloop of 8 guns with a crew of twenty men, but Yeats had then deserted him and sent a message to the Governor of South Carolina that he and his crew wished to surrender and take advantage of the King's Pardon, 'which being granted, they all came up and received certificates'.[13]

On 30 August the large merchant ship *Neptune* and three other vessels set sail from Carolina bound for London. What happened next was recorded in a long and complicated deposition which John King, the commander of the *Neptune*, swore before Rogers several months later.[14] Four hours out from the American coast the merchant vessels were intercepted by Vane's brigantine, which came alongside Captain King's *Neptune* 'with a black flag flying, and after having fired several guns, demanded him to strike'.[15] Vane put prize crews on board each of the merchantmen and led them to Green Turtle Key. There the pirates careened the brigantine and proceeded to plunder their prizes. The arrival of a sloop with bad news from New Providence prompted the pirates to maroon and attempt to destroy the *Neptune* by cutting away her masts and rigging and then firing a gun down into her hold.

Meanwhile Hornigold and Cockram had located Vane but had decided that he was too powerful for them to risk an attack. They kept him under observation and when he sailed away they put in an appearance. They told King that they would go back to New Providence and return with more sloops so that they could recover his cargo. Eventually King and his ship and most of his cargo were rescued and brought into Nassau. It was around this time that Vane sent word to Rogers that he intended to visit him and burn his guard-ship in revenge for the Governor having sent two sloops after him.

This was his final act of defiance. In November his refusal to attack a French warship led his crew to vote him out of his command. John Rackam, his quartermaster, replaced him as commander of the brigantine and sailed away, leaving Vane in a sloop with the remnants of his crew. In the winter or early spring of 1719 Vane ran into a storm and was shipwrecked on a deserted island off the Bay of Honduras. He was later captured, and was hanged in Jamaica.[16]

Rogers had heard nothing from Hornigold for three weeks. 'I was afraid he was either taken by Vane or [had] begun his old practice of pirating again which was the general opinion here in his absence.'[17] He was therefore delighted when Hornigold returned, bringing with him the sloop which had been trading with Vane at Green Turtle Key. A few weeks later Rogers despatched Hornigold and Cockram on another pirate-hunting expedition and this time they intercepted a pirate sloop off the coast of Exuma, which lay to the south of Nassau. A brief fight took place in which three of the pirates were killed but the remaining ten men were brought back to Nassau and delivered up to the Governor. On 24 December 1718 Rogers despatched the first of his letters to James Craggs the Younger, who was Secretary of State for the South and his main contact in London. In his letter he expressed his full confidence in the behaviour of the two reformed pirate captains. In particular, 'I am glad of this new proof Capt Hornigold had given the world to wipe off the infamous name he has hitherto been known by, though in the very acts of piracy he committed most people speak well of his generosity.'[18]

The pirates captured by Hornigold presented Rogers with some problems. The first was to find a suitable place to confine the prisoners because there was no jail on the island and a shortage of soldiers to guard them. This problem was addressed by imprisoning them on board the guardship *Delicia* out in the harbour. A more serious problem was that Rogers did not believe he had the legal powers to order a trial for piracy. There was also a danger that 'should any fear be shewn on our part, it might animate several now here, to invite the pirates without to attempt a rescue of these in custody'. Given the number of former pirates around, as well as those who had rejected the royal pardon and were on ships in the vicinity, there was every likelihood that they might combine together to mount a rescue attempt. Rogers was also aware that if he diverted too many soldiers or sailors to act as guards the all-important work on the fortifications would be jeopardised.

A private meeting of Rogers' senior officers and legal advisers on 28 November 1718 noted that the Government of Carolina had recently executed twenty-two pirates, and decided that Rogers' instructions and directions as Governor, Captain-General and Vice-Admiral did give him the authority to order a trial. The meeting reached the conclusion that 'We are entirely of opinion his Majesty will approve of the necessity for the Governor's judicial proceeding with these pirates, by a trial in the best manner we can according to law; and do verily believe the speediest execution for those who shall be found guilty, will conduce most to the welfare of this Government.'[19] The stage was set for an event of high drama which would have repercussions across the Caribbean.

Hanged on the Waterfront

The trial of the ten men accused of mutiny and piracy took place on Tuesday 9 and Wednesday 10 December 1718 at a special Admiralty Sessions sitting in accordance with an Act of Parliament which had been passed in 1700.[1] Before that date all pirates captured in the British colonies had had to be sent back to London to be tried under the jurisdiction of the High Court of Admiralty. If found guilty the pirates were hanged at Execution Dock on the Thames waterfront near the Tower of London. The 'Act for the More Effectual Suppression of Piracy' ended the requirement to send the accused men back to England and enabled Admiralty Courts to be held overseas. These courts were usually presided over by the colonial governor sitting with a judge and six or seven local merchants, planters or the captains, lieutenants or warrant officers of British warships in the vicinity. They had the authority to impose the death sentence. There had been very few pirate trials in the colonies during the War of the Spanish Succession but from 1717 a number of pirate trials were held at Boston, Massachusetts; Charleston, South Carolina; James Town, Jamaica; Newport, Rhode Island; and Williamsburg, Virginia. It was usual for the pirates to be hanged on the waterfront and the dead bodies of the more notorious pirates were displayed on gibbets set up at a harbour entrance as a warning to sailors.

Woodes Rogers presided over the trial at Nassau and was assisted by William Fairfax, who acted as Judge of the Admiralty, and by six others, including Robert Beauchamp, Thomas Walker and Captain Wingate Gale, the commander of the *Delicia*. The setting of the trial was grandly described as 'his Majesty's Guard-Room in the City of Nassau'. We know from a later description that the guard room was a simple timber building which had been erected within the walls of the fort. It had been built on the orders of Rogers soon after his arrival. It measured thirty-six feet in length and was nineteen feet wide and sixteen feet high. It cannot have been a very solid structure because it was totally demolished in a hurricane in 1729.[2]

The ten accused men were brought into the room and ordered to stand at the bar while the lengthy accusation against them was read out. They were aged between eighteen and forty-five and were a mixed bunch of seamen. The oldest of them, William Cunningham, had been a gunner with Blackbeard. William Lewis, aged thirty-four, was a former prizefighter. Thomas Morris, twenty-two, was described as an incorrigible youth. He would prove defiant and unrepentant to the end.

The formal accusation against the men was couched in such tortuous legal language that it must have been almost incomprehensible to them. The most serious charge was that most of them had 'lately received the benefit of his Majesty's most gracious pardon, for your former offences and acts of robbery and piracy' but, 'not having the fear of God before your eyes, nor any regard to your oaths of allegiance to your Sovereign, nor to the performance of loyalty, truth and justice; but being instigated and deluded by the Devil', had been persuaded 'to return to your former unlawful evil courses of robbery and piracy'.[3] This preamble was followed by a detailed description of their offences. In brief they were accused of mutiny on board three vessels at anchor at Green Key; they had combined together to rob the cargoes of the vessels and had sailed away with one of the vessels; and they had marooned five men on Green Key, a deserted island seventy miles south of New Providence. On being asked how they intended to plea, all of them pleaded not guilty. The witnesses for the prosecution included all five of the men who had been marooned, with the addition of Captain Greenaway, the commander of one of the vessels, who provided the clearest description of what had taken place.

According to Greenaway, the schooner *Batchelor's Adventure* and the sloops *Mary* and *Lancaster* were anchored at Green Key on 6 October when the mutiny took place. Greenaway had rowed across to the schooner to inform her commander that he intended to sail that night. He had been confronted by Phineas Bunce, who had ordered him down into the cabin and told him he was a prisoner. Dennis Macarty then 'presented a pistol at this deponent's breast, and told him if he spoke a word he was a dead man'.[4] Bunce, the leader of the mutiny (subsequently killed when the mutineers were intercepted by Hornigold), told Greenaway that most of the crew of the *Mary* were on his side and he was taking command of the vessel. Five of the sailors refused to join Bunce and they were put ashore on Green Key. Greenaway was not marooned with them because the mutineers thought that because he was a Bermudian he would be able to swim back to one of the anchored vessels. He was therefore made a prisoner while they plundered his vessel. As they sailed away they warned Greenaway that he must remain where he was for twenty-four hours. Greenaway ignored this direction and set sail for New Providence the next morning. He was sighted by the pirates, who took him back to Green Key and cut away the mast of his vessel and scuttled it. While they were doing this Greenaway escaped and hid on the island until the pirates departed.

The other witnesses provided additional information. During the mutiny Bunce had demanded and drunk two bottles of beer and had struck a man with his cutlass. And John Hipps, Captain Greenaway's boatswain (and now one of the prisoners at the bar), had been forced to join the pirates by threats that he would otherwise be beaten and marooned on a deserted island. After hearing all the evidence the court adjourned for lunch. At 3 p.m. the trial continued and the afternoon was devoted to hearing the defence of the prisoners. A number of witnesses spoke in favour of Hipps and confirmed that he had been compelled to join the pirates and that he intended to desert them at the first opportunity. The other prisoners could offer little or nothing in their defence. Macarty had been heard to say that 'he was sorry for his unadvisedness, which might bring great troubles on his poor wife, having a small child'.[5]

The court assembled at ten o'clock the next morning. The prisoners were brought in and each was asked if he had anything further to say in his defence. Hipps again produced witnesses to speak in his favour, but the eighteen-year-old George Bendall had been heard to say that he wished he had become a pirate sooner because he thought it a pleasant life. The evidence for and against the prisoners was then debated and considered. All except Hipps were unanimously found guilty. It was agreed that judgement on Hipps should be delayed till the following week. The remaining nine prisoners were then informed that they had been found guilty of mutiny, felony and piracy. Their names were read out and the awful words of the death sentence were pronounced. They were to be 'carried to prison from whence you came, and from thence to the place of execution, where you shall be hanged by the neck till you are dead, dead, dead; and God have mercy on your souls'.[6] Rogers, as president of the court, announced that their execution would take place in two days' time at 10 a.m.

Early on the morning of 12 December each of the pirates was asked if he had anything to confess which might be a 'load upon their spirits' but none of them had anything to declare. At ten o'clock they were released from their irons. The Provost Marshal pinioned their hands and ordered the guards to take them up to the ramparts of the fort, which looked out across the harbour and the sea beyond. In the presence of about 100 soldiers and supporters of the Governor a service was held with prayers and psalms selected at the prisoners' request. When the service was finished the pirates were taken down a ladder to the ground at the foot of the walls, where a gallows had been erected. A black flag had been hoisted above the gallows and below was a temporary stage resting on three large barrels. The condemned men climbed another ladder to get on the stage and the hangman fastened a noose around each man's neck. Three-quarters of an hour passed while some more psalms were sung and the men were allowed to take a final drink and say any last words. John Augur, aged forty, who had spent many years in command of vessels at Jamaica, appeared extremely penitent. He was unwashed, unshaven and wearing his old clothes. He had been given a small glass of wine on the ramparts which he drank 'with wishes for the good success of the Bahama Islands and the Governor'.

William Golding and William Ling also behaved in a penitent manner and George Bendall was sullen. By contrast the 28-year-old Dennis Macarty had changed his clothes and wore long blue ribbons at his wrists, knees and on his cap in the manner of a prize-fighter. He appeared cheerful and defiant. Up on the ramparts he had declared that there was a time when the many brave fellows on the island would not have allowed him to die like a dog 'and at the same time pulled off his shoes, kicking them over the parapet of the fort, saying he had promised not to die with his shoes on'.[7] Three of the others were equally defiant. Thomas Morris, aged twenty-two, wore ribbons like Macarty but in his case they were red ribbons. 'We have a new governor,' he said, 'but a harsh one.' And he wished that he had been a greater plague to the islands than he had been. William Lewis, thirty-four, who had actually been a prizefighter, appeared unconcerned about his imminent death and asked for liquor to drink with his sufferers on the stage and with the onlookers. William Dowling, twenty-four, who was reputed to have lived a wicked life and spent much time among the pirates, had confessed that he had murdered his mother before he left Ireland. His behaviour on the stage was described as 'very loose'.

At the last moment, just as the condemned men were expecting the order for the hanging to be given, Rogers asked for young George Rounseval to be untied and led off the stage. He was the son of 'loyal and good parents at Weymouth in Dorsetshire', and Rogers, who had been born and raised in that county, must have felt some sympathy for him.[8] He later wrote on his behalf to London in the hope that the royal pardon could be extended to him. As soon as Rounseval was clear of the gallows the barrels holding up the stage were hauled away, 'upon which, the stage fell, and the prisoners were suspended'.

The hangings at Nassau have become one of the best-known and most often quoted events in the history of the pirates of this period.[9] This is partly because full details of the trial and execution of these pirates have been preserved, but also because it was one of the landmarks in the British Government's campaign against piracy. It marked the end of Nassau and the island of New Providence as a base for the pirates and it was a clear signal to the hundreds of pirates still operating in the Caribbean that the Bahamas were no longer a free zone for piracy. Rogers still had many setbacks and misfortunes ahead of him but the pirates were no longer a major problem. It would be for other colonial governors and the Royal Navy to track down and bring to trial the pirates who had dispersed. Some had headed south to the Windward Passage and the eastern Caribbean, some to the east coast of North America and a few to the west coast of Africa.

Three weeks before the hangings at Nassau another key event in the campaign against the pirates had taken place among the mudbanks and shallows of Ocracoke Inlet off North Carolina. This was the death of Blackbeard. His career as a pirate leader had lasted no more than two years and yet in that time he had established a reputation which eclipsed those of all other pirates of his day. His exploits were reported in the newspapers and subsequently inspired eighteenth- and nineteenth-century plays and melodramas and later several Hollywood movies.[10] He continues to be the subject of books and documentary films, the interest in him no doubt boosted by the discovery in 1996 of the remains of a ship which is almost certainly the *Queen Anne's Revenge*. Unlike with pirates such as Charles Vane, Edward Low and Bartholomew Roberts, there is no evidence to show that Blackbeard or his crew killed or wounded anyone during their attacks on shipping, nor is there any record of his torturing his victims. His fame seems to have been largely due to the violent and dramatic circumstances of his death and the vivid account of his brief life and ferocious appearance which appears in Captain Johnson's *General History of the Pyrates*. We know from several sources that Blackbeard had a long black beard but it is Johnson who supplies the other memorable details about him. According to Johnson, he would go into battle with three brace of pistols hanging in holsters from a sling round his shoulders and would stick lighted matches under his hat 'which appearing on each side of his face, his eyes naturally looking fierce and wild, made him altogether such a figure, that imagination cannot form an idea of a fury from hell to look more frightful'.[11]

It is Johnson who tells us that Blackbeard married a young girl of sixteen, this being his fourteenth wife, and that after he had lain with her at night it was his custom to force her to prostitute herself with five or six of his crew while he watched. And Johnson also has the story of Blackbeard drinking one night with Israel Hands and two others in his cabin. Unobserved by them, he draws and cocks two pistols under the table, blows out the candle, crosses his hands and fires, shooting Israel Hands through the knee. When asked why he did this his only answer is to swear at them and tell them 'that if he did not now and then kill one of them, they would forget who he was'.[12]

While some of this may be the product of Johnson's imagination, there is reliable evidence for Blackbeard's brazen attack on the town of Charleston, South Carolina. On 22 May 1718 the *Queen Anne's Revenge* and three pirate sloops appeared off the harbour bar of the busy port. When a pilot boat went out to meet them the pilot and his crew were taken captive. During the course of the next few days Blackbeard and his men intercepted and plundered eight merchant ships as they entered or left the harbour. These included the ship *Crowley*, commanded by Captain Clark, which was bound for London; the *William* from Weymouth, Captain Hewes; a brigantine with a cargo of African slaves; and a ship from Boston. With a number of Charleston's citizens held hostage on board his pirate ships, Blackbeard made an unusual demand. In the words of Robert Johnson, the Governor of South Carolina, 'Several of the best inhabitants of this place . . . then sent me word that if I did not immediately send them a chest of medicines they would put every prisoner to death.'[13] Several theories have been put forward to explain the pirates' urgent need for medicines, the most likely theory being that some of Blackbeard's crew were suffering from venereal disease. The usual treatment for syphilis at this period was an injection of mercury – and one of the objects recovered from the wreck of the *Queen Anne's Revenge* was a metal syringe which proved on analysis to contain a high concentration of mercury.

Captain Richards, who commanded one of the pirate sloops, was despatched by Blackbeard to fetch the medicines. He was accompanied by Mr Marks, a local resident, and Blackbeard made it clear that if Richards or Marks failed to return he would sail over the bar and burn all the ships in the harbour. To save the lives of the hostages Governor Johnson and his council 'complied with the necessity and sent aboard a chest valued at between £300 and £400, and the pirates went back safe to their ships'. After stripping the hostages of their valuables and sending them ashore, the pirate flotilla lifted the blockade of the town and sailed away.

Blackbeard now came up with a devious plan to rid himself of his flagship and most of his crew. We can only guess at his motives. He may have realised that his recent exploits were likely to spur the authorities into hunting him down (which would prove to be the case). The *Queen Anne's Revenge* was too conspicuous a target and her deep draft made her unsuitable for hiding among the shallow creeks of Pamlico Sound or Chesapeake Bay. He may have decided that after his relatively successful stint as a pirate he wanted to pursue a quiet life. He was certainly intending to apply for the royal pardon at some time in the near future. Whatever Blackbeard's motives his solution was a drastic one. Around the beginning of June his flotilla arrived off Topsail Inlet (now called Beaufort Inlet), a relatively narrow channel between the sand dunes leading to the town of Beaufort, which was then a small village. The *Queen Anne's Revenge* led the way up the channel and as she drew level with Beaufort she was deliberately run aground on a submerged sand bar. Israel Hands, in command of the sloop *Adventure*, was asked to help tow her off but, since he was part of Blackbeard's plot, he simply towed the big ship further on to the sand bar, and then ran his own vessel aground. Both vessels were wrecked beyond repair.

Major Stede Bonnet, who was still aboard the *Queen Anne's Revenge* in an honorary capacity, was persuaded by Blackbeard to seek the royal pardon from Governor Eden of North Carolina. While Bonnet was away Blackbeard and twenty or thirty selected members of his company fitted out one of the two remaining sloops, plundered the other vessels of loot, provisions and gear and then sailed out of Topsail Inlet, leaving more than 200 of his pirates behind. For some reason Blackbeard wanted to teach a lesson to one group of pirates. According to Captain Johnson's account he arranged for seventeen members of his company to be marooned on a small sandy island 'where there was neither bird, beast or herb for their subsistence, and where they must have perished if Major Bonnet had not two days after taken them off'. Bonnet returned to find a lot of disgruntled pirates marooned on the island or abandoned ashore at Beaufort. He had been granted a pardon by Governor Eden but foolishly, and fatally, decided to return to piracy. With some loyal followers in the sloop *Revenge* (later renamed the *Royal James*) he set off to find Blackbeard but, failing to find him, he cruised off the mouth of the Delaware River, where he captured and looted a number of small merchant vessels.

In September 1718 Bonnet was tracked down by a pirate-hunting expedition led by Colonel William Rhett, a war hero and a leading member of the South Carolina Assembly. Rhett's two armed sloops found Bonnet's *Revenge* with two of her prizes at anchor in Cape Fear River. A confused and hard-fought action followed on a falling tide among the shoals. Three of the vessels ran aground. The sloop with Rhett aboard and Bonnet's *Revenge* were grounded within musket shot of each other. For nearly six hours 'they were engaged very warmly, until the water rising set our sloops afloat, about an hour before the pirate, when Col. Rhett making the signal, and they prepared to board him, which the pirate seeing, sent a white flag, and after a short time surrendered'.[14] Rhett's privateers lost fourteen men killed and sixteen wounded in the action; the pirates had seven killed and five wounded.

Bonnet and his crew were put on trial at Charleston on 28 October. The judge described Bonnet as 'a gentleman that have had the advantage of a liberal education, and being generally esteemed a man of letters' but, far from helping the defendant's case, this was held against him.[15] Bonnet was found guilty of piracy and sentenced to death. He was overwhelmed by the verdict. 'His piteous behaviour under sentence very much affected the people of the province, particularly the women, and great application was made to the Governor for saving his life, but in vain.'[16] Twenty-nine members of Bonnet's crew were executed on 8 November and Bonnet himself was hanged on the waterfront at Charleston a month later.

11

Blackbeard's Last Stand

After abandoning his flagship and most of his crew Blackbeard sailed
north-east along the Outer Banks of North Carolina to Ocracoke
Island. This was a remote and deserted place surrounded by shoals
and sandbanks. The southern shores of the island faced the breaking waves of the Atlantic Ocean, but on the side facing the sheltered
waters of Pamlico Sound was the narrow channel of Ocracoke Inlet.
Here, in the summer of 1718, Blackbeard dropped anchor. For the
next few months he used this as a base for his sloop *Adventure*. He
also took a house in Bath Town, then a small settlement on the banks
of a creek on the other side of Pamlico Sound. By the end of June
he had secured a meeting with Governor Eden and had obtained the
royal pardon for himself and his pirates.[1] For about two months he
seems to have lived a settled and respectable life, dividing his time
between Bath Town and Ocracoke, but by August he had returned
to plundering passing merchant ships. He was now in the sights of
Alexander Spotswood, Lieutenant Governor of the nearby colony
of Virginia.

Spotswood, like Captain Woodes Rogers, was a resolute and
determined man with an interesting past. He was born in 1676, the

son of an army surgeon serving in the English military garrison at Tangier.[2] At the age of seven he came to England and was educated at Westminster School. He joined the army in 1693 and spent the next seventeen years as an officer. He served under Marlborough in Flanders, was wounded at the Battle of Blenheim and was captured but later exchanged at the Battle of Oudenarde. In 1710 George Hamilton, Earl of Orkney and one of Marlborough's most able generals, was appointed Governor of Virginia. Not wishing to leave Britain, he selected Spotswood as his Lieutenant Governor with full authority to run the colony. Spotswood proved an energetic Governor. As we have seen earlier, he had warned the British Government of the growing danger to the American colonies posed by the pirates and he now decided that Blackbeard was such a threat that he must be hunted down. As he later wrote to the Council of Trade and Plantations, 'I judged it high time to destroy that crew of villains, and not to suffer them to gather strength in the neighbourhood of so valuable a trade as that of this colony.'[3]

There were two warships assigned to the Virginia station and they were currently anchored in the James River, not far from Williamsburg, the capital of Virginia. The largest of the ships was the 40-gun *Pearl*, commanded by Captain Ellis Brand. The other ship was the *Lyme*, 24 guns, commanded by Captain George Gordon. Both ships had orders from the Admiralty, 'To correspond and act in concert against the pirates.'[4] When Captain Brand and Captain Gordon were summoned to a meeting with Governor Spotswood and told that he wished to mount an expedition against Blackbeard they were happy to give him their support. The warships were too big to negotiate the shallows around Ocracoke, so Spotswood hired two local sloops, the *Ranger* and the *Jane*, and the navy provided the men – thirty-three from the *Pearl* and twenty-four from the *Lyme*. They were put under the overall command of Robert Maynard, the first lieutenant of the *Pearl*, and each sloop had a local pilot to guide them through the channels of the Outer Banks. Lieutenant Maynard's log survives and his entry for Monday 17 November 1718 marks the day that the expedition set sail:

> Modt. gales & fair Weather, this day I recd. from Capt. Gordon, an Order to Command 60 men out of his Majesties Ships Pearle & Lyme, on board two small sloops, in Order to destroy some pyrates, who resided in Nº Carolina. This day Weigh'd, & Sail'd hence, with ye Sloops undr. my Command, having on board a month Proviso. Of all species, with Arms, & Ammunition Suitable for ye Occasion.[5]

It was not known whether Blackbeard was on his sloop at Ocracoke or was staying in Bath Town, so while Maynard's sloops sailed down the James River and along the coast, Captain Brand led an overland expedition to Bath Town. He had around 200 men under his command, including sailors from the warships and a company of Virginia militiamen. As it happened, Blackbeard was at Ocracoke with twenty-five of his pirates. (Israel Hands and the rest of his crew were across the Sound in Bath Town.) When Lieutenant Maynard arrived on the seaward side of Ocracoke Island on the evening of 21 November there was a local trading sloop anchored in the channel near Blackbeard's *Adventure*. Samuel Odell, the master of the local sloop, and two or three of his crew were being entertained by Blackbeard and his men. Maynard decided to delay his attack till the next morning.

At dawn on 22 November Maynard commenced his approach. The sea was calm, the sky overcast and there was only the lightest of breezes to help them on their way. A boat was sent ahead with a sailor taking soundings. If heavy casualties were to be avoided it was essential to surprise the pirates because Maynard's sloops had no guns and his men had weapons suitable only for a boarding action: muskets, pistols, cutlasses and boarding axes. The *Adventure* was armed with nine carriage guns which could do a great deal of damage before the attackers were within musket shot of the pirates. Although the various accounts of the action differ in many respects it seems that the element of surprise was lost because the pirates spotted the attackers while they were still some way off and fired a shot in their direction. A shouted exchange took place between Maynard and Blackbeard with Maynard telling the pirate that he intended to board him.

'Teach understanding his design, told him that if he would let him alone, he would not meddle with him; Maynard answered that it was him he wanted, and that he would have him dead or alive; whereupon Teach called for a glass of wine, and swore damnation to himself if he either took or gave quarters.'[6] Blackbeard ordered several of his carriage guns to be fired at the approaching sloops. These apparently did less damage than a discharge from a swivel gun loaded with swan shot, nails and pieces of old iron. The attacking force was decimated. Midshipman Hyde, commanding the sloop *Ranger*, was killed instantly and twenty other men were either killed or wounded. According to Maynard, the *Ranger*, having no one to command her, fell astern and took no further part in the action until it was almost over.

Blackbeard had cut his anchor cable and was intending to sail out of the channel but the attackers managed to shoot away the jib and fore halyards of the *Adventure*, which drifted on to a shoal and grounded. To save further casualties Maynard hid most of his men below deck as he approached the pirate sloop, so that Blackbeard, 'seeing so few on the deck said to his men, the rogues were all killed except two or three and he would go on board and kill them himself'.[7] It is not clear whether the final battle took place on board the *Adventure* or the sloop *Jane*, but what is in no doubt is that Blackbeard and Maynard engaged in a hand-to-hand fight as the rest of the British sailors swarmed on deck and took on the pirates. Maynard attacked Blackbeard with his sword but bent it on the pirate's cartridge box. When Blackbeard's sword broke the naval officer's guard and wounded his fingers Maynard was forced to step back and use his pistol. His shot found its mark but had no immediate effect on Blackbeard, who was now surrounded by Maynard's men. According to Captain Johnson's vivid account of the action, 'he stood his ground and fought with great fury'.[8] The final blow came from a Scottish Highlander who struck Blackbeard with such force that he cut off his head.

There were several black Africans in Blackbeard's crew and one of them had remained below, ready to blow up the ship if the order was given. He was prevented from doing so by two of the men from the trading sloop who had also remained below during the fighting. Blackbeard's death marked the end of action. His headless body was thrown overboard and those pirates who were still alive surrendered. Every account of the action gives different figures for the casualties but it is evident that the fighting was exceedingly fierce and the deck must have been running with blood. According to Maynard, 'I had eight Men killed and 18 wounded. We kill'd 12, besides Blackbeard, who fell with five Shot in him, and 20 dismal Cuts in several Parts of his Body. I took nine prisoners, mostly Negroes, all wounded.'[9]

Maynard took command of the *Adventure* and, with Blackbeard's head hung from the bowsprit, he sailed back to Virginia to rejoin his ship and report on the success of his mission. He reached the James River on 3 January 1719. It was a fine winter's day with a light breeze. The warships *Pearl* and *Lyme* were still lying at anchor in the river. Lieutenant John Hicks of the *Pearl* recorded the occasion in his logbook, 'Little wind & fair weather. Tache ye Pyrate

Sloop commanded by Lieut Maynard anch'd here & Saluted us with 9 Guns we Answ'd with ye same number he brought Tache ye pyrates head undr his Bowsprette.'[10]

Displaying the pirate's head so prominently as a war trophy was an unusual action for a British naval crew but it was in line with the custom of displaying the dead bodies of notorious highwaymen, thieves and pirates in prominent public places as a warning to others. And Maynard needed to bring back the head of the notorious pirate as proof of his death and to enable him and his men to claim the reward. Back in November Governor Spotswood had issued a proclamation to encourage the capture or killing of any pirate or pirates within the vicinity of Virginia or North Carolina:

> for Edward Teach, commonly called Captain Teach, or Black-beard, one hundred Pounds, for every other Commander of a Pyrate Ship, Sloop, or Vessel, forty Pounds; for every Lieutenant, Master, or Quarter-Master, Boatswain, or Carpenter, twenty pounds; for every other inferior Officer, fifteen pounds, and for every private Man taken on board such Ship, Sloop, or Vessel, ten pounds.[11]

Political considerations and bureaucratic delays held up the payment of the rewards for several years. There was less delay in the trial and execution of the pirates. Captain Brand had rounded up Israel Hands and one or two others in the vicinity of Bath Town and on 12 March 1719 sixteen men were put on trial in the Capitol building at Williamsburg. Samuel Odell, the captain of the trading vessel which had been anchored alongside Blackbeard's sloop, was acquitted. Hands was allowed the benefit of the royal pardon, probably because he had agreed to testify against his shipmates. According to Johnson, writing in 1724, Hands 'was alive some time ago in London, begging his bread'.[12] The fourteen remaining members of

Blackbeard's crew, including five black Africans, were hanged on the road leading out of Williamsburg.

These executions, together with the executions of Stede Bonnet and his crew at Charleston, and the executions at Nassau, were significant events in the campaign against the pirates but they did not relieve the pressure on Rogers. His reports and letters to London indicate the many problems he was facing. He had been so ill for weeks after arriving in Nassau that he had had difficulty in carrying out some of his duties. The local inhabitants continued to prove lazy and so unproductive that it was hard to find sufficient provisions to feed the soldiers of the garrison. But his chief concern was the withdrawal of the naval ships which had accompanied him to the Bahamas. In a letter to Secretary James Craggs he pointed out that the lack of a ship of war was likely to have grave consequences 'by encouraging the loose people here and even some of my own soldiers'. He had uncovered a plot 'to seize or destroy me and my officers and then deliver up the fort for ye use of the pirates'.[13] He had dealt with the ringleaders of the plot by having them severely flogged but he continued to worry that the former pirates in the community would turn against him.

He was equally concerned that the absence of a warship in the harbour left the settlement extremely vulnerable to an attack by the Spanish. There had been growing hostilities between Spain and the other European powers throughout the summer of 1718 owing to the territorial ambitions of King Philip V of Spain and his forceful Italian wife Elizabeth Farnese. A Spanish expedition sent to conquer Sicily prompted the British to send a powerful naval force to the Mediterranean under the command of Sir George Byng. Although there had been no formal declaration of war Byng attacked the Spanish fleet off Cape Passaro on 31 July 1718. The Spanish were outnumbered and outmanoeuvred and by the end of an extended action stretching over several days twenty-two of their warships had been captured, burnt or sunk. War was officially declared on 17 December. Known as the War of the Quadruple Alliance, it pitched Spain against Britain, France, Austria and the Netherlands. Brief as it was the war had repercussions in the West Indies and the American colonies. By February 1719 Rogers had received news that the Spanish intended to attack and conquer the Bahamas.[14] In May a Spanish invasion fleet sailed from Cuba. With four warships, eight sloops and around 3,000 troops this posed a formidable threat to New Providence, where the fortifications were still incomplete and there was only the *Delicia* and a few armed sloops to defend the harbour. Fortunately the Spanish fleet was diverted to Florida because the French had seized a strategically important fortress at Pensacola. Not till the following year did the Spanish make an attempt on the Bahamas, by which time Rogers was in a much stronger position.

When the invasion force arrived off Nassau on 24 February 1720 Rogers had at his disposal 100 soldiers and nearly 500 local militiamen; the fort was armed with fifty mounted guns and the 10-gun eastern battery had been completed; and in addition to his 40-gun guardship *Delicia*, there was a naval warship in the harbour – HMS *Flamborough*, 24 guns, which happened to be paying a visit. The logbook of the *Flamborough* recorded the first sighting and approach of the Spanish fleet: 'at 6 AM saw 12 Sail in the Offing standing for the harbour mouth, We made 'em to be 3 Ships, 1 Brigantine and the rest Sloops, At noon the Ships anchored off the Bar and the Brig & Sloops sailed to the E end of Hogg Island & there anchored, They all hoisted Spanish Colours.'[15]

Later information revealed that the Spanish invasion fleet was led by the flagship *San José* of 36 guns; she was accompanied by the *San Cristóforo*, 20 guns; a third ship of 14 guns; a 12-gun brigantine; and eight armed sloops. They were carrying a military force of between 1,200 and 1,300 men. In theory the Spanish were considerably superior in ships and men to the British defenders, but an amphibious invasion force was invariably at a disadvantage when faced with well-manned forts and gun emplacements; and on this occasion the Spanish also had to contend with the weather. For some reason the Spanish admiral decided against launching an immediate attack but waited until the next day. And the next day a strong north wind built up during the morning so that the fleet found itself on a lee shore with waves breaking on the shoals and reefs off the harbour entrance. By 3 p.m. the situation had become so hazardous that the vessels in the fleet cut their anchor cables and headed for the open sea. The three ships never came back but at around eleven that night the brigantine and the sloops returned and, according to the *Flamborough*'s log, 'attempted to land their men but two Negroes firing into their Boats they put back again to their vessels'.[16] That was the end of the invasion. Some of the sloops remained off the coast for the next few days but on 1 March they headed back to Cuba. Several weeks later Rogers received a letter from two Englishmen in Havana who had been informed that the Spanish fleet had been hit by a storm two hours after arriving off Nassau and had been forced to lose their anchors and bear away. The Englishmen had some doubts about this version of events and reported that most of the ships 'have all returned again to their safe harbour whether it was distress of weather or fear (which we are more apt to believe) that hath thus baulked their attempt we doubt not . . .'.[17] However, the danger from the storm was very real because on the return voyage the *San Cristóforo* was wrecked on the Bahama Banks.[18]

Having successfully prevented a Spanish invasion and having expelled the pirates from New Providence, Rogers had every reason to expect a favourable reaction to the reports he sent home. He also

deserved a sympathetic and practical response to his requests for
the reimbursement of the money he and the copartners had spent
on defending the island. Instead he heard nothing and received
nothing. There was no response from the Council of Trade and
Plantations to his first detailed report, and no replies to the many
letters he wrote to Secretary Craggs updating him on progress. It is
little wonder that the opening sentence of his second report to the
Council, written two months after the abortive Spanish invasion,
revealed his sense of abandonment: 'My Lords, Its about twenty one
months since my first arrival here attended with as great disappoint-
ments, sickness and other misfortunes as almost can be imagined of
which I have continually advised in the best manner I could, and
I have yet no account from home what is or will not be done for
the preservation of this settlement.'[19] He went on to point out that
'having no news of my bills being paid at home I am forced to run
into too much debt and its with great difficulty that I have hitherto
supported myself and the garrison'. In December of the previous
year Samuel Buck, on behalf of the copartners, had sent a petition
to their lordships pointing out that they had already spent £11,394
on the fortifications, and further sums on the seamen's wages for
the guardship *Delicia* and on commissioning the sloops and crews
which had been despatched to track down the pirates. The total sum
to date was more than £20,000 and he humbly besought their lordships to present the estimates to Parliament for payment.[20]

During the summer of 1720 an incident took place which was
minor in itself but revealed the tensions which Rogers was under. On
the evening of 10 July the sentry on the eastern bastion challenged
a boat which had set off from the shore and was heading across the
harbour. The sentry challenged fifteen times without receiving an
answer, and was therefore ordered by Rogers to fire two shots at
the boat. The crew promptly yelled back that they were from the

Delicia. Rogers immediately summoned Captain Wingate Gale, the commander of the guardship, to come ashore. When Gale refused to do so, Rogers collected his Provost Marshal and twelve soldiers and went out to the ship with a warrant to put its commander under arrest. Rogers' justification for this was that Gale had disobeyed his commands and 'I was driven to apprehend him myself by force to prevent the mischievous consequences of his ill example, or his raising a mutiny against me.'[21] According to one witness, Captain Gale armed his men in order to resist the soldiers coming on board but several other witnesses denied that the captain or his men were armed and that Captain Gale 'offered no resistance until Governor Rogers called him a rascal and struck him with his pistol upon the head'.[22] Rogers ordered Gale to be put in close confinement all night and the next morning called a Council, which agreed that if Gale gave his word for his future good behaviour he could be released from custody.

The incident gives added credence to the remarks of Dr Thomas Dover, who, it will be recalled, noted several instances of Rogers' hot temper and his violent threats to those who opposed him. But it is clear from Rogers' correspondence that it was not the Spanish, or problems with his Council or his colleagues, which were proving an intolerable burden. It was his grave concerns about the finances of the islands, and his own ever-increasing debts, which were making him ill. Soon he would be driven to seek leave of absence in order to recover his health. Before he did so the pirates caused another diversion. It was a diversion which had its origins in the Bahamas but would reach its much publicised conclusion on the island of Jamaica.

12

Calico Jack and the Female Pirates

It was Woodes Rogers who first alerted the outside world to the presence of women among the pirates of the Caribbean. On 10 October 1720 *The Boston Gazette* printed a news item and two proclamations which had been despatched from New Providence a month earlier. The news item informed readers that among the pirates on the coast of the Bahamas was 'one Rackum who run away with a sloop of 6 guns and took with him 12 men, and two women'. It went on to say that the Governor of the Bahamas had sent a sloop with forty-five men after them, and some time later Dr Rowan with his 12-gun sloop and fifty-four men had also set out to track down the pirates.

The first of the two proclamations issued by Rogers concerned a pirate attack on the sloop *Recovery* of Nassau by a company of pirates led by John Lewis. The second proclamation provided further details of the piracy committed by John Rackam and his associates. It announced that on 22 August 'John Rackum, George Featherstone, John Davis, Andrew Gibson, John Howell, Noah Patrick, &c. and two Women, by Name, Ann Fulford alias Bonny, & Mary Read' had stolen and run away with a sloop called the *William*, of about twelve tons, 'mounted with 4 great Guns and 2 swivel ones, also ammunition, sails, rigging, anchor, cables, and a canoe owned by and belonging to Capt. John Ham'. The pirates had gone on to rob a boat on the south side of New Providence as well as a sloop riding at Berry Islands, some thirty miles to the north. The proclamation concluded that John Rackam and his company 'are hereby proclaimed pirates and enemies to the Crown of Great Britain, and are to be so treated and deemed by all his Majesty's subjects'.[1]

This was a sensational announcement because seafaring was then regarded as an exclusively male occupation. Women went to sea as passengers, of course, and it was not uncommon for wives on naval and merchant ships to accompany their husbands on ocean-going passages. A few examples have come to light of young women dressing as men in order to spend months and sometimes years at sea working as sailors but they were so rare that when their sex was revealed they tended to become minor celebrities – Hannah Snell, who served in the British army and the navy in the eighteenth century, later performed on the London stage. Women pirates were an even greater rarity. There was Alwilda, the daughter of a Scandinavian king who had taken command of a company of pirates and roamed the Baltic in the fifth century AD. She had fought a battle in the Gulf of Finland and had eventually become Queen of Denmark. And there was the brave and resourceful Grace O'Malley, whose exploits along the west coast of Ireland in the sixteenth century are well documented. From her base at Rockfleet Castle, overlooking Clew Bay in County Mayo, she led a fleet of around twenty galleys on punitive raids against rival chieftains. She attacked and plundered passing merchant ships, provoking such a storm of protest that the English governor of the province sent an expedition to besiege her castle. She fought off this challenge but in 1577 was caught during a raid and imprisoned in Limerick gaol for eighteen months. Constantly forced to defend her territory from aggressive neighbours she famously appealed to Queen Elizabeth I. They met at Greenwich Palace in September 1593 and O'Malley made such an impression on the English queen that she was granted 'some maintenance for the rest of her living of her old years'.[2] She died at Rockfleet in her seventies and her son eventually became Viscount Mayo.

Apart from these isolated examples there are no documented accounts of women pirates in the western world until the appearance of Anne Bonny and Mary Read, so it is not surprising that when Captain Johnson came to write his history of the pirates he devoted considerable space to their lives and drew particular attention to 'the remarkable actions and adventures of the two female pyrates' on the title page of his book. Although the printed record of their trial provides us with detailed information about their appearance and behaviour while they were members of Rackam's crew, the only information we have about their early lives comes from Johnson. No evidence has come to light to substantiate his colourful account, which is a pity because, as he himself admits, 'the odd incidents of their rambling lives are such, that some may be tempted to think the whole story no better than a novel or romance'.[3]

According to Johnson, Mary Read was born in England. Her mother had married a sailor and had a son, but the sailor went away to sea and never returned. Left on her own, the young mother had a brief affair and became pregnant. To conceal this from her relations she went to stay with friends in the country, where she gave birth to Mary. Soon after this her son died and she decided to pass her daughter off as her son and to ask her wealthy mother-in-law for financial assistance. Mary was brought up as a boy and when she was thirteen she was sent out to work as a footboy for a French lady. She soon grew tired of this menial life and, having 'a roving mind', she travelled to Flanders and joined a foot regiment as a cadet. She fought in several engagements, fell in love with a handsome Flemish soldier with whom she was sharing a tent and duly married him. After leaving the army they set up as proprietors of a public house near Breda called the Three Horse Shoes. Mary's husband died shortly after this, so she assumed men's clothing again and after a spell in another foot regiment she boarded a ship and sailed to the West Indies. Her ship was captured by pirates and after further adventures she found herself on the ship commanded by Rackam with Anne Bonny among the crew.

Anne Bonny was born near Cork in Ireland. Her father was a lawyer and her mother was a maid in the lawyer's household. When the lawyer's wife learnt of her husband's affair they separated. The lawyer was so fond of the girl he had by the maid that he decided that she should live with him. He dressed her as a boy and pretended that he was training her to be a lawyer's clerk. When the true circumstances were revealed the scandal affected his practice, so he emigrated to Carolina, taking the maid and their daughter Anne with him. Anne grew up to be a bold and headstrong young woman and in 1718 she married a penniless sailor named James Bonny. This so upset her father, who was now a successful merchant and plantation owner, that he threw her out of the house. Anne and her sailor husband sailed to New Providence, where he hoped to find employment. According to Johnson, it was in Nassau that James Bonny found that his wife, 'who was very young, turned a libertine upon his hands, so that he once surprised her lying in a hammock with another man'. She also attracted the attention of John Rackam, 'who making courtship to her, soon found means of withdrawing her affections from her husband'.

It will be recalled that Rackam had been a member of Charles Vane's crew. He had taken part in the spate of pirate attacks which

Vane had undertaken in the weeks before Rogers' arrival, and he was with Vane when he escaped from the harbour at Nassau after the fire-ship attack on the warships which had escorted the new Governor to the Bahamas. In November 1718 Vane had broken off an action with a French warship against the wishes of the majority of his crew. The next day, by a general vote of the pirates, Vane had been replaced as captain by Rackam, his quartermaster. Rackam took command of the pirate brigantine and sailed away, leaving Vane with a sloop and the remnants of the crew. Rackam had headed for Jamaica. On 11 December he captured the merchant ship *Kingston* off the harbour of Port Royal and in sight of the inhabitants. The ship had such a valuable cargo that her owners promptly fitted out two privateers and set off in pursuit. They tracked Rackam to the Isle of Pines, off the south coast of Cuba. From Sir Nicholas Lawes, the Governor of Jamaica, we learn that, upon the approach of the privateers, 'the pirates who were on board the ship, made their escape on shore in a canoe, and the two sloops are returned into Port Royal harbour with the ship and the greatest part of her cargo'.[4] Rackam and his men eventually managed to make their way to Nassau, where they persuaded Rogers to grant them the royal pardon.

At some point Rackam had acquired the memorable nickname of Calico Jack 'because his jackets and drawers were always made of calico'.[5] He would now acquire lasting fame by his association with the female pirates. His recent piracies had provided him with enough loot to live in some luxury and his generosity towards Anne Bonny evidently contributed to her wish to leave her sailor husband. In the Appendix to the first volume of his history Johnson includes a curious description of what happened next. It seems that Anne wished Rackam to give James Bonny a sum of money in order to persuade him to give up his claim on her so she could live with Rackam. Furthermore she wanted this arrangement to be put in writing and confirmed by witnesses. Word soon got round the small community of Nassau 'so that the Governor hearing of it, sent for her and one Anne Fulworth, who came with her from Carolina, and passed for her mother, and was privy to all her loose behaviour, and examining them both upon it, and finding they could not deny it, he threatened if they proceeded further in it, to commit them both to prison, and order them both to be whipped'. Anne thereupon promised to be very good, to live with her husband and to avoid loose company in the future.

Anne did not keep her promise for very long. Having run out of money, Rackam decided to return to piracy. He had his eye on John Ham's 6-gun sloop *William*, which was noted for its speed and was currently at anchor in the harbour. On his behalf Anne went on board the vessel on several occasions to find out how many men were usually on the vessel and what sort of watch was kept. She learnt that the owner slept on shore at night and that only two men remained on board to keep watch. Armed with this useful information, Rackam decided to act at once. He assembled fourteen pirates, including Anne Bonny and Mary Read, and at midnight they rowed out to the *William*, which was lying very close to the shore. The night was dark and it was raining so they got on board without anyone raising the alarm. They had no difficulty in overcoming the men on watch. Anne went straight to their cabin with a drawn sword in one hand and a pistol in the other, and 'swore that if they pretended to resist, or make a noise, she would blow out their brains'. One anchor was heaved in, the other anchor cable was let loose and a small sail was set to give them steerage way. Passing close to the fort, they were challenged and asked where they were going. They explained that their anchor cable had parted and they told the same story to the men on the guardship. When they reached the harbour mouth, and reckoned that they could not be seen because of the darkness of the night, they hoisted all sail and stood out to sea. John Ham's two seamen were unwilling to join the pirates, so they were given a boat to enable them to row ashore.

From Nassau they sailed east to Eleuthera and along its low-lying coast until they sighted the settlement of wooden houses on Harbour Island. A mile or so off the white sandy beaches of that beautiful island they intercepted seven fishing boats and systematically robbed the local fishermen of their fish and fishing tackle and any money and valuables they could find. To avoid any search parties sent out by Rogers they headed south to the great island of Hispaniola, where they landed to steal some cattle and then attacked two British sloops which they found sailing offshore. According to witnesses, they 'did make an assault in and upon one James Dobbin, and certain other mariners' and then plundered the vessels of gear and tackle 'of the value of one thousand pounds of current money of Jamaica'.[6] Continuing their passage south, they sailed through the Windward Passage to the north coast of Jamaica, where they proceeded to plunder any easy target they came across. On 19 October they intercepted the schooner of Thomas Spenlow a few miles off Port Maria. They assaulted Spenlow and his crew, putting them 'in corporeal fear of their lives', and seized fifty rolls of tobacco and nine bags of pimiento (sweet pepper). They kept Spenlow and his men prisoner for forty-eight hours before releasing them and their schooner.

Sailing into the bay of Dry Harbour, they fired a gun at the merchant sloop *Mary and Sarah*. Thomas Dillon, the master of the vessel, and his crew escaped ashore in a boat to the accompaniment of shots from Rackam's sloop. When Dillon hailed the attackers he was told that they were English pirates, that he need not be afraid, and they urged him to return to his ship. Dillon later swore on oath that there were two women on the pirate sloop and that 'they were both very profligate, cursing and swearing much, and ready and willing to do any thing on board'.[7] According to Dillon, the pirates then took over the merchant sloop and her cargo and 'carried her with them to sea'. It is not clear whether he was forced to accompany them or whether he returned to shore. From Dry Harbour they continued sailing west and the last of their victims was Dorothy Thomas, a Jamaican woman who was in a canoe filled with provisions. As Rackam's sloop came alongside, the female pirates encouraged their shipmates to kill the woman 'to prevent her coming against them'. Dorothy Thomas would later provide the most damning evidence against Mary Read and Anne Bonny. She said that they 'wore men's jackets and long trousers, and handkerchiefs tied about their heads; and that each of them had a machet and pistol in their hands, and cursed and swore at the men, to murder the deponent'.[8] She further said that she knew them to be women by the largeness of their breasts.

By the beginning of November the pirates were off Negril Bay at the western end of Jamaica. Today this is a tourist resort and the seven-mile expanse of beach is lined with smart hotels, but in the eighteenth century it was a desolate spot. Beyond the beach was nothing but swamps and mangroves. Towards evening two sloops on a trading voyage to Cuba hove in sight. One of them was commanded by Captain Bonnevie, the other by Captain Jonathan Barnet. Back in 1715 Barnet had applied to Lord Hamilton, then Governor of Jamaica, for a commission to capture pirates. He was granted the commission on condition that he keep a fair journal of his proceedings; that he did not attack any British ships or those of His Majesty's allies, friends or neutral nations; that before he set sail from Port Royal he deliver a list containing the names of his crew to the chief officer of the customs; and that he fly a union flag which was distinguished from those worn by His Majesty's ships by a white square or escutcheon in the middle of the flag.[9] It is not known whether Barnet had renewed his commission, but the new Governor of Jamaica, Sir Nicholas Lawes, would later inform London that a trading sloop 'being well manned and commanded by a brisk fellow one Jonathan Barnet did us a very good piece of service . . .'.[10]

Bonnevie hailed Barnet and told him he could see a sloop lying close inshore which had fired a gun. Barnet, whose vessel was well armed, decided to go and investigate. At around 10 p.m. he came up with the anchored vessel and hailed her. The response was, 'John Rackam of Cuba.' Barnet ordered him to strike immediately to the King of England's colours. One of the pirates replied that they would strike no strikes and immediately fired a swivel gun at Barnet's sloop. At this Barnet ordered his men to fire a full broadside and a volley of small shot. The effect of this was to carry away the boom of the pirate sloop, which effectively disabled her. The pirates called for quarter and surrendered to Barnet and his men. They were taken ashore at Davis's Cove, a few miles beyond Negril Point, and were delivered into the custody of Major Richard James, a militia officer.[11] The major assembled some men to guard the pirates and took them across the island to the jail in Spanish Town (then known as St Jago de la Vega).

The trial of the pirates was held before Sir Nicholas Lawes as President of the Admiralty Court and twelve commissioners. These included two naval captains, one of whom was Captain Edward Vernon, who was commander-in-chief of British naval ships on the Jamaica station and later, as Admiral Vernon, led British attacks on Portobello and Cartagena. Calico Jack and the ten male members of his crew were tried on Wednesday 16 November 1720. The female pirates were tried twelve days later. The charges concerned the attacks off Harbour Island, off Hispaniola and off the north coast of Jamaica. Because the prosecution was able to call eyewitnesses to confirm the 'piracies, felonies, and robberies committed by them on the high sea' the result was a foregone conclusion and all the men on trial were found guilty and condemned to death. The day after the trial five of the pirates were hanged at Gallows Point, and the rest were hanged the next day. The bodies of Calico Jack, George Fetherston and Richard Corner were taken down from the gallows and hanged in chains at Gun Key, Bush Key and Plumb Point, where they could be seen by the sailors on ships sailing into and out of the harbour of Port Royal.

The trial of Anne Bonny and Mary Read followed similar lines because the charges against them were exactly the same. What the court had to determine was whether the women had played an active part in the piracies and, as we have already noted, Thomas Dillon and Dorothy Thomas were in no doubt about their role. Two Frenchmen, speaking through an interpreter, confirmed that both women were very active in the attacks on Spenlow's schooner and Dillon's sloop, and went on to say, 'Anne Bonny, one of the prisoners at the bar, handed gun-powder to the men, that when they saw any vessel, gave chase, or attacked they wore men's clothes; and at other times, they wore women's clothes; that they did not seem to be kept, or detained by force, but by their own free will and consent.' After all the witnesses had been examined the president of the court asked the two women whether they had any defence to make or any witnesses to speak on their behalf, but they had nothing to offer on either score. After consulting with the twelve commissioners sitting alongside him, the president informed the women that they had unanimously been found guilty and told them, 'you shall be severally hanged by the neck, till you are severally dead. And God of his infinite mercy be merciful to both your souls.'[12]

Not till after they had heard these words did the women make the shock announcement that they were both pregnant, and they asked that there might be a stay of execution. An examination showed that both of them were indeed 'quick with child' and the sentence was suspended. They were returned to prison, where Mary Read was 'seized with a violent fever' and died in custody. The parish register for the district of St Catherine in Jamaica records her burial on 28 April 1721.[13] The fate of Anne Bonny is a mystery. According to Captain Johnson, she remained in prison until she gave birth to her child and was 'afterwards reprieved from time to time. But what is become of her since, we cannot tell.' Some evidence has come to light which suggests that her father, William Cormac, managed to get her released from jail and took her back to Charleston, where she married a local man, had eight children by him and died in 1782 at the age of eighty-four. What is certain is that over the years the story of the female pirates joined the other stories of warrior women and they have become feminist icons, their lives providing the inspiration for ballads, plays, novels and several Hollywood films.[14]

In the Epilogue the links between *Robinson Crusoe* and Woodes Rogers' account of Alexander Selkirk will be explored in some detail but it is worth noting here the similarities between another classic work of fiction by Daniel Defoe and real historical events. As the historian Marcus Rediker has pointed out, Anne Bonny and Mary Read were real-life versions of the heroine of Defoe's *Moll Flanders*, which was published in 1722, less than two years after the trial of the pirates.[15] Moll Flanders was a thief, a whore and a spirited adventurer rather than a pirate, but Rediker notes that in common with Read and Bonny she was illegitimate, poor at birth and, like them, she did cross-dress at one point in her life. All three of them experienced homelessness, a roving existence, found themselves on the wrong side of the law and faced the gallows. Defoe might have seen brief references to the capture and trial of the female pirates in the newspapers and it is possible that he saw the printed transcript of the trial before he wrote *Moll Flanders*. But he would not have seen Johnson's detailed account of the early lives of Bonny and Read (the *General History of the Pyrates* was not published until 1724) – unless, of course, he was the real author of Johnson's history.[16]

Charles Vane was executed in Jamaica soon after the hanging of Calico Jack and his men. After being voted out of his command by his crew and replaced as captain by Calico Jack, Vane had sailed away to the Bay of Honduras in a small sloop with a few of his supporters. They had captured three more sloops and were sailing in the seas off Jamaica when they were hit by a violent tornado. Vane's sloop was driven on to the shore of a deserted island and wrecked. Vane survived but most of his companions were drowned. After a few weeks a ship called by to take in water. She was commanded by Captain Holford, an old buccaneer who was a former acquaintance of Vane. Holford refused to take Vane on board his ship because he believed that he would conspire with his crew, 'knock me on the head, and run away with my ship a pyrating'. Soon after Holford had departed another ship dropped anchor off the island and the captain allowed Vane to join his crew. Unfortunately for Vane this ship happened to cross the course of Holford's ship and the captain invited Holford to come aboard. When Holford spotted Vane working down in the hold he told his fellow captain that the seaman he had rescued was none other than Vane the notorious pirate. The captain agreed to hand him over and Holford took him in irons to Jamaica, where he was delivered up to the authorities. In March 1721 Vane was tried, convicted and sentenced to death.[17] In his *General History of the Pyrates* Captain Johnson noted that Vane proved a coward on the scaffold and 'died in agonies equal to his villainies'.[18] A gentleman who witnessed the execution at Gallows Point informed Johnson that Vane showed not the least remorse for his crimes.

13

Great Debts and Bills

The hanging of Calico Jack and Charles Vane in Jamaica was another victory for the authorities in the war against the pirates but it was no consolation for Woodes Rogers. He had already requested leave of absence in order to go home 'to settle the affairs of this neglected colony'.[1] On 26 November 1720 he authorised his Council to send a letter to Secretary Craggs in London. It is a letter which reveals Rogers to be so worn down by his responsibilities and his financial concerns that his health has been affected. Craggs was informed that the Governor's bills were being refused everywhere; that he had sacrificed his utmost fortune to maintain the garrison, and 'the trouble which our hardships has given Governor Rogers has occasioned in him a great decay of health, which has induced him to go for South Carolina with hopes to recover himself'.[2] After appointing William Fairfax as Deputy Governor to take charge of the government of the Bahamas in his absence, Rogers embarked on a ship for South Carolina and arrived in Charleston on 6 December.

At this stage in its development Charleston (still called Charles Town in honour of King Charles II) was a relatively small settlement at the junction of the Ashley and Cooper rivers. It had been established by English settlers as recently as 1670 and in its early years was under constant threat of attack by the French and Spanish as well as by marauding tribes of Native Americans. The fortifications surrounding the town looked more impressive than they were and its chief defence was its position. Situated on a peninsula between two rivers, it was surrounded by water on three sides; and the entrance to the spacious harbour was notoriously difficult to navigate because it was protected by an extensive harbour bar and shifting shoals. By the time of Blackbeard's raid in 1718 Charleston had become a thriving port, with a rapidly growing export trade in rice, indigo, timber and hides. It would be some years before the town developed the streets of elegant Georgian buildings for which it is well known today, but as Rogers sailed into the harbour he would have been impressed by the number and variety of ships lying at anchor. Among them was HMS *Flamborough*. Rogers had tried to prevent her commander, Captain John Hildesley, from leaving Nassau in the aftermath of the abortive Spanish invasion but had failed to do so. Hildesley had received an urgent request from South Carolina to take his warship there. He had left Nassau on 1 May 1720 and arrived at Charleston two weeks later.

If he was hoping for a rest from the troubles of the Bahamas, Rogers was disappointed. In the interval between the departure of Governor Robert Johnson and the arrival of the next Governor there was considerable unrest in the town. Captain Hildesley attempted to take charge but he was an abrasive character and only made things worse. He quarrelled with Colonel Rhett, the man who had fought and captured Stede Bonnet. He openly criticised the way the place was being run, and he caused a riot on the waterfront when he ordered his lieutenant to seize the chief mate of the merchant ship *Samuel* and had him flogged with '24 severe lashes on his bare back'. All this and more was reported to Secretary Craggs, who was also told that 'Governor Rogers of Providence was here for about six weeks and fought a duel with Capt. Hildesley upon some disputes they had at Providence, they were both slightly wounded.'[3] A search through the letters of naval captains to the Admiralty has revealed a letter from Hildesley which explains the origins of this duel. Since he is reporting events to his superior officers in London, it is not surprising to find that Hildesley blames Rogers for the disputes that arose between them.

The root of the problem was that Rogers needed warships for the defence of New Providence and believed he had the authority to dictate terms to naval captains. In the words of Hildesley, 'all men of war which should happen to come into this port were subject to his orders . . . he did not value the Lords of the Admiralty for his commission was signed by the King'.[4] When the Spanish invasion fleet had arrived off Nassau, Hildesley had insisted that all the vessels in the harbour should come under his command, and when he discovered that no watch was being kept on the guardship *Delicia* he had sent his first lieutenant across to take possession of the ship. This had so annoyed Rogers that he had put Hildesley and his lieutenant under arrest on the *Delicia* and threatened to imprison the naval captain in the fort. Later, when Hildesley punished a member of the *Delicia*'s crew for attempting to throw his first lieutenant overboard, Rogers 'pointed the Fort guns at His Majesty's ship and encouraged the mob to rise which ye next day assaulted my lieutenant ashore'.[5] Rogers was also angry when Hildesley refused to take his warship with two sloops and 300 men to attack Moors Castle, the great fortress which protected the entrance to the harbour of Havana. The disputes led Rogers to challenge Hildesley to a duel with sword and pistol and to appoint a time and place to meet. Hildesley had arrived punctually to meet the challenge but Rogers, 'wisely considering what would of consequence follow', had sent his Attorney-General in his place, and the duel had been postponed for another time and another place.

Hildesley also criticised Rogers for ruling the island in a despotic manner. He observed that the island's Council was 'obliged to say, write and sign as he directs for his Government is absolute as will appear to all the world when his conduct is called into question'.[6] In October of the previous year Captain Whitney, commander of HMS *Rose*, had called in at New Providence to take in water and he had subsequently informed the Admiralty, 'I found the Governor complaining for want of help . . . I observed a general dissatisfaction at the Governor, and believe it had ended to the disadvantage of the Proprietors of the Islands.'[7] It may be that Rogers' despotic and sometimes bullying behaviour was due to the pressures he was under, the isolation of his position and the breakdown in his health, but there does seem to be a pattern to his behaviour when under stress. The observations made by Dr Thomas Dover concerning Rogers' violent outbursts during the latter stages of the circumnavigation, as well as his treatment of Hildesley and his assault on Captain Wingate Gale, suggest that he was a man with a short fuse and a hot temper.

Writing to Secretary Craggs from Charleston on 20 December, Rogers was able to report that he was now feeling much better, thanks to the sea air during his voyage and the cold weather he experienced on his arrival. He made no mention of his dispute with Captain Hildesley but did express his concern about two matters he had learnt about during his stay at Charleston. The first was his discovery that a new copartnership had been set up for improving the Bahama Islands. He was surprised that he had not been informed of this. The second was more worrying. Some months previously Rogers had sent Lieutenant Robert Beauchamp to England to let people know about the state of the island and its defences. At this critical time in his life Rogers needed friends in London but he now learnt that Beauchamp had been speaking out against him. 'I hear he has acted to my disadvantage, I pray God forgive him . . . if what I hear is true he is a most ungrateful man.'[8] Beauchamp had come out to the Bahamas with Rogers in 1718 and one of the Governor's first acts had been to appoint him First Lieutenant of the Independent Company and Secretary General of all the islands.

Rogers did not improve his situation by writing a second letter to Craggs from Charleston in which he announced that it was his intention to return to New Providence and, having put his affairs in order, set out for London at the beginning of April, whether or not he was granted leave to do so. The Lords of Trade and Plantations had ignored Rogers' numerous requests for assistance but they were not going to ignore the fact that he was intending to leave his post as Governor. It was unfortunate for Rogers that he now lost his principal contact in London. On 16 February 1721 James Craggs died of smallpox. He was succeeded as Secretary for the South by Lord Carteret, an energetic and ambitious young man of thirty. John Carteret had inherited a barony at the age of five, been educated at Westminster School and Oxford and taken his seat in the House of Lords in 1711. He had been one of the Lords Proprietors of the Carolinas and served briefly as ambassador to Sweden. He would ensure that the post of Governor of the Bahamas did not remain vacant for long.

Rogers was back in Nassau by the end of January 1721 and in February he sent his third report to the Lords of Trade and Plantations. He reminded them of the problems he had faced on his arrival and his distress at being abandoned by the naval ships. He listed some of the measures taken to safeguard the islands from the Spanish, the costs he had incurred in feeding and clothing the men in the garrison and those of fitting out and manning several vessels to suppress the pirates. 'By doing all this I have contracted great debts and the bills I drew to defray several of these expenses which ought to have been immediately paid, have been protested . . .'[9] Thanks to his efforts the islands were now secure but it had been at the expense of his health. He was now determined to return to England, by way of Carolina, and would leave the government of the Bahamas in the hands of Mr Fairfax.

On 19 April Lord Carteret wrote to the Council of Trade and Plantations enclosing a petition to the King from the copartners in which they set out their costs and requested further powers and a charter. Carteret explained that further powers were absolutely necessary 'especially in regard Governor Rogers has signified his intention to leave Providence in April, which may be attended with very fatal consequences, by leaving the islands exposed to the Spaniards or Pyrates'.[10] There must have been some urgent consultations in the corridors of power in London because on 12 June Carteret informed their lordships that the King had appointed George Phenney to be Governor of the Bahamas in place of Rogers.

We can only speculate on the reasons behind the decision to terminate Rogers' appointment. The members of the Council of Trade and Plantations may have lost patience with his failure to increase the trade and prosperity of the islands. His pessimistic reports, his ill health and his absences from his post would not have helped his cause, and nor would the adverse reports on his behaviour from Captain Whitney, Captain Hildesley and Lieutenant Beauchamp. Rogers himself believed that it was his copartners who were responsible for ousting him from the governorship. Several years later he maintained that he arrived back in England in the middle of the year 1721, 'in a very low state of health, almost worn out, when to his great surprise he found another Governor appointed in his stead, at the instance of his CoPartners'.[11]

Rogers had been away for three years and he returned to London in the aftermath of the South Sea Bubble – the fevered speculation in the shares of the South Sea Company which had been followed by the crash in the company's shares.[12] This had ruined thousands of men and women from all walks of life. The South Sea Company had been set up in 1711 with the twin aims of trading with Spain's South American colonies and providing a mechanism to finance Britain's national debt. In 1719 the company had proposed to take on more of the national debt and there had been considerable bribery at court and in Parliament to secure the necessary political backing for this. The fact that King George I, as well as prominent courtiers and politicians, had shares in the company gave the venture an air of respectability. Rumours of the huge profits to be made from the trade with the New World circulated and provoked a speculating frenzy. The price of the company's stock rose from £130 a share in January 1720 to £1,000 in August. At this point the increasing doubts about the future prospects of the company caused people to start selling. As the value of the stocks began to fall, selling continued at such a pace that, by the end of the year, the share price had dropped to £100.

The repercussions of the crash were widespread. The King lost £56,000 and his physician lost £80,000. Banks and goldsmiths went out of business and hundreds of people became bankrupt. Suicides in London were 40 per cent higher than usual.[13] An investigation into the recent operations of the South Sea Company by a House of Commons Committee led to the downfall and disgrace of a number of politicians. The Chancellor of the Exchequer, John Aislabie, was found guilty of 'the most notorious, dangerous and infamous corruption'.[14] He was expelled from Parliament and sent to the Tower of London. Lord Stanhope, Secretary of State, died after bursting a blood vessel while defending his actions during a debate in the House of Lords. The Postmaster General, James Craggs the Elder, was found to have received £30,000 of stocks which he had not paid for. His son James Craggs the Younger was also implicated – which might explain why Rogers had received no replies to his recent letters. Secretary Craggs died on the very day he was due to give evidence. His death so affected his father that he died a month later, apparently of apoplexy, although it was rumoured that it was suicide.

A few people did benefit from the South Sea Bubble. Among those more cautious investors who sold out before the share prices plummeted were the Duchess of Marlborough and the bookseller and philanthropist Thomas Guy. The Duchess was able to finance the completion of John Vanbrugh's magnificent Blenheim Palace, which had been commissioned by the nation to honour the military victories of her husband. Thomas Guy, who was already a wealthy man and a governor of St Thomas's Hospital, used his windfall to found Guy's Hospital. The man who profited most from the repercussions of the South Sea Bubble was the Whig politician Robert Walpole. Although he had bought shares in the company he had got rid of them at an early stage and so was never under suspicion of corrupt practices. His measures to mitigate the effects of the crash were accepted by Parliament in December 1720 and in April of the following year he became First Lord of the Treasury and Chancellor of the Exchequer. In fact, if not in name, he became prime minister and for the next twenty-one years he was the dominant figure in English politics.

News of the turmoil in London had reached Rogers while he was in Charleston, and in his letter of 21 December 1720 to James Craggs he had mentioned 'my great concern hearing the vast confusion ye fall of stocks has made . . .'.[15] On his return to London he would have found that his own financial problems were put into perspective by the troubles of so many others. Professional people, tradesmen and shopkeepers had lost their houses, businesses and livelihoods. Aristocrats and landed gentry had lost estates which had been in their family for generations. Sir Gilbert Heathcote, former Lord Mayor of London, wrote that he 'was sorry to see great estates acquired by miscreants, who, twelve months ago, were not fit to be valets to the gentlemen they have ruined'.[16]

Very little is known about Rogers' life during the first few years following his return to England. It is certain that he spent some time in a debtor's prison because one document makes it clear that he was compelled to declare himself bankrupt (for the second time), 'there being no other method to free him from a prison'.[17] A search of the surviving records of Marshalsea Prison, Fleet Prison and King's Bench and Queen's Bench Prisons has failed to reveal which one he was in and for how long he was confined.[18] Hogarth's pictures and other sources suggest that life in a debtor's prison at this period was harder than it was in Dickens' day, especially if the prisoner had no means of bribing the jailers. However, Daniel Defoe, who was frequently in financial trouble and twice filed for bankruptcy, had survived imprisonment on three occasions without any apparent ill effects. In 1692 he had been imprisoned in Fleet Prison and he had spent several weeks in the more notorious Newgate in 1702 and 1706. For Rogers the conditions could not have been any worse than his more gruelling experiences during his voyage round the world.

The notice of his bankruptcy was posted in the *London Gazette* of 30 January 1724 and described him as 'Woods Rogers, of London, Merchant'. This freed him from prison, cancelled his debts and marked the first step in the recovery of his reputation. His cause was much helped at this stage by the publication of Captain Johnson's *General History of the Pyrates*. This was first published in London on 14 May that same year. A second edition was published a few months later because 'the first impression having been received with so much success by the public, occasioned a very earnest demand for a second'. A third edition appeared in 1725 and a fourth and much enlarged edition followed in 1726. The extent of Rogers' possible contribution to the book will be considered in a later chapter but the numerous passages devoted to his role in the dispersal of the pirates at Nassau placed him in a most favourable light and also reminded the authorities of his previous exploits in the Pacific. His bluff manner and lack of diplomatic skills may have put him at a disadvantage among the politicians, diplomats and civil servants in London but his resilience in the face of setbacks and his persistence in arguing his case began to yield results.

A crucial step forward was a long letter sent to the King on his behalf by eight senior army officers based at Horse Guards in Whitehall. Dated 15 July 1726 and headed 'The case of Captain Woodes Rogers, late Governor of the Bahama Islands', this summarised the difficulties he had faced and overcome to clear the pirates out of Nassau and stave off a Spanish invasion. It explained that he had been given no powers to raise money locally as other colonial governors were able to do, and so had had no option but to cover many of the costs himself. The letter noted that he had sunk more than £3,000 of his own money in maintaining the defences of the colony and was now double that sum in debt. He had no way of extricating himself from this situation 'till at last with the consent of his creditors he received what his CoPartners were pleased to allow him for his share, what was but fifteen hundred pounds, and a bond of five hundred more'. He was obliged to deliver this up to his creditors, 'who, being fully convinced of the unexampled hardships he endured, left him four hundred pounds out of his money for what he expended to support himself after he came from his Government'.[19] The letter concluded by recommending that he be allowed half pay as Captain of Foot from the time he was superseded as Governor. At the end of the letter it was noted that Rogers had received his arrears of pay as Captain of Foot. He was still without a job but at least his debts had been written off and he had some form of income. Later in the year his advice was sought by the Government on the likely route and timing of a Spanish treasure convoy which was due to return to Europe from Panama – further proof of the revival of his fortunes.[20]

Two more years passed during which we must assume he continued to lobby his friends and supporters. In February 1728 he sent a carefully worded petition to King George II, who had succeeded to the throne a few months previously. He stressed the importance of the Bahamas for the commerce of Britain and humbly prayed that His Majesty would be 'graciously pleased to restore him to his former station of Governor, and Captain of an Independent Company of these Islands'.[21] To coincide with this letter a testimonial on his behalf was sent to the leader of the ruling Whig party, Sir Robert Walpole.[22] This bore the signatures of twenty-nine influential names, including Sir Hans Sloane, several prominent London and Bristol merchants and three men who knew at first hand the problems which Rogers had faced during his time in the Caribbean. They were Alexander Spotswood, Benjamin Bennet and Samuel Shute, the former colonial governors of Virginia, Bermuda and Massachusetts. Further support came from Sir Charles Wager, the distinguished and much respected admiral who was MP for Portsmouth. He had made his name while in command of the British fleet in the West Indies and had been one of the copartners behind the venture which had sent Rogers to the Bahamas in 1718. On 10 August he wrote a testimonial for Rogers to pass on to the Duke of Newcastle, who was at Hampton Court in attendance on the King.[23]

The campaign to reinstate Rogers as Governor of the Bahamas was greatly assisted by the fact that George Phenney, the man who had replaced him in 1721, had been having a difficult time in Nassau. He had begun with the best of intentions. He had supervised the building of a small church – in March 1723 he had sent back to London a drawing of 'the Church as now building'.[24] His Council had passed measures to encourage churchgoing and discourage 'rash oaths, cursings, execrations, drunkenness, uncleanness or other scandalous actions'. Every soldier was to be properly equipped and officers must train and exercise their men regularly. Phenney had improved the island's defences by bringing out from England twenty-four eighteen-pounder guns and mounting them in a line to the west of Fort Nassau; he had completed the building of a wooden palisade around the fort; and he had rebuilt two of the fort's corner bastions. These improvements can be seen on a plan of the fort which he despatched to the Board of Trade in December 1723.[25] Unfortunately he failed to maintain the defences and, at the end of his term as Governor, the lieutenant and gunner of the garrison compiled a damning report on the state of the guns, the fort and the various buildings within the walls.[26] Like Rogers before him, Phenney found most of the local people to be unproductive, and reluctant to assist him in governing the island; he complained that he was sometimes unable to get enough members of his Council together to form a quorum. His governance was also fatally hampered by his wife, who abused her position by taking charge of much of the trade of the island and setting her own exorbitant prices. She was accused of frequently browbeating juries 'and insulted even the justice on the bench'. Her high-handed behaviour was reported back to England and did much to undermine Phenney's position.

On 4 December 1728 the King formally approved a recommendation by the Council of Trade and Plantations that Rogers be appointed Captain General and Governor in Chief of the Bahama Islands. This time he was given the authority to call General Assemblies and was granted an annual income of £400. To mark the final restoration of his fortunes Rogers commissioned a family portrait by the 31-year-old William Hogarth. The artist had already established a reputation with engravings which wickedly satirised contemporary themes and events such as the South Sea Bubble, but he had yet to make his name as a painter. Very few oil paintings can be attributed to him before 1728, so his picture for Rogers is among the first of the conversation pieces which he embarked on around this time.[27] The painting is so small and the face of Rogers so obscured by his wig that it is of little use as a likeness, but the picture does reveal his motto which is inscribed on the walls of Fort Nassau behind his seated figure. 'Dum spiro, spero' ('While I breathe, I hope') is entirely appropriate for a man of such determination. The globe beside Rogers, the pair of dividers in his hand and the distant ship represent his circumnavigation in command of the *Duke* and *Dutchess*. Opposite the newly appointed Governor are his son William, who is displaying a map of New Providence, and his daughter Sarah, who has a book in her hand (perhaps intended to be *A Cruising Voyage Round the World*). Beside her is the family's spaniel and behind her is a maidservant holding a dish of fruit. Rogers' wife is conspicuous by her absence.

14

Death on the Coast of Guinea

While Woodes Rogers had been struggling with debts and bankruptcy on his return to London, the man he had rescued from Juan
Fernández was in a ship some 3,000 miles to the south. Following
his marriage to Francis Candish in Plymouth, Alexander Selkirk
had sailed to Portsmouth as mate of the *Weymouth*. At Spithead
the *Weymouth* had joined the 50-gun ship *Swallow*, whose
commander, Captain Chaloner Ogle, had orders to cruise against
the pirates on the coast of Guinea – the name commonly given to
central west Africa at this period. For six weeks the two warships
lay at anchor in the lee of the Isle of Wight while they took on
provisions and waited for a small convoy of merchantmen to
gather. At 4 p.m. on 5 February 1721 the *Swallow* made the signal
to weigh anchor and the two warships set sail, accompanied by
the three merchant ships, *Cape Coast*, *Martha* and *Whidah*, and
by three sloops. They made good progress as they headed south.
They reached Madeira on 10 March, and were off Cape Verde
on the 31st. Here they parted, the *Weymouth* heading due east to
the River Gambier and the *Swallow* heading south-east to Sierra
Leone.

The surgeon on the *Swallow* was John Atkins, who had joined the navy in 1701 and had considerable experience of treating men wounded in action. When he retired from the navy in 1723 he produced two interesting books. The first was entitled *The Navy Surgeon, or, Practical System of Surgery* and was notable for being the first publication to provide detailed descriptions of tropical diseases such as cerebral malaria, Guinea-worm and African sleeping sickness.[1] His second book, *A Voyage to Guinea, Brasil and the West Indies*, was a journal of the voyage of the *Swallow* and *Weymouth*. Atkins' descriptions of the places and peoples seen en route provide a vivid accompaniment to the typically brief comments to be found in the logbooks of the two warships. He described the River Sierra Leone as being as tidal at its mouth as the English Channel but after ten miles or so narrowing to half the breadth of the Thames at London. The banks were thickly lined with mangroves and the waters were infested with crocodiles and sharks, 'the most bold and ravenous of the watery tribe'. He noted that the sharks would eat anything, including canvas and blankets. If a corpse was committed to the deep, the sharks would tear and devour it, 'and the hammock that shrouded it, without suffering it once to sink, tho' a great weight of ballast in it'.[2]

The *Weymouth* arrived at the entrance of the River Gambia on 2 April but ran aground on a sandy shoal in the middle of the estuary. The master's log noted the part played by Selkirk in getting the ship afloat. 'Mr Barnsly took the first Mate (Mr Selkirk) with him and went a sounding the Depth of water this morn: the Boates was sent to lay on the sands by directions of Mr Selkirk.' To lighten the ship some of the fresh water was jettisoned overboard, and an anchor and hawsers were laid out astern so the ship could be heaved off. The ship was eventually floated off on the morning of 4 April but remained in the river for several more days while the crew went ashore to stock up on wood and water. They too were troubled by sharks. On one occasion the ship's barge was attacked by a shark which seized one of the oars in its mouth and snapped it in two.

By the beginning of June the *Swallow* was sailing along the Ivory Coast, which Atkins observed was low, lined with trees and very straight, without bays and inlets. This made it difficult to distinguish landmarks and it was dangerous to send boats ashore because there was no shelter from the high surf caused by the heavy Atlantic swell. Only the natives were able to push their way safely through the surf in their long canoes, each carved out of a single cotton tree and carrying up to twenty rowers. At Cape Three Points the *Swallow* was reunited with the *Weymouth* and the two ships proceeded along the Gold Coast, where there was a series of trading posts guarded by forts or large castles. The oldest of these was at Elmina and had been established by the Portuguese in 1482. To the west of Elmina were smaller trading stations at Dixcove and Shama, and to the east was the massive structure of Cape Coast Castle. This was originally a Swedish trading post but it had been captured by the British in 1664 and had become the headquarters of the Royal Africa Company.

At the slave port of Whydah the two warships dropped anchor for two weeks in order to take in wood and water. There were several merchant vessels lying in the roadstead and the union flag was flying from the fort. On 20 July the *Swallow* and *Weymouth* sailed south-east across the Gulf of Guinea to the Portuguese island of Principe. They anchored in a deep-water harbour in a long, narrow inlet which was sheltered from the wind and was protected by a small fort. At the head of the inlet was a settlement of timber houses along two or three streets where the Portuguese Governor and the chief residents lived. Beyond was a thickly wooded landscape of hills and valleys echoing with the cries of parrots and monkeys. In the valleys were the villages of the black Africans who had been brought over by the Portuguese and who cultivated the plantations of yams, pineapples, bananas and Indian corn.

The *Swallow* and *Weymouth* remained at Principe for seven weeks, the crew living ashore in tents while the ships were heeled and careened. It was during this time that the deaths began. Surgeon Atkins blamed the deaths on the excessive heat and the debauches of the seamen, who drank large quantities of palm-wine so that 'they soon run into excess, which brought on an epidemical malignant fever'.[3] Whether it was malaria or yellow fever is not known but the effects were devastating, particularly on the crew of the *Weymouth*. The first death took place on 3 September. The victim was John Herdman, who was presumably a relative of Captain Mungo Herdman. By 21 September twenty-six members of the crew were dead and so many seriously ill that they had to borrow men from the *Swallow* and take on some black African slaves to enable them to weigh anchor and set sail.

They made first for the larger Portuguese island of St Thomas (São Tomé) and then headed back to the Gold Coast. As they anchored off Cape Coast Castle on 22 October they received a salute of thirteen guns, which they answered with the same number. By now the *Weymouth* had buried forty-five men and the deaths continued inexorably for the next four months. On 10 December the ship moved a few miles west to Elmina and dropped anchor in eleven fathoms in the roadstead overlooked by the castle. According to the French merchant Jean Barbot, the castle was 'justly famed for beauty and strength, having no equal in all the coasts of Guinea. It is built square, with very high walls of a dark brown stone, so very firm that it may be said to be cannon-proof.'[4] All the stone for the construction of the castle had been transported in ships from Portugal but in 1637 the Dutch had seized the castle from the Portuguese and the Dutch flag flew over the battlements for the next 200 years.

It was while the *Weymouth* was anchored off Elmina that Alexander Selkirk's name was added to the list of victims of the tropical fever which was decimating the crew. On 13 December 1721 the captain's log recorded, 'Little wind and fair weather . . . Mr Alexr. Selkirk died.' He was forty-five years old. He had circumnavigated the world, lived through storms and mutinies, and had famously survived for four years as a castaway on an island in the South Pacific, but like so many sailors it was his fate to die of a tropical disease in a remote location thousands of miles from home. It is not known whether he was buried ashore or was buried at sea according to the usual custom of the Royal Navy. Captain Herdman later recorded that he buried no fewer than 196 men during the voyage.[5] Atkins gave a much larger figure and noted that the *Weymouth* 'brought out of England a compliment of 240 men, having at the end of the voyage 280 dead upon her books'.[6] The additional numbers needed to sail the ship were made up by impressing men from merchant ships and by purchasing more African slaves. When he got back to England at the end of the voyage Captain Herdman set out his problems in a letter to the Admiralty:

In my late voyage to Guinea, there happened such an unusual sickness and mortality among the ship's company under my command; that when I was upon my departure from thence in April 1722, I had not men enough in health to weigh my anchors or sail the ship; not above forty being able to come upon deck at a time to do their duty. In this extremity to comply with the orders I received to return home, I was obliged to purchase fifty negroes of General Phipps, the commanding officer at Cape Coast Castle.[7]

The *Swallow* had also suffered deaths from fever but to a lesser extent, and Captain Ogle was determined that the search for the pirates must continue. He ordered the *Weymouth* to cruise between Cape Three Points and Cape Palmas, while he took the *Swallow* eastwards and patrolled the coast between Cape Coast Castle and Whydah. On 10 January 1722 he learnt from General Phipps that two pirate ships had taken a French ship in the vicinity. As he was making his way along the coast he encountered several trading vessels and one of them sent a boat across to the *Swallow* with news that the pirates were at Whydah. 'On my arrival at Whydah I was informed that two pyrate ships one of 40 and another of 24 guns commanded by one Roberts had been there and had sailed about 36 hours before.'[8] There were ten sailing ships at anchor in the roadstead, two of which were English, three French and five Portuguese. In order to save their ships each of the captains had been forced by the pirates to pay a ransom of eight pounds' weight of gold or gold dust. The only ship to refuse to pay was the English slave ship *Porcupine*, commanded by Captain Fletcher. This provoked the pirates to cover the decks of the ship with tar and set her alight. They made no attempt to release the eighty black slaves who were on the ship, chained together in pairs. The terrified slaves had to choose between drowning or being burnt alive. Those who decided to jump overboard were seized by sharks and torn apart.

Roberts, the pirate leader mentioned by Captain Ogle, was Bartholomew Roberts, who was the most formidable and the most successful of the pirates who operated on both sides of the Atlantic in the period between 1715 and 1725. He was believed to have taken some 400 vessels during his two and a half years as a pirate, and this may not have been an exaggeration. A study of the many newspaper reports of his raids; the accounts of his activities in the Colonial

Office papers; and the extensive and well-documented account of his life in Captain Johnson's history indicates the range of his operations as well as his constant activity. His plundering cruises can be seen as the high point but also the final flourish of the Golden Age of piracy.

A stern and somewhat puritanical Welshman, Roberts was described as being tall, dark and 'of good natural parts and personal bravery'. Born in the village of Newydd Bach (Little Newcastle), near Fishguard in Pembrokeshire, he had gone to sea as a merchant seaman. In June 1719 he was second mate of the ship *Princess* of London, which was taking on slaves near Cape Coast Castle when his ship was attacked by a pirate ship commanded by Howell Davis, another Welshman. Eight members of the crew of the *Princess*, including Roberts, were forced to join the pirates. Roberts had no intention of remaining with the pirates at first but he soon became reconciled to life on a pirate ship, which was considerably easier and more rewarding than life on a merchant ship engaged in the slave trade. When Howell Davis was killed in an ambush during a visit to the island of Principe the crew took a vote and chose Roberts as their new captain.

After capturing a Dutch Guineaman and an English ship off Cape Lopez, Roberts took his ship across the Atlantic to Brazil. For nine unproductive weeks he cruised along the Brazilian coast until he came to the town of Bahia (now known as Salvador da Bahia) which was situated on a peninsula at the entrance of a great bay, the Bahia de Todos os Santos. Lying at anchor was the Portuguese treasure fleet of thirty-two armed merchantmen, together with two 70-gun warships which were to escort the fleet to Lisbon. Roberts' ship, the 32-gun *Royal Rover*, was no match for the warships and was outgunned by many of the merchant ships, but Roberts managed to convince his crew that an attack was possible. Keeping most of his men hidden, he picked out one of the ships and headed towards her. As he came alongside he ordered her captain to come quietly aboard the *Royal Rover* and threatened to kill his whole crew if any of them offered any resistance. The pirates now appeared on deck and the sight of this alarming bunch of men flourishing cutlasses was enough to persuade the Portuguese captain to do as he was told. Once he was on board Roberts' ship, he was asked, on pain of death, to reveal which was the richest ship in the fleet. He told them it was the *Sagrada Familia*, a ship of 40 guns.

Roberts sailed his ship to within hailing distance of the *Sagrada Familia* and got his captured Portuguese captain to invite her commander on board the *Royal Rover*. This time the element of surprise failed. The captain and crew of the intended victim became suspicious and took defensive action. Roberts and his men acted swiftly: 'without further delay, they poured in a broadside, boarded and grappled her; the dispute was short and warm, wherein many of the Portuguese fell, and two only of the pirates.'[9] So ferocious was the pirates' attack that the *Sagrada Familia* soon surrendered. By now the rest of the fleet was alert to the trouble in their midst but they were far too slow to react. When the first of the warships bore down on the *Royal Rover*, Roberts swung her round and prepared for battle, which caused the warship to fall back and wait for her consort to join her. By the time both ships were ready to give chase the *Royal Rover* and her prize were clear of the anchorage and on their way.

In a daring attack worthy of Francis Drake or Henry Morgan, Bartholomew Roberts had got his piratical career off to a flying start and his crew were able to share the spoils, which included 90,000 gold moidores, jewels, a cross set with diamonds and a cargo of sugar, skins and tobacco. From Brazil they headed north to the Caribbean, taking a brigantine and a Bristol ship in the vicinity of

Barbados. Towards the end of June 1720 Roberts sailed 2,500 miles north to Newfoundland and in the harbour of Trepassey he caused havoc, burning and sinking twenty-two vessels before moving on to the Newfoundland Banks, where he destroyed nine or ten fishing vessels and seized a French ship of 26 guns which he took over and named the *Fortune*. With this ship he attacked the *Samuel* of London, and then a Bristol snow, a Virginia ship, a brigantine and a sloop. By July Roberts was back in the West Indies, where he captured a French ship from Martinique which became his new flagship and was given the name *Royal Fortune*. At Martinique his men destroyed some twenty vessels, and off the island of Dominica they took a Dutch ship of 22 guns and a brigantine. These relentless and indiscriminate attacks on merchantmen in the West Indies continued until the crew voted to head for the Guinea coast, 'where they thought to buy gold-dust very cheap. In their passage thither they took numbers of ships of all nations, some of which they burnt or sunk.'[10]

Roberts, like a few other pirate leaders such as Blackbeard and William Moody, usually operated with a flotilla of two or three vessels, which meant that most merchant ships had neither the firepower nor the crew numbers to offer any resistance. A notable feature of Roberts' cruises was that any opposition to his attacks invariably provoked a savage response. A Dutch merchantman of 30 guns which was attacked by Roberts off St Lucia managed to hold off the pirates and kill a great number of them during a four-hour battle. When the Dutch crew eventually surrendered 'what men the pirates found alive on board they put to death after several cruel methods'.[11] And after the raid on shipping off Martinique 'the men they took they barbarously abused, some they almost whip't to death, others had their ears cut off, others they fixed to the yard arms and fired at them as a mark . . .'.[12]

By June 1721 Roberts and his pirates had crossed the Atlantic and arrived on the African coast near the River Senegal. From there they sailed to Sierra Leone and on to Jacqueville, 'plundering every ship they met of what was valuable in her, and sometimes to be more mischievously wicked, would throw what they did not want overboard . . .'.[13] At Cestos they found a fine frigate-built ship called the *Onslow* lying at anchor. She belonged to the Royal Africa Company and her commander, Captain Gee, and most of his crew were ashore. The pirates were able to come alongside and capture the ship with no resistance from those on board – several of whom subsequently joined the pirates. Roberts handed his French ship over to Captain Gee and commandeered the *Onslow*. Renamed the *Royal Fortune* and mounted with 40 guns, she became his new flagship. With this powerful ship and a much smaller ship (the *Little Ranger*) he made the murderous attack on Whydah which resulted in the burning and drowning of the black slaves. After six months of raids on shipping along the Guinea Coast, Roberts sailed south-east across the Gulf of Guinea to Cape Lopez, where there was a sheltered, deep-water anchorage in the lee of the cape. It was there that he was finally tracked down by Captain Chaloner Ogle.

The *Swallow* had sailed from Cape Coast Castle during the first week of January 1722. Leaving the *Weymouth*, with her much depleted crew, to patrol the coast in the vicinity of Cape Three Points, Captain Ogle took the *Swallow* across the Gulf of Guinea in the tracks of Roberts. He had learnt that Roberts had seized a French ship at Whydah and believed that the pirates intended to adapt her for their own use: 'Therefore I judged they must go to some place in the Bight to clean and fit the French ship before they would think of cruising again.' There was no sign of the pirates at the mouth of the River Gabon but at daybreak on 5 February, 'I saw

Cape Lopas bearing WSW about 3 leagues and at the same time discovered three ships at anchor under the Cape which I believed to be the pyrates . . .'[14]

The dramatic events of that day and those that followed were recorded by many of the participants and appear in their logbooks and letters, as well as in the transcript of the trial which took place at Cape Coast Castle seven weeks later.[15] Captain Ogle wanted to lure the pirates out to sea and he succeeded in doing so. As his ship neared Cape Lopez he was forced to bear away to avoid an off-lying shoal called Frenchman's Bank. The sight of the *Swallow* heading out to sea caused one of the pirate ships to weigh anchor and give chase. With smooth water and a brisk breeze from the south-east, the *Swallow* ran before the wind but Captain Ogle deliberately slowed her down, 'keeping our main tack on board, our main sheets aft and our main yard braced to give him the opportunity of coming up with us'.[16] The pirate ship was the French ship of 32 guns which Roberts had seized at Whydah. Now named the *French Ranger* to differentiate her from the *Little Ranger*, she was flying a Dutch pennant from her main masthead and an English ensign jack. By 10.30 a.m. she was within gunshot distance and fired several shots with her chase guns which splashed in the water alongside the *Swallow*. The pirates now hoisted a black flag at their mizzen peak, and the crew of the warship could see that she had her spritsail yard slung under her bowsprit ready for boarding when she came alongside.

Captain Ogle waited until she came within musket shot distance and then 'we starboard our helm and ran out our lower guns'.[17] As the *Swallow* swung round the pirates discovered too late that their prey was not a large merchantman but a 50-gun British warship. It was an unequal contest. The pirates survived the first broadside and swept past so that for a while the *Swallow* was unable to bring her guns to bear. Ogle noted that the pirate ship 'sailed rather better than us' but was steered so badly that the *Swallow* slowly closed the distance. At around 2 p.m. the warship's guns brought down the pirate's maintopmast and soon after that the pirates surrendered. Of the 123 men on board twenty-three were black.[18] Twenty-six of the pirates were killed or seriously wounded, including the captain, James Skyrm, a 44-year-old former merchant seaman from Somerset. He had a leg shot off during the action but 'his temper was so warm as to refuse going off the deck, till he found all was lost'.[19] There were no serious casualties on the *Swallow*.

When emergency repairs had been carried out on the pirate ship, Captain Ogle put a prize crew on board and sent her off to wait for him at the island of Principe while he returned to Cape Lopez. He arrived within sight of the cape on the evening of 10 February. The weather had deteriorated. Fresh south-westerly gales and rain were sweeping across the sea. With darkness approaching Ogle had to stand off the land and sail to windward all night. At dawn he sailed back to Cape Lopez and saw three vessels at anchor. He knew from questioning some of the captured pirates that the largest ship was the 40-gun *Royal Fortune* and one of the others was the 24-gun *Little Ranger*. He would later learn that the third vessel was a trading pink called the *Neptune*, Captain Hill, of London.

The *Swallow*, which was flying a French ensign to confuse the pirates, had to make two long tacks and it was not till around 10 a.m. that she was in a position to bear down on the anchorage. On board the *Royal Fortune* there was much debate among the pirates as to the identity of the ship they could see heading their way. Some of them thought she was a Portuguese ship, some a French slave ship, and some thought she was the *French Ranger* returning. As she got closer a pirate named Thomas Armstrong, who was a deserter from the *Swallow*, correctly identified her as his former ship. Roberts was apparently undaunted by this news and ordered his men to prepare for action. At 10.30 a.m. the *Royal Fortune* slipped her anchor cable and got under sail. According to Captain Ogle, the pirate ship 'came down upon me with English ensign and jack and a black pendant flying at her maintopmast head, and I showing him a French ensign, when he came within pistol shot I hoisted my proper colours, and gave him a broadside which he returned and endeavoured to get from me by making all the sail he could'.[20]

From Captain Johnson we learn that Bartholomew Roberts made a gallant figure on this, his last fight. He was dressed in a crimson damask waistcoat and breeches, with a red feather in his hat, a diamond cross hanging from a gold chain around his neck, a sword in his hand, and two pairs of pistols slung from his shoulders on a silk sling 'according to the fashion of the pyrates'. He was killed in the first or second of the *Swallow*'s broadsides, struck in the throat by grapeshot. He collapsed across the rope tackles of a gun, and his body was thrown overboard 'according to the repeated request he made in his lifetime'.[21] The drama of the occasion was heightened by the weather. According to Captain Ogle's logbook (and this is confirmed by the logs of the *Swallow*'s first and second lieutenants), around noon there was 'much rain, lightning & thunder A small tornado about ½ past 1 o clock the pyrates mainmast came by the board being shott just below the parrell The Mizn topmast ye same the first broadside . . .'. At 2 p.m. the pirates surrendered. Of the 152 men on board fifty-two were black.[22] Only three pirates were killed in this action and again the *Swallow* had none killed or injured. Surgeon Atkins observed that the pirates, 'tho' singly fellows of courage', were a contemptible enemy owing to their drunkenness and disorder.[23]

Two days later the *Swallow* and her prize anchored at Cape Lopez. The *Neptune* had disappeared and it soon became apparent that her crew had plundered the *Little Ranger*, which had been left at anchor with no crew on board – Roberts had ordered all the pirates to join the *Royal Fortune* before she sailed into battle. The captured pirates were dismayed to find that they had been robbed of several thousand pounds of gold and gold dust stored in their sea chests.

The weather continued to be stormy with heavy rain, more tornadoes and thunderstorms so fierce that on one occasion the *Swallow*'s fore topmast was split by a lightning strike. Atkins described the tornadoes as 'fierce and violent gusts of wind that give warning for some hours by a gradual lowering and blackening of the sky to windward whence they come, accompanied with darkness, terrible shocks of thunder and lightning, and ends in rains and calms'.[24] They stayed a week at Cape Lopez, replenishing their supply of water and heeling the *Swallow* so that they could scrub off the weed and barnacles. Apart from the weather it was a pleasant location. There were plenty of fish in the anchorage and grey parrots in the trees. The surrounding countryside was mostly savannah with wandering herds of buffalo. The local people were friendly and were pleased to trade goats, chickens and honey in exchange for linen, calico, pewter spoons and knives.

On 18 February they set sail with the *Royal Fortune* and the *Little Ranger*. They called in at Principe to collect the *French Ranger* and on 16 March they anchored off Cape Coast Castle. The captured pirates were sent ashore and were presumably confined in the cells built to hold African slaves. These cells were underground vaults situated in the large quadrangle in the centre of the castle. They had iron gratings at the surface 'to let in light and air on those poor wretches, the slaves, who are chained and confined there till the demand comes'.[25] In the surrounding buildings, protected by massive walls and battlements, were lodgings for General Phipps and his officers, and for merchants, soldiers, miners and tradesmen. The castle had workshops for blacksmiths and coopers as well as a chapel and a large hall which would be the setting for the trial of the pirates

The *Weymouth* had been patrolling the coast some eighty miles away and did not learn of the *Swallow*'s success until 25 March. When Captain Herdman received the news he immediately headed east and at 2 p.m. on 27 March the *Weymouth* anchored off the castle. Events now moved rapidly. Within a day of his arrival Captain Herdman was appointed President of the Admiralty Court which was convened to try the pirates. (Captain Ogle was disqualified from taking part because he was the captor of the pirates.) Captain Herdman was assisted in his deliberations by James Phipps, the governor of the castle; by Edward Hyde, who was Secretary of the Royal Africa Company; and by Lieutenant Barnsley and Lieutenant Fanshaw of the *Weymouth*; and two merchants, Mr Dodson and Mr Boye. Surgeon Atkins was appointed Register of the court and later claimed expenses for twenty-six days' attendance. The task before the court was daunting. Two hundred and sixty-two men had been captured by the *Swallow*. Seventy-five of these were black Africans and they were excluded from the trial. Several men had died from their wounds, but this still left a total of 168 men to be cross-examined and their innocence or guilt determined. In terms of the numbers of men accused it was the largest pirate trial of the period, and it would also break records for the number of men found guilty and hanged.

The charges varied slightly according to which ship the men were serving on when captured, but in summary they were accused of being 'wickedly united, and articled together for the annoyance and destruction of His Majesty's trading subjects by sea'. They were also accused of 'sinking, burning and destroying such goods, and vessels as then happened in your way'. And most seriously they were indicted as 'traitors, robbers, pirates and common enemies of all mankind' because they had hoisted a piratical flag and fired upon His Majesty's ship *Swallow* with the intention of 'distressing the said King's ship and murdering His Majesty's good subjects'.

The full transcript of the trial is in the collections of the National Archives at Kew, and Captain Johnson reproduced much of the transcript in his *General History of the Pyrates*. The statements of the accused and of the witnesses provide a fascinating glimpse into the world of the pirates: who they were and where they came from; and how and why they found themselves on pirate ships. Almost all the men captured were former merchant seamen. There were a few men who had been pirates for three or four years, some of whom had served with Howell Davis, but the majority had joined the pirates voluntarily or involuntarily during Roberts' recent cruises along the coast of West Africa. Apart from a group of eighteen Frenchmen and seven Dutch seamen, almost all the rest were British. Most came from major English ports such as London, Bristol and Plymouth but there were also men from Scotland, Wales, Ireland, the Isle of Man, the Channel Islands and the West Indies. Of the fifty-two men found guilty of piracy the average age was twenty-eight, a figure which is in line with several studies made of the pirates of this period, and is similar to the average age of men in the eighteenth-century Royal Navy.[26] The oldest of the pirates was forty-five and the youngest was nineteen. A common thread running through the pirates' statements is the emphasis on drink. Many men seem to have spent most of their time drunk. John Jaynson 'was more busy at drinking than anything else'. Michael Lemmon was 'as often drunk as the rest of the crew'. A witness said of Robert Devins that he never saw him sober or fit for any duty, and Joseph Mansfield admitted that it was drink that had drawn him into the company of the pirates, 'the love of drink and a lazy life having been stronger motives with him than gold'.[27]

In spite of the numbers involved, the members of the Admiralty Court made a point of questioning all the accused men individually and seem to have done their best to get evidence from eyewitnesses. At this period, and for decades to come, the response of the authorities to crimes against property was draconian. It was common for men and women to be hanged for a variety of petty crimes such as the theft of a silver tankard and a silver spoon, or the theft of three bedsheets and fifteen napkins. Highway robbery was invariably punished by death.[28] Given this background the Admiralty Court showed considerable sympathy towards most of the poor seamen who came before them. Captain Herdman, in his role as President, particularly admonished the hard core of seasoned pirates who were on trial, for robbing honest and needy seamen 'who are purchasing their livelihoods through hazards and difficulties' and who were then forced to join the pirates 'to their own and families ruin, removing them from their wives and children, and by that, from the means that should support them from misery and want'.[29]

Anyone who could prove that he had been forced to join the pirates against his will and had refrained from taking an active role in robbing ships was acquitted. This particularly applied to those men with specialist skills useful to the pirates such as carpenters, caulkers and coopers. John Lane, a boatswain's mate, was told by Bartholomew Roberts that 'such men we want, and you shall go with us'. John Johnson was another skilled man and the pirates, 'hearing he was a tailor and wanting such a man very much, did oblige him to continue on board them'. Nicholas Brattle, who played the fiddle and was one of four musicians captured, 'was only made use of, as musick, which he dared not refuse'. All these men were acquitted.

On the other hand the court was merciless towards those who were found guilty of actively plundering ships; or showed violence towards their shipmates; handled swords, cutlasses or pistols, or fired the guns when going into action. In the words of Captain Herdman, 'To a trading nation, nothing can be so destructive as pyracy, or call for more exemplary punishment.' And the punishment was indeed exemplary. Those found guilty were hanged in batches of between four and fourteen men within a day of their sentence being pronounced. The gallows were set up on the beach in front of the castle's gates and between the high- and low-water marks. After the execution the Provost Marshal was directed to cut down the bodies, to secure them in chains and to hang them on 'the gibbets already erected on the adjacent hillock'.

Thomas Armstrong, the 34-year-old deserter from the *Swallow*, was executed in the manner reserved for naval deserters. On 24 April he was hanged from the fore yardarm of the *Weymouth*. He spent his last hour bewailing his sins, urging the spectators to lead an honest and good life and asking them to join him in singing two or three verses of Psalm 140. This psalm begins: 'Deliver me, O Lord, from the evil man: preserve me from the violent man.' After this warning the psalm concludes with some reassuring words: 'I know that the Lord will maintain the cause of the afflicted, and the right of the poor. Surely the righteous shall give thanks unto thy name: the upright shall dwell in thy presence.'

The trial lasted for four weeks. In a letter which he sent to the Admiralty a few months later Captain Ogle included a summary account of the fate of the men taken by the *Swallow* off Cape Lopez. Of the 262 men found alive on the pirate ships, seventy-five were black Africans excluded from the trial, nineteen died of their wounds before they came to trial, seventy-seven were acquitted, fifty-two were hanged, twenty were condemned to seven years' servitude in the Cape Coast mines, seventeen were sentenced to imprisonment in London's Marshalsea Prison and two had their execution 'respited till the Kings pleasure is further known'.[30]

Early in May 1722 the *Swallow* and *Weymouth* left Cape Coast and sailed across the Atlantic to Brazil and then north to the Caribbean. They called in at Barbados and then headed for Jamaica. On 24 August they dropped anchor in the harbour of Port Royal. Four days later a hurricane swept across the island, causing almost as much damage as the great earthquake and tidal wave of 1692 in which a whole section of the town had slid beneath the sea.

Captain Ogle reported that the wind began to blow very hard at half past eight on the morning of 28 August. Lying at anchor in the harbour were nearly thirty merchant vessels as well as the *Swallow*, the *Weymouth* and two other warships, the *Falkland* and the sloop *Happy*. As the wind increased to hurricane force the crews of the naval vessels put out more anchors and then cut away their masts to prevent the ships heeling over. By eleven o'clock the harbour was lashed by torrential rain and Ogle reported 'as much wind in my opinion as could possible blow out of the heavens'.[31] Prodigious waves were throwing up tons of stones and rocks over the sea wall at the eastern end of the town and the streets of Port Royal were flooded to a depth of five feet. Apart from the naval vessels only two merchant ships and a sloop remained at anchor. The rest were blown ashore or sank on their moorings. The ships of Bartholomew Roberts came to a suitably violent end. 'The Royal Fortune formerly called the Onslow, and Little Ranger pyrate prizes both drove ashore on the rocks under Salt Pan Hill and were cast all to pieces in less than an hour.'[32]

The death toll of between 400 and 500 was not comparable with the 1692 earthquake, when more than 2,000 people died, but according to Ogle, 'the island received more damage by this hurricane than ever was known'. In Kingston more than half the houses were destroyed.[33] Sugar mills across the island were blown down, plantations were flattened and the streets of Port Royal were strewn with the wrecks of ships, the debris of buildings and dead bodies.

15

Back to the Bahamas

Seven years later Woodes Rogers was faced with the aftermath of another hurricane when he returned to the Bahamas to take up his role as Governor for the second time. He had left England at the end of May 1729 and arrived in Nassau on 25 August after a stormy crossing of the Atlantic. At first sight the appearance of the harbour and the town was a considerable improvement on the scene which had greeted his squadron of warships and merchantmen back in 1718. This time there was no sign of any pirate ships or burnt-out and plundered hulks. Dominating the waterfront were the ramparts and bastions of Fort Nassau, which, when seen from a distance, appeared to be in good order. Many of the houses had lost their roofs or been badly damaged by the hurricane which had swept across the island three weeks before but rising up behind them was the steeply pitched roof and bell tower of the new church.

On going ashore Rogers soon discovered that conditions on the island were not much better than they had been when he had left the place in 1721. So many people had gone down with 'an ague and fever' that the Assembly had not been able to sit for several weeks.[1] The island's defences were in a parlous state. The wooden gun carriages of the fifteen guns in Fort Nassau were so rotten that three of them collapsed when a salute was fired to mark Rogers' arrival. The carriages of the twenty-four guns brought out from the Tower of London by Phenney had disintegrated, leaving the gun barrels lying uselessly on the ground. The timber guard room and officers' rooms built by Rogers had been demolished by the recent hurricane, while the magazine, prison and cook room built under the ramparts were so badly decayed that they were unusable, 'so that it is thought best to fill up under the ramparts and make them solid for a support to the outer wall'.[2] The Independent Company, which comprised the garrison and was the island's only defence force, numbered no more than 110 men including the officers. This might have been sufficient to repel a pirate raid if the guns had been serviceable, but would have had little chance against a serious invasion mounted by France or Spain.

A recent survey of the trade of the islands carried out by George Phenney at the request of London suggested that the island was nearly self-sufficient in food and produce. Local turtles and fruit were bartered for provisions with traders in South Carolina. The natural produce of New Providence was listed as: large sugar canes; the finest cotton in the world; mahogany, cedar and pine suitable for ship building; lignum vitae, brown ebony and various dye woods; a variety of fruits, 'the pineapples here being the best kind in America'; and hats made by the local women from palm leaves, small quantities of which were exported.[3] The reality behind Phenney's optimistic report was that the Bahamas were languishing far behind Britain's other West Indian colonies. Only 800 acres of land were under cultivation on New Providence. New settlers had failed to materialise in significant numbers and the population remained tiny. A census carried out in 1731 revealed that the total population of New Providence, Harbour Island and Eleuthera was 1,388. Of the 1,042 people living on New Providence there were 409 black slaves, and the white population consisted of 190 males, 135 females and 308 children.[4] This compared with Barbados, which had a population of around 61,000 (16,000 whites and 45,000 blacks) and Jamaica with 62,000 (7,000 whites and 55,000 blacks).[5] Both these islands had thriving sugar-cane plantations, with Jamaica exporting 10,249 tons of sugar to Britain in 1725.[6] It is no wonder that the Board of Trade took little interest in the reports received from the Bahamas.

Rogers had brought out to Nassau his 22-year-old son William, and also two men he hoped would assist him in governing the islands. John Colebrooke, who was to be appointed Speaker of the new Assembly, was a former merchant with considerable experience of wheeler-dealing in Europe. He was variously described as being 'of pleasant conversation and good sense' and 'a cunning man and perfect master in the art of stock-jobbing'.[7] He was accompanied by John White, a long-time associate of his who was shortly to become the islands' Treasurer and Chief Justice. These two would form an alliance which would seriously undermine Rogers' authority and make his life a misery.

The day following his arrival Rogers convened a Council meeting at which George Phenney was present. The superseded governor handed over the great seal of the islands and Rogers produced the communion silver and furnishings for the church which he had brought over with him. These were a gift from the King and included a silver chalice, paten, small flagons and an alms dish; a large bible and two prayer books; and a cushion and altar frontal of crimson damask with silk fringes. A month later, on 29 September, the first Assembly was held. It consisted of twenty-four members and included representatives from Eleuthera and Harbour Island. During the next few months various Acts were passed to improve the appearance of Nassau and help the economy of the islands. The public highways were to be cleared and a straight street was to be constructed from east to west in Nassau 'with a space left in the middle of the town for a square'. Measures were agreed to prevent the stealing of fruit and to stop the destruction of trees whose timber could be used for shipbuilding; the planting of cotton was to be encouraged; cattle were to be restrained from damaging crops and plantations; and an Act was passed 'for the encouragement of foreigners and strangers settling in these islands'.[8]

George Phenney, who was keen to divorce his troublesome wife, tried to persuade Rogers to detain her in Nassau while he escaped to England but this came to nothing when she discovered her husband's plan. After several difficult months the two of them left the island in November and returned to London, where, as Rogers anticipated, they conspired against him. Two years later Phenney moved to Virginia to take up the position of Surveyor General of Customs for the southern part of the American colonies.[9]

The one positive aspect of Rogers' second term as Governor was the disappearance of the pirates. When he had first arrived at Nassau in August 1718 the number of pirates operating in the Caribbean and along the eastern shores of North America was between 1,500 and 2,000. This increased to between 1,800 and 2,400 in the years 1719 to 1722 but successful operations against some of the pirate companies had spread them further afield and, as we have seen, several pirate companies, such as those led by Bartholomew Roberts, had shifted their operations to the coast of West Africa. But from 1723 onwards there was a dramatic decline in pirate numbers. By 1724 there were no more than 500 or so pirates prowling around the coasts of the North Atlantic and by 1726 the total had dwindled to less than 200.[10] The decline was due to the capture, trial and execution of pirate crews, and the deaths, usually violent, of their most prominent leaders. The historian Peter Earle has noted that, of the

55 pirate captains of the period whose fates are known, 26 were hanged, 6 were killed in action, 4 were drowned in shipwrecks, 4 were shot by their own men, one shot himself, one was set adrift in an open boat, and one retired to a life of poverty in Madagascar. Only 12 of those who surrendered were fortunate enough to live on after the end of their piratical careers.[11]

The response of the authorities to the pirate companies that were captured had been and continued to be as harsh as it was towards highwaymen, burglars or petty thieves. Marcus Rediker has estimated that no fewer than 400 and as many as 600 pirates were hanged in the years between 1716 and 1726.[12] Mass hangings were not unusual. We have already noted the fifty-two men of Roberts' company who were hanged at Cape Coast Castle. Of the fifty-eight pirates led by Matthew Luke who were captured by HMS *Launceston* in 1722, no fewer than 41 were hanged at Jamaica. Twenty-six of the thirty-six pirates captured by HMS *Greyhound* in 1723 were hanged. Eighteen of the nineteen men led by Lyne were hanged in 1726, and eleven of the sixteen men of Lowther's crew were hanged at St Kitts in 1724. Hangings were always treated as public spectacles and provided grisly entertainment for the large crowds which gathered on the waterfront to hear the last words of the condemned men and watch them die. To further dissuade sailors from taking up piracy the bodies of well-known pirate leaders were hanged on gibbets at the entrance to harbours, in the same way that Calico Jack's body had been put on display in Jamaica after his execution at Gallows Point. Five pirates taken by HMS *Winchelsea* in 1723 were hanged at the high-water mark at St John's in Antigua, and afterwards the body of Finn, their leader, was hung in chains on Rat Island. After they had been hanged at Boston in 1724 the bodies of pirate quartermaster John Rose Archer and William White 'were conveyed in boats down to an island where White was buried, and the quartermaster was hung up in irons to be a spectacle, and so a warning to others'.[13] A naval or merchant seaman in the 1720s was likely to see the decaying bodies of pirates prominently displayed along the banks of the River Thames in London, at Leith Sands outside Edinburgh, at Newport, Rhode Island, in Boston harbour, at Charleston, South Carolina, at St Kitts, at Port Royal and at several other West Indian harbours.

The colonial governors were in no doubt that the trials and executions of pirates were a deterrent and would lead to a decline in pirate attacks. The executions carried out by Rogers certainly marked the end of Nassau as a pirate headquarters. After the hanging of Calico Jack and his crew, Governor Lawes of Jamaica reported that the 'trial of the pirates executed here which has had good effect these seas having been more free of late from such villains than for some time before'.[14] After the hanging of Matthew Luke and his pirates he wrote, 'I make no question but the example that has been made of these rogues will deter others in these parts.'[15] And writing to Lord Carteret to inform him of the capture of pirates off New York by HMS *Greyhound* in 1723, Governor Burnet concluded, 'This blow, with what they received from Captain Ogle will I hope clear the seas of these accomplished villains.'[16]

Although the warships of the British Navy played a prominent role in hunting down the pirates, it had taken some time for the Admiralty to respond to the pirate threat. It will be recalled that the pirates hanged by Rogers had been brought in by the former pirate Ben Hornigold. Calico Jack and his crew had been captured by Jonathan Barnet, a merchant sea captain. Stede Bonnet and his crew were taken by private vessels commanded by Colonel Rhett, and Charles Vane had been handed over to the Jamaican authorities by Captain Holford, a retired buccaneer. Not till May 1718 did the Admiralty specifically order the nine warships based at Jamaica,

Barbados, the Leeward Islands, Virginia, New York and New England, 'To correspond and act in concert against the pirates'.[17] Even then some naval captains showed a marked reluctance to get involved. We have already seen how Rogers was deserted by the naval ships which had accompanied him to the Bahamas in spite of his strenuous demands that they stay while the islands were still under threat from pirates. And there is evidence to show that some naval captains preferred to use their ships for trading rather than to look for pirates among the dangerous shoals and coral reefs of the Caribbean.[18] However, when the Royal Navy did go into action against the pirates it certainly achieved results, the most notable examples being the hunting down of Blackbeard and Bartholomew Roberts and HMS *Greyhound*'s actions off New York.

By 1726 all the leading pirate captains described in Captain Johnson's *General History of the Pyrates* and almost all those whose names featured in the newspapers or colonial office reports of the period had been executed, killed or had retired. This did not mean the end of piracy in the Caribbean. There were still occasional attacks on merchant vessels (usually by rogue elements of the Spanish coastguard) but pirates were no longer a serious threat to the trade of the region.

The only mention of pirates in the Council meetings and Assembly meetings called by Rogers during his second term as Governor appeared in 'a Humble Address to the Kings most excellent Majesty' which was drawn up by the Assembly on 30 October 1729. This thanked the King for appointing Woodes Rogers as Governor and pointed out that 'the experience we formerly had of his justice, conduct and valour not only in the defence but in rescuing this island from pirates the worst of enemies, leaves us in no doubt, but that under his present administration these islands will soon be in as flourishing a condition as any of your Majesty's colonies in

America'.[19] However, Rogers faced an uphill task to achieve the results he was hoping for. He was particularly concerned about the islands' defences and on 26 November 1730, fifteen months after his arrival, he addressed the Assembly and warned the members that the fortifications were still in a very bad condition and the Bahamas were vulnerable to attack. There might be peace in Europe but he was concerned about a possible rupture with the Spanish or the French.

All Rogers' efforts to improve the fortifications of the islands were hampered by the sinister alliance of John Colebrooke and John White. Colebrooke was in a powerful position as Speaker of the Assembly, while White, 'being a great talker in the Council most of which were old inhabitants and illiterate, they two always being together consulted their measures with the Assembly so as to be continually pushing forward their own views, by which means they soon began to lord it over the people in a very haughty and imperious manner and to oppose the Governor in everything they could'.[20]

By the end of 1730 Rogers decided he must put an end to their machinations and on 1 December he suspended the meetings of the Assembly. This prompted Colebrooke to launch a personal attack on Rogers. He threatened to ask the King to replace their tyrannical and arbitrary governor with an honest governor, and he seized all the Assembly's books and papers and refused to hand them over. A few weeks later Rogers wrote to the Council of Trade and Plantations to inform them that the state of his health obliged him to travel to South Carolina 'for a change of air, from whence I hope to return in three weeks or a month'.[21] By the beginning of April he was in Charleston and was soon sufficiently recovered to be planning a visit to Cat Island, which was considered to be more fertile than the other islands and might prove a suitable location for more plantations. He was back in Nassau by early May, accompanied by a lawyer who was made Attorney-General and who assisted him in bringing Colebrooke before a Grand Jury. Colebrooke had continued to stir up trouble but at a sessions held towards the end of May he was tried and found guilty of vexatious litigation and disturbing the public peace. He was fined £750 and ordered to be 'confined during his Majesty's pleasure'.

On 14 October 1731 Rogers wrote to London for the last time. He enclosed details of the trial of Colebrooke and the relevant proceedings of the Council and Assembly. He said that he was sending his son to England to explain the urgent need to repair the fortifications to prevent the islands becoming an easy prey to their powerful neighbours. The Council of Trade and Plantations received no further communications from the Bahamas for the next nine months. On 20 July 1732 a brief statement was sent to the Duke of Newcastle which began:

> Whereas it pleased Almighty God to take unto himself the soul of Woodes Rogers Esqr. our late Governr. on the fiveteenth day of this Instant.
>
> We the President and the rest of his Majestys Council for these Bahama Islands being on this Occasion Assembled in Council have thought fit to Acquaint yr. Lordship therewith, which with all Possible Submission we now do . . .[22]

No records have survived to indicate the cause and circumstances of Woodes Rogers' death. All we know is that he died at the age of fifty-three. Did he succumb to one of the tropical diseases which caused the death of so many in the West Indies? Were his son and daughter present at his deathbed and his funeral in Nassau? Was he buried beside the church built by his predecessor or within the walls of the fort which he had restored and had struggled to maintain in good order? There was no mention of his death in the London newspapers but the September issue of *The Gentleman's Magazine* contained the following information: 'Came Advice of the Death of Woods Rogers, Esq; Governour of the Bahama Islands July 16. He, and Capt.Cook lately drowned, made a cruizing Voyage to the South Seas and round the Globe in the *Duke and Dutchess*, in the Wars of Q.Anne.'[23]

It is strange but not inappropriate that the death of Captain Edward Cooke, who, like Rogers, had published an account of their circumnavigation, should be recorded in the same issue of the same magazine. Where and exactly when Cooke was drowned is not known. Rogers had made his will on 26 May 1729, shortly before setting off for the Bahamas, and it was proved in London on 24 November 1732. The probate act described him as 'late of the parish of St Margaret, Westminster, but dying at the Bahama Islands, a widower'.[24] He left his estate to his son William and his daughter Sarah. His son became a member of the Council of the Bahamas the following year and then went out to the Guinea Coast as a merchant for the Royal Africa Company. He died in 1735 at Whydah, a victim of one of the tropical diseases which had killed Alexander Selkirk in the same region fourteen years earlier.

Epilogue

The death of Woodes Rogers may have passed almost unnoticed in London, but his name would live on long after the names of the civil servants in Whitehall and the other colonial governors of his day had been forgotten. This was partly due to his voyage round the world and his capture of the Manila galleon. His expedition in the *Duke* and *Dutchess* may not have been as successful as it has sometimes been portrayed but it gave Rogers a buccaneering image and linked him with Drake, Cavendish, Anson and other plunderers of Spanish ships in the Pacific. His other claim to fame was the restoration of law and order in the Bahamas – an achievement which for many years was reflected in the islands' motto: *Expulsit pirates, restituta commercia* (Pirates expelled, commerce restored).[1] But it was his rescue of Alexander Selkirk, and his description of how Selkirk survived his solitary years on Juan Fernández, which ensured that Rogers achieved a measure of immortality out of all proportion to his own exploits.

This was due to the publication on 23 April 1719 of *Robinson Crusoe*, Daniel Defoe's masterpiece.[2] The book proved instantly popular among all classes of the reading public in London and beyond. The initial edition of 1,000 copies was followed by a second edition on 9 May and a third edition on 6 June. A fourth edition came out shortly before the publication in August 1719 of Defoe's rapidly compiled sequel, *The Further Adventures of Robinson Crusoe*. Within a year the book had been published in French, Dutch and German. Generally regarded by literary critics as the first English novel, *Robinson Crusoe* is a study of survival, written with such conviction and attention to detail that it is hard to believe it is a work of fiction. It has a universal appeal and has been admired for different reasons by people as various as Benjamin Franklin, Jean-Jacques Rousseau, Karl Marx and Virginia Woolf. As Coleridge famously pointed out, Crusoe is a representative of humanity in general, 'the person for whom every reader could substitute himself',[3] and a more recent commentator has observed that Crusoe, in common with a few other characters such as Don Quixote, Hamlet and Faust, has 'passed into the collective understanding of western humanity'.[4]

To what extent was Rogers' account of Selkirk's adventures responsible for Defoe's memorable creation? In his book of 1712 *A Cruising Voyage Round the World* Rogers provided what has come to be accepted as the definitive account of Selkirk's experiences on Juan Fernández, and it is worth noting that a second edition was published in 1718, the year before Defoe's novel was published. There was also Edward Cooke's account in *A Voyage to the South Sea and Round the World*, which covers much of the same ground as Rogers' book. And there was the article in *The Englishman* by Richard Steele which added some additional information gleaned from his interview with Selkirk. Within a few months after the return of the Bristol ships with the captured Manila galleon, we can assume that Selkirk's story was well known in London. Defoe, with his keen interest in voyages and travel, and the South Seas in particular, would certainly have taken a close interest in the story.

The American academic Arthur Secord (who persuasively argued the case that another castaway was the model for Crusoe) was in no doubt that 'when Londoners talked of desert island adventures they naturally thought of Selkirk. Not only was his case the most recent one, but it had also been given much wider publicity than any of the others, through the interest aroused by his return.' And he concluded that 'Selkirk undoubtedly furnished Defoe with the central theme of the story'.[5]

It is not surprising, therefore, that for a long time it was taken for granted that Selkirk's marooning not only provided the original idea for *Robinson Crusoe* but that Selkirk was the model and prototype for Crusoe. The similarities were obvious: they both hunted goats on foot when the powder for their guns ran out; they both wore clothes made from goat-skins; they both built two huts from tree branches and assigned separate purposes for each one; they both ingeniously adapted the tools and equipment they had at their disposal. After an early period of despair Selkirk recovered and kept up his spirits by singing psalms and reciting from the Bible and in doing so made himself a better person – as did Crusoe. They both attempted to impose order on their existence by marking trees to note the passing days. Selkirk hid in a tree to prevent his discovery by Spaniards who landed on the island and might have enslaved him, and Crusoe did the same. And although the location of Crusoe's island was thousands of miles from Juan Fernández, the landscape and topography of his island were very similar to descriptions which Defoe would have read of Juan Fernández.

The similarities are offset by a number of differences in the stories of Selkirk and Crusoe. These have led to what Glyn Williams has described as 'the thickets of scholarship that surround the issue of the sources used by Defoe'.[6] The discussion has been most intense among Defoe scholars but doubts were expressed as early as the

1820s by Sir Walter Scott, who wrote, 'The assistance which De Foe derived from Selkirk's history seems of a very meagre kind. It is not certain that he was obliged to the real hermit of Juan Fernandez even for the original hint . . .'7 Scott does acknowledge that Defoe probably borrowed from Rogers' account the abundance of goats, the clothing made from their skins and the circumstance of the two huts. John Robert Moore, who was for many years considered the leading expert on Defoe, echoed this view when he wrote, 'It has often been supposed that Crusoe was almost identical with Alexander Selkirk, but the influence of the Selkirk story on Robinson Crusoe has been greatly exaggerated.'8

It has to be said that some of the differences between Selkirk's story and Crusoe's story are considerable. Selkirk was marooned after an argument with his captain but Crusoe was shipwrecked in a storm and cast on to the beach. Selkirk was a castaway on Juan Fernández for four years and four months, while Crusoe was on his island for twenty-eight years. Selkirk had an extremely limited supply of tools and equipment at his disposal but Crusoe was able to make numerous journeys out to his wrecked ship and recovered ships biscuit, Dutch cheeses, rice, rum, rigging, sails, an arsenal of weapons with powder and shot, the carpenter's chest, 'three bags full of nails and spikes, a great screw-jack, a dozen or so hatchets, and above all, that most useful thing called a grindstone'. Crusoe is constantly trying to improve his situation by growing corn, by attempting to make baskets and pots, and by carrying out improvements to the safety and appearance of his dwelling, but Selkirk remains in his crude huts and is content to rely on goats, fish, turtles and the turnips and cabbage trees already available on the island. Crusoe hopes to escape from his island by making a canoe, but Selkirk feels he has no alternative but to await rescue by the ship of a friendly nation. Selkirk had no human companions during his time

A GENERAL
HISTORY
OF THE
Robberies and Murders
Of the moſt notorious
PYRATES,
AND ALSO
Their *Policies, Diſcipline* and *Government,*

From their firſt RISE and SETTLEMENT in the Iſland of *Providence,* in 1717, to the preſent Year 1724.

WITH

The remarkable ACTIONS and ADVENTURES of the two Female Pyrates, *Mary Read* and *Anne Bonny.*

To which is prefix'd

An ACCOUNT of the famous Captain *Avery* and his Companions; with the Manner of his Death in *England.*

The Whole digeſted into the following CHAPTERS;

To which is added,

A ſhort ABSTRACT of the Statute and Civil Law, in Relation to PYRACY.

By Captain CHARLES JOHNSON.

LONDON, Printed for *Ch. Rivington* at the *Bible* and *Crown* in St. *Paul's Church-Yard, J. Lacy* at the *Ship* near the *Temple-Gate,* and *J. Stone* next the *Crown* Coffee-houſe the back of *Greys-Inn,* 1724.

Title-page of the First Edition, 1724

on the island, but Crusoe was joined by Man Friday, who plays an important part in the last part of the book. Perhaps the most significant difference is the geographical setting of the two islands. Juan Fernández (Isla Róbinson Crusoe) is of course in the Pacific and is some 400 miles away from the mainland of South America. Crusoe's island is on the Atlantic coast of Venezuela, near the mouth of the River Orinoco, and is close enough to the mainland to receive visits from native 'savages' who have rowed across in canoes.

If the differences seem to cast doubts on Selkirk being a credible model for Crusoe, where did Defoe get his idea and his information? The first and most obvious source was the work of William Dampier. Defoe was certainly familiar with *A New Voyage Round the World* because in his book *The Compleat English Gentleman* he pointed out the advantages of travel and advised young men to 'go round the Globe with Dampier and Rogers'.[9] Dampier's description of the marooning and subsequent rescue of Will the Miskito Indian was one of several accounts of castaways available to Defoe and was a possible source for Man Friday. On three occasions Dampier described how native peoples made large canoes or piraguas by hollowing out the trunks of trees. He noted how sailors would collect parrots and keep them as pets, and he described several islands off the north coast of Venezuela which were stocked with goats and turtles. Taken as a whole Dampier's writings provided an encyclopaedic store of information about life at sea, navigational methods, shipwrecks, tropical islands, savage Indians and exotic fauna and flora.

A number of scholars have suggested that the most likely alternative source for Robinson Crusoe is the life of Henry Pitman, which has the merit of being set in a location not too far from the mouth of the Orinoco. Pitman was a surgeon who, like Defoe himself, took part in Monmouth's Rebellion against King James II. He was arrested after the Battle of Sedgemoor, and was tried for treason before 'Hanging' Judge Jeffreys. He was sentenced to transportation and was despatched to Barbados to work as a convict slave on the plantations. In May 1687 he escaped from Barbados in a small open boat with seven companions. Their destination was the Dutch island of Curaçao but after a nightmare journey they landed on the island of Salt Tortuga, which was being used as a base by a group of pirates. During the course of his enforced stay on the island Pitman lived on turtle meat and turtle eggs; he attempted to make a stewing pot out of fine sand and egg yolks bound together with goat hair; and he acquired a Man Friday figure – an Indian he had ransomed from the pirates: 'I went abroad with my Indian a-fishing, at which he was so dextrous that with his bow and arrow he would shoot a small fish at a great distance.' Eventually Pitman was rescued from his island existence and in 1689 he published an account of his adventures entitled *A Relation of the Great Sufferings and Strange Adventures of Henry Pitman, Surgeon to the Late Duke of Monmouth*.

In the research for his book *Seeking Robinson Crusoe* the writer and explorer Tim Severin travelled to many of the places where likely models for Crusoe had spent months or years. His travels took him to Juan Fernández, to the Mosquito Coast of Nicaragua, to the Isthmus of Panama and to various islands off the River Orinoco, including Salt Tortuga, where Pitman had been marooned. Ironically it was in the British Library, after he had returned from his intrepid journeys, that Severin discovered the closest link between Pitman and Defoe. For some years Pitman had been a lodger at the premises of his publisher John Taylor 'at the Sign of the Ship in St Paul's Churchyard, London'. And it was his publisher's son, William Taylor, who published *Robinson Crusoe* round the corner 'at the Ship in Paternoster Row'. Pitman and Defoe were similar in age, could well have met and, even if they did not, Severin suggests that

William Taylor would surely have shown Defoe a copy of Pitman's book, which had been produced by the family firm.

Another possible model for Crusoe was Robert Knox, a sailor who was shipwrecked on the coast of Ceylon and published an account of his experiences in 1681 entitled *Historical Relation of Ceylon*. Although Ceylon is far from the Orinoco, and Knox was not alone on the populous island, Arthur Secord has drawn attention to remarkable similarities in the lives of Knox and Crusoe. In the first place their dates correspond closely. Defoe has Crusoe shipwrecked on 30 September 1659, and Knox was shipwrecked in November 1659. Both Knox and Crusoe had gone to sea against the wishes of their respective fathers. On his return to England after twenty-eight years away, Crusoe finds 'all his family extinct' except two sisters and the children of one of his brothers. Knox returns after nineteen years of captivity and finds that his only living relatives are his brother and sister and her children. The island experiences of the two castaways have several points in common: Knox, like Crusoe, built two or three huts and he surrounded one with a hedge to hide it from hostile intruders. Both Knox and Crusoe had bibles and spent much time in prayer and uplifting religious meditation. They both had lamps, Knox using coconut oil for his and Crusoe making use of goat's tallow. Knox, like Crusoe, created pits covered with vegetation as traps for goats, and he made pens to keep the captured goats in the vicinity of his dwelling. Secord reaches the conclusion that 'If we think of Selkirk as having suggested the idea of writing a story of desert island life, and of Knox as having provided him with a concrete embodiment of that idea, we shall not go far astray.'[10]

This is not the place to list all the castaways who have been proposed as models for Crusoe, but there is one other who has a strong claim to be included and that is Robert Drury. He was the son of one of Defoe's neighbours in Stoke Newington, at that time a village just north of London. He was shipwrecked on the southern coast of Madagascar in 1703. His companions were killed by hostile natives but Drury survived and spent nearly fourteen years on the island as a captive. He returned to England in 1717. His experiences were not published until 1729 but if Defoe was the author of *Madagascar; or Robert Drury's Journal*, as has sometimes been suggested, then he would have got the story at first hand from Drury himself.

The debate over the sources for *Robinson Crusoe* will no doubt continue but, as many commentators have pointed out, it is not the sources that matter so much as the force of Defoe's imagination. In the words of Pat Rogers, 'Background can never explain a great book; for the genesis of creative literature is, in the last analysis, internal rather than external . . .'[11] For many of the details in his first novel Defoe was able to draw on his own past experiences and interests. Like Crusoe (and like Dampier) he had a rambling nature and was 'inured to a wandering life'. He was an inveterate traveller all his life and although his travels were limited to the British Isles and the continent, his reading of books of voyages was extensive. He knew about ships and shipbuilding, and his two brothers-in-law, who were shipwrights, would have been able to supply him with further information if he needed it. His ownership of a tile factory near Tilbury enabled him to give an authentic account of the difficulties involved in the making of clay pots and tobacco pipes. His observations of the effects of the Great Storm of 1703 (which he had published) furnished him with material for Crusoe's various shipwrecks. He may even have taken the name of his hero from a classmate at Morton's Academy who was called Timothy Cruso or Crusoe.

Whether he drew on his own background or on the lives of castaways like Henry Pitman, it seems that it was economic necessity which prompted the 59-year-old Defoe to embark on a book which purported to be the true story of a shipwrecked sailor. He was constantly in financial difficulties and needed the money to support his large family. He would have been well aware that stories of voyages and adventures overseas were among the best-selling books of his day. Selkirk may or may not have provided the model for Crusoe himself but it is generally acknowledged that it was his story which provided the initial spark which got Defoe going on the first and most successful of all his novels.

Apart from his association with *Robinson Crusoe* through his rescue of Selkirk, Woodes Rogers has one other claim to fame and that is his role in another book which was a best-seller in its day and has since become a classic in its field. Captain Charles Johnson's *General History of the Robberies and Murders of the Most Notorious Pyrates* has been frequently quoted in this book, as it has been in all books concerned with the Golden Age of Piracy. Indeed it could be argued that Johnson created the idea of a Golden Age by his detailed and vivid account of the lives of those western pirates who were operating from around 1700 (Captain Kidd was hanged at Execution Dock in London in 1701) to about 1726, when William Fly and two of his crew were hanged on the banks of the Charles River at Boston. In the two volumes of his history Johnson described the lives of some thirty pirate leaders, including Blackbeard, Bartholomew Roberts, Charles Vane, Sam Bellamy, Calico Jack Rackam and the female pirates Mary Read and Anne Bonny. While the identity of Captain Johnson remains a mystery, there is no doubt about the authenticity of most of the material in his book because it echoes contemporary reports from colonial governors, the depositions of sea captains and sailors captured by pirates and the surviving transcripts of pirate trials. Johnson certainly made use of these sources as well as reports in the newspapers of his day. In the preface to his book he assured

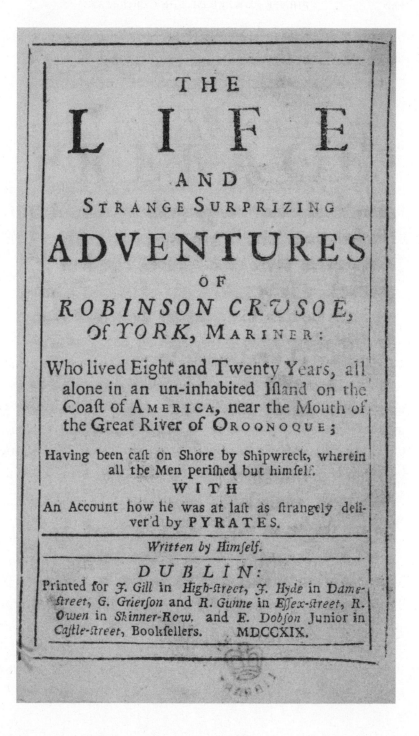

THE
LIFE

AND
STRANGE SURPRIZING

ADVENTURES

OF

ROBINSON CRUSOE,
Of YORK, MARINER:

Who lived Eight and Twenty Years, all
alone in an un-inhabited Island on the
Coast of AMERICA, near the Mouth of
the Great River of OROONOQUE;

Having been cast on Shore by Shipwreck, wherein
all the Men perished but himself.

WITH

An Account how he was at last as strangely deliver'd by PYRATES.

Written by Himself.

DUBLIN:
Printed for *J.* Gill in *High-street, J. Hyde* in *Dame-
street,* G. *Grierson* and R. *Gunne* in *Essex-street,* R.
Owen in *Skinner-Row.* and E. *Dobson* Junior in
Castle-street, Booksellers. MDCCXIX.

his readers that 'those facts which he himself was not an eye-witness of, he had from the authentic relations of the persons concerned in taking the pirates, as well as from the mouths of the pirates themselves, after they were taken . . .'.[12]

Johnson devoted a considerable amount of space to Woodes Rogers in his book. He described the circumstances of his appointment as Governor of the Bahamas and covered his arrival at Nassau in great detail. He described the measures Rogers took to put down the pirates and included the full transcript of the pirate trial at Nassau presided over by Rogers. All these facts would have been available to Johnson without too much difficulty but he also included other facts which suggest that Rogers may well have supplied him with the information himself.

The first edition of volume one of Johnson's history was published in May 1724. It included an introduction to the rise of piracy in the West Indies and contained biographies of seventeen pirate leaders and their crews. In July 1728 a second volume was published which contained the biographies of fifteen more pirate leaders and it was to this second volume that Johnson added an appendix giving additional information about Rogers and events which took place during his first period as Governor of the Bahamas. It will be recalled that Rogers returned to London from his first term as Governor in the summer of 1721. As far as we know he remained in London for the next eight years until he was reinstated as Governor and sailed for the Bahamas in May 1729. During that period he spent some time in a debtors' prison (where he would have been allowed visitors) but for the rest of the time his primary aim was to clear his debts and gather support for his reinstatement as Governor. Although Johnson makes no reference to consulting Rogers, it would be surprising if he did not contact such a key player in the campaign against the pirates.

There are two passages in particular in the *General History of the Pyrates* which suggest that Johnson may have got his information direct from Rogers. The first concerns Rogers' voyage to Madagascar in 1714. We know that Rogers had applied to the East India Company to sail the merchant ship *Delicia* from London to Madagascar, where he proposed to buy slaves whom he would sell in the East Indies. In his chapter on Captain Avery and his exploits in the Indian Ocean, Johnson described Rogers' visit to Madagascar in considerable detail. He noted the miserable state of the pirate colony on the island and the pathetic appearance of the pirates and their children. The pirates were persuaded to sell some of their Negro slaves in exchange for clothes, knives, saws, gunpowder and musket balls. During the course of the negotiations Rogers realised that the pirates were planning to overcome his crew and seize his ship. He took the necessary precautions to prevent this and sailed on to the East Indies. Johnson tells us that one of the Madagascar pirates 'had formerly been a waterman upon the Thames, where having committed a murder he fled to the West Indies'. The rest of the pirates had all been foremast men or ordinary seamen, 'nor was there a man amongst them who could either read or write'.[13]

The other passage which contains the sort of first-hand detail which might have been supplied by Rogers concerns the piracies of Charles Vane. In the first volume of his history Johnson had described Vane's attempt to disrupt Rogers' landing at Nassau in 1718. In the appendix to his second volume Johnson wrote that 'we have since had some particulars sent us, which relate to pyracies, both before and after that date'.[14] He then supplied a much more detailed account of Vane's exploits around the time of Rogers' arrival as Governor. In particular he reproduced a letter which Vane had written to Rogers on 24 July 1718, the day before Rogers' ships entered the harbour. The letter was addressed 'To his Excellency the Governor of New Providence' and it began: 'Your Excellency may please to understand that we are willing to accept his Majesty's most gracious Pardon on the following Terms, viz. That you will suffer us to dispose of all our Goods now in our Possession . . .' Vane informed Rogers that he would accept the pardon if his terms were agreed upon, otherwise 'we are obliged to stand on our Defence'. The letter was signed by 'Charles Vane and Company' and included the postscript, 'We wait a speedy answer.'[15]

During the previous weeks Vane and his men had captured and brought into Nassau no fewer than seven ships and sloops, many of them laden with rich cargoes, so his terms would have been totally unacceptable. As we know, Vane subsequently sent a fireship against one of Rogers' ships and fled the harbour. According to Johnson, he then sent word to Rogers that 'he would make him a visit, and burn his guardship, for sending two sloops to chase him instead of answering his letter'.[16]

The amount of detail contained in both the above passages suggests that the information must have been supplied by someone who took part in Rogers' voyage to Madagascar in 1714 and his expedition to Nassau in 1718. Since Rogers was in London while Johnson was compiling his book, he would seem to be the obvious source.[17]

Although he lives on in the pages of the *General History of the Pyrates*, and in the colonial office records of the period, and in his spirited account of his circumnavigation, Rogers remains an elusive figure. There are no descriptions of his physical appearance. The seated figure in Hogarth's family portrait could be anyone. What is remarkable about Rogers is the way in which his life touched so many aspects of the world in which he lived. It was an age during which the maritime nations of Europe fought for the possession of overseas islands and territories; an age of privateering and piracy, of voyages and books about voyages. It was also an age of merchants and entrepreneurs; of sugar plantations and the slave trade; of speculations and bankruptcies. As a sea captain, privateer, slave trader and colonial governor Rogers was involved in all these things.

We may have no idea of his appearance but we do know that Woodes Rogers was a man of great determination who refused to be cast down by the troubles and setbacks he faced during the course of his life. There is a passage in *A Cruising Voyage Round the World* which has already been quoted but is worth repeating because it could well serve as his epitaph: 'I begun this voyage with a resolution to go through with it, and the greatest misfortune or obstacle shall not deter me; I'll as much as possible avoid being thoughtful and afflicting myself for what can't be recalled, but indefatigably pursue the concerns of the voyage.'

Glossary

aft, after Situated at the back or stern part of a vessel.

bark A sailing vessel which was used for trading or fishing, sometimes ship-rigged with three masts or rigged as a brig or snow with two masts.

boatswain, or bosun The warrant officer in charge of sails, rigging, anchors and associated gear.

bow The front part of a vessel as it widens from the leading edge or stem.

bowsprit A heavy spar pointing forward from the stem or front of the vessel.

brace A rope used to control the horizontal movement of a square-sailed yard.

brig A two-masted vessel, fully square-rigged on both masts, with a fore-and-aft sail on the lower part of the mainmast.

brigantine A two-masted vessel having a fully square-rigged foremast and a fore-and-aft rigged mainmast with squaresails on the main topmast.

broadside The simultaneous firing of all the guns on one side of a ship.

bulkhead A vertical partition inside a ship.

bumboat A small boat used to bring out and sell fruit, vegetables and other produce to the sailors on ships anchored some distance from the shore.

cable A measure of distance based on the usual length of a ship's anchor cable which was 120 fathoms.

careen To heave a ship over to expose the bottom for cleaning and repairs.

carriage gun A cannon, mounted on a wheeled gun carriage, which usually required several men to load, aim and fire it. Guns were classified by the weight of ball they fired and in the eighteenth century ranged from three- or four-pounders to forty-two-pounders.

caulk To seal the gaps between the planks with oakum and pitch.

collier A sturdy, flat-bottomed sailing vessel for carrying coal.

colours The flags worn by a vessel to show her nationality.

corsair (French *corsaire*; Italian *corsaro*) Pirates or privateers who were based in the Mediterranean.

cutter A small one-masted vessel rigged with a fore-and-aft mainsail, foresail and jib. In the eighteenth century a cutter usually had a square topsail as well.

East Indiaman A large ship engaged in trade with the East Indies.

ensign The national flag usually flown by ships at or near the stern of the vessel.

fathom A measure of six feet, used to describe the depth of water.

flag captain The captain of a ship carrying an admiral and flying his flag.

flagship A ship commanded by an admiral and flying the admiral's distinguishing flag.

fore Situated in front; the front part of a vessel at the bow.

fore-and-aft At bow and stern; backwards and forwards or along the length of the ship.

fore-and-aft rig Having mainly fore-and-aft sails, i.e. sails set lengthwise (and not at right-angles to the ship's hull, as is the case with square-rigged sails).

forecastle, fo'c's'le The short deck built over the fore part of the main deck; the forward part of a ship where the sailors lived.

foremast The mast at the front of the vessel.

frigate In the early eighteenth century the term could be applied to an armed merchantman with all the carriage guns on a single gun deck. Later the term was used to describe a fast cruising warship, less heavily armed than a ship of the line.

galleon A large three- or four-masted warship or armed merchantman which came into existence around 1570. Most of the Spanish and English ships which took part in the Armada campaign of 1588 were galleons and so were the treasure ships used by the Spanish in the seventeenth century and early eighteenth century.

gig A light, clinker-built boat carried by a warship and often favoured by captains for their own use.

grape, grapeshot Anti-personnel shot made up of small balls secured in a cylindrical canvas bag which flew apart on firing, scattering the shot over a wide area.

great cabin A large cabin at the stern of the ship reserved for the use of the captain or senior officer on board.

gunwale The upper planking along the sides of the vessel.

halyard A rope for raising and lowering a sail or yard.

heave to (past tense: hove to) To check the course of a vessel and bring her to a standstill by heading her into the wind and backing some of the sails.

helm The tiller or wheel which controls the rudder and enables a vessel to be steered.

hulk An old ship taken out of service and moored in harbour. Hulks were used as prison ships, convict ships, hospitals, floating barracks and receiving ships for pressed men.

larboard An old word for *port* (the left side of a vessel facing forward) which was preferred for helm orders. It was abandoned in 1844.

launch Originally a dockyard boat, the launch was used, like the longboat, for carrying heavy loads such as anchors, casks and barrels.

league A measure of distance: 3 miles (5 km).

lee The side or direction away from the wind, or downwind.

lee shore The shore on to which the wind is blowing; a hazardous shore for a sailing vessel, particularly in strong or gale force winds.

letter of marque A licence issued by the Lord High Admiral or the High Court of Admiralty which authorised an armed merchant vessel which was privately owned to attack the shipping of a named enemy in wartime.

log, logbook A journal or diary which recorded the ship's position, speed and course, with notes on the wind direction, weather, sail changes, flag signals and other vessels met en route. The official logbook in a British warship was kept by the ship's master (navigator) but the captain and lieutenants also kept logbooks and so did the midshipmen.

longboat The largest and heaviest boat carried by a ship and used for laying out anchors, and carrying water casks and other heavy loads.

mainmast 1. The mast at the centre of the ship or vessel, always the largest in square-rigged ships. 2. The name of the first and lowest section of the main-mast in a square-rigged ship; the others are the maintopmast, maintopgal-lant mast and main royalmast.

mainsheet The rope at the lower corner of the mainsail for regulating its position.

man-of-war An armed ship belonging to the navy of a country.

mess A division of a ship's company for the distribution of victuals; any group of officers or crew who eat, drink and associate together on a regular basis.

mizzenmast The mast at the stern or back of a vessel.

muster book A book containing the names of the ship's company.

pendant (pronounced 'pennant') The term can be used for any long tapering flag. The commissioning pendant of a naval ship was a very long flag like a streamer flown from the main masthead and it distinguished a warship in commission from a merchant ship.

pennant See pendant.

pinnace A ship's boat, ranging in size from twenty-three to thirty feet in length, which was mostly used to carry officers and men from ship to shore.

piragua A dugout canoe used by the native peoples of South and Central America. They were rowed or paddled and sometimes sailed with a single sail.

poop deck The aftermost and highest deck of a ship.

port The left side of a vessel facing forward.

privateer A privately owned warship (or the commander and crew of that vessel) licensed by a letter of marque to capture enemy shipping for profit in time of war.

prize A ship or smaller vessel captured from the enemy in time of war.

quarter The side of a ship towards the stern.

quarterdeck A deck above the main deck which stretched from the stern to about halfway along the length of the ship. It was from this deck that the captain and officers controlled the ship.

rate (as in first rate, second rate, etc.) Warships were grouped into six different categories according to the number of guns they carried. In the eighteenth century a first-rate ship had 100 guns, a second-rate ship had 90 guns, a third-rate had between 80 and 70 guns, a fourth-rate had between 64 and 50 guns, a fifth-rate had between 40 and 28 guns, and a sixth-rate had between 24 and 12 guns.

reef To reduce the area of a sail by rolling it up or bundling part of it and securing that part with short lines.

road, roadstead An open anchorage.

running rigging Ropes which run through blocks or are moved in any way to operate the sails and gear of a vessel – as distinct from standing rigging.

scuppers Holes in a ship's side for carrying off water from the deck.

sheet A rope made fast to the lower corner or corners of a sail to control its position.

ship 1. A vessel with three or more masts and fully square-rigged throughout. 2. The term is also used to describe any large sea-going vessel.

ship of the line A warship large enough to take her place in the line of battle.

shrouds The set of ropes forming part of the standing rigging and supporting the mast or topmast.

sloop 1. A vessel having one fore-and-aft rigged mast with mainsail and a single foresail. 2. In the Royal Navy any ship or vessel commanded by an officer with the rank of master and commander, usually rigged as a ship or brig with 16 to 18 guns.

snow A two-masted vessel similar to a brig and square-rigged on both masts but with an additional trysail mast stepped close behind the mainmast on which was set a fore-and-aft sail.

sound (or take a sounding) To measure the depth of water beneath a ship, usually with the aid of a lead weight and a line marked at regular intervals.

spar A stout wooden pole used for the mast or yard of a sailing vessel.

square-rigged The principal sails set at right angles to the length of the ship and extended by horizontal yards slung to the mast (as opposed to fore-and-aft rigged).

standing rigging That part of the rigging which supports the masts and spars and which is not moved when operating the vessel – as distinct from running rigging.

starboard The right side of a vessel facing forward.

stem, stempost The main timber forming the leading edge at the very front of a vessel.

stern The back or aft part of a vessel.

swivel gun, swivel-cannon A small piece of artillery, firing a shot of half a pound or less, which was fixed in a socket on the top of a ship's sides, stern or bow. The gun could be swivelled by hand to direct it up or down or sideways.

tack To change the direction of a sailing vessel's course by turning her bows into the wind until the wind blows on her other side.

tender A vessel attending a larger vessel and used to supply stores or convey passengers.

three-decker The largest class of warship with upwards of 90 guns on three gun decks.

two-decker A ship of the line having two complete gun decks.

van The foremost or leading ships of a fleet.

warp (noun) A rope used in towing or warping.

warp (verb) In calms or contrary winds it was often necessary to warp a vessel in and out of harbour or along a river. This was done by taking a rope or ropes from the ship to a fixed point ashore, or to a heavy post or pile driven into the river bed alongside the channel, and then heaving in the rope to haul the ship along.

warrant officers These ranked below the commissioned officers (the captain and lieutenants) and included the master, purser, surgeon, gunner, boatswain, carpenter and cook.

wear (as in to wear ship) To change the direction of a sailing vessel's course by turning her bows away from the wind until the wind blows on her other side (the opposite manoeuvre from tacking when the bows are turned into the wind).

weather (adjective) The side facing the wind. The weather column of a fleet is that to windward or nearest the direction from which the wind is blowing.

weigh To pull up the anchor.

yard A long spar suspended from the mast of a vessel to extend the sails.

yardarm Either end of a yard.

yawl A ship's boat of medium size (eighteen to twenty-six feet in length) which was developed from the seaworthy, clinker-built boats built at Deal in Kent to service the ships anchored in the Downs.

Notes

List of abbreviations

ADM	Admiralty documents
C	Chancery documents
CO	Colonial Office documents
CSPC	Calendar of State Papers, Colonial, America, and West Indies
Oxford DNB	*Oxford Dictionary of National Biography*
NMM	National Maritime Museum, London
PRO	Public Record Office, Kew, London

Prologue

1. *Post Boy*, London, Thursday, 24 October 1717.
2. Nathaniel Uring, quoted from *The Voyages and Travels of Captain Nathaniel Uring*, ed. A. Dewar (London, 1928), p. 241.
3. Governor Johnson to Council of Trade and Plantations, Charles Town, South Carolina, 18 June 1718. CSPC, vol. 1717–1718.
4. Sir Nicholas Lawes to Council of Trade and Plantations, Jamaica, 21 June 1718. CSPC, vol. 1717–1718.

5. Council of Trade and Plantations to Secretary Addison, Whitehall, 21 November 1717. CSPC, vol. 1717–1718.

6. Captain Woodes Rogers, *A Cruising Voyage Round the World*, ed. G. E. Manwaring (New York and London, 1928), p. 91.

7. Hugh Thomas, *The Slave Trade: The History of the Atlantic Slave Trade 1440–1870* (London, 1997; edn. cited 1998), pp. 211, 794; and O. H. K. Spate, *The Spanish Lake* (London, 1979), p. 193.

8. Neville Williams, *The Sea Dogs: Privateers, Plunder and Piracy in the Elizabethan Age* (London, 1975), p. 130.

9. *Calendar of State Papers, Spanish*, IV, 1587–1603, pp. 491–2.

10. For the origins and early history of the buccaneers see John Esquemeling, *Bucaniers of America* (London, 1684), vol. 1, part 1.

11. Quoted by the French missionary the Abbé Jean Baptiste Du Tertre. Peter Wood, *The Spanish Main* (Amsterdam, 1980), p. 110.

12. The Treaty of Madrid had been signed in July 1670. The sacking of Panama took place in January 1671. For a detailed account of Morgan's campaigns see Peter Earle, *The Sack of Panama* (London, 1981) and Dudley Pope, *Harry Morgan's Way: The Biography of Sir Henry Morgan* (London, 1977).

13. Quoted in *A Buccaneer's Atlas: Basil Ringrose's South Sea Waggoner*, ed. Derek Howse and Norman Thrower (Berkeley and Oxford, 1992), p. 29.

Chapter One: Raiding the South Seas

1. The printed edition of the journal of Basil Ringrose in *Bucaniers of America*, by John Esquemeling (London, 1684), vol. 2, p. 33.

2. Ringrose, in *Bucaniers of America*, vol. 2, pp. 15–16.

3. John Cox, in *The Voyages and Adventures of Capt. Barth. Sharp, and Others in the South Sea* (London, 1684), p. 13.

4. For a detailed description of the buccaneers' muskets and other weapons see William Gilkerson, *Boarders Away II: Firearms of the Age of Fighting Sail* (Lincoln, Rhode Island, 1993), pp. 160–2, 171–3.

5. Ringrose, in Esquemeling, *Bucaniers of America*, vol. 2, p. 29.

6. Ibid., p. 30.

7. Ibid., p. 31.

8. *A Collection of Original Voyages . . . published by Capt. William Hacke* (London, 1699), p. 12.

9. Ringrose, in Esquemeling, *Bucaniers of America*, vol. 2, p. 30.

10. Peter Bradley, *The Lure of Peru: Maritime Intrusions into the South Sea, 1598–1710* (London, 1989), pp. 126–7.

11. The principal source for the democratic methods of the buccaneers is John Exquemeling, *Bucaniers of America*, vol. 1, part 1, p. 42.

12. From Woodes Rogers' Introduction in the Narrative Press edn. of *A Cruising Voyage Round the World* (Santa Barbara, California, 2004), p. 5.

13. Ringrose in *Bucaniers of America*, vol. 2, p. 119.

14. For an excellent description of the Miskito Indians see Tim Severin, *Seeking Robinson Crusoe* (London, 2002), pp. 103–87. Severin tracked down the descendants of Will and his companions on the Caribbean coast of Nicaragua.

15. John Masefield (ed.), *Dampier's Voyages* (London, 1906), vol. 1, p. 39.

16. Dampier, quoted in Howse and Thrower, *A Buccaneer's Atlas*, p. 19.

17. Ibid., p. 22.

18. Ibid., p. 22.

19. Masefield (ed.), *Dampier's Voyages*, vol. 1, pp. 285–6.

20. Ibid., p. 114.

21. Ibid., p. 112.

22. See Joel H. Baer, 'William Dampier at the Crossroads: New Light on the "Missing Years," 1691–1697', *International Journal of Maritime History*, 8 (1996), pp. 97–117; and Diana and Michael Preston, *A Pirate of Exquisite Mind: Explorer, Naturalist and Buccaneer: The Life of William Dampier* (New York, 2004), pp. 220–4.

23. John Evelyn, *Diary* (Oxford, 1959), p. 1027.

Chapter Two: The Sea Captain

1. John Callander, *Terra Australis Cognita: or Voyages to the Terra Australis or Southern Hemisphere* (Edinburgh, 1768), vol. 3, p. 232.

2. Glyndwr Williams, in *The Great South Sea: English Voyages and Encounters, 1570–1750* (London and New Haven, 1997), points out the shortcomings in Rogers' character which are entirely overlooked in Brian Little's *Crusoe's Captain: Being the Life of Woodes Rogers, Seaman, Trader, Colonial Governor* (London, 1960) and other accounts of Rogers' life.

3. Dr Thomas Dover to John Batchelor & Company . . . Cape of Good Hope, 11 February 1711. PRO: C.104/160.

4. John Masefield (ed.), *Dampier's Voyages* (London, 1906), vol. 2, p. 321. The other references to Captain Rogers are in vol. 2, pp. 202, 246.

5. Captain Woodes Rogers, *A Cruising Voyage Round the World*, ed. G. E. Manwaring (New York and London, 1928), p. 99.

6. Daniel Defoe, *A Tour through the Whole Island of Great Britain* (London, 1724–7), vol. II, letter III, p. 54.

7. John Macky, *A Journey through England* (London, 1722), vol. 2, pp. 133–4.

8. The logbooks of the *Dreadnought* indicate that Whetstone was in command of the ship from July 1696 to June 1699. PRO: ADM.51/4170.

9. Benbow's Action of 1702 and the subsequent court martial proved controversial and have been the subject of some debate among naval historians. The transcript of the court martial and related documents are bound into one volume and make fascinating reading. PRO: ADM.1/5263.

10. *Observator*, quoted by David J. Starkey, *British Privateering Enterprise in the Eighteenth Century* (Exeter, 1990), p. 86.

11. Starkey, *British Privateering Enterprise*, p. 100.

12. An Act for the better securing the Trade of this Kingdom by Cruisers and Convoys (6 Annae, c.65, AD.1707), *Statutes of the Realm*, vol. VIII, pp. 811–13.

13. Capt. Edward Cooke, *A Voyage to the South Sea, and Round the World* (London, 1712), vol. 1, p. xv.

14. Callander, *Terra Australis Cognita*, vol. 3, p. 231.

15. Declaration by Woodes Rogers before William Whitehead, Mayor, 26 April 1708. PRO: HCA.25/20.

16. PRO: HCA.25/20.

17. PRO: C.104/36, part 2.

18. Ibid.

19. Callander, *Terra Australis Cognita*, vol. 3, p. 232.

20. Deposition of Alexander Selkirk, 18 July 1712. This is mostly devoted to the voyage of the *St George* and the *Cinque Ports* and is somewhat confused and illegible in places. It does contain the memorable passage that Selkirk thought 'that Dampier & Morgan & Stradling . . . managed all things hugger mugger among themselves without the knowledge of any of the ships company . . .'. PRO: C.24/13221, part 1.

21. Richard Steele's interview with Selkirk was published in *The Englishman* in December 1713. The text is also reproduced in R. L. Mégroz, *The Real Robinson Crusoe: Being the Life and Strange Surprising Adventures of Alexander Selkirk of Largo, Fife, Mariner* (London, 1939), pp. 193–7.

Chapter Three: From Bristol to Cape Horn

1. Thomas Cox, *Magna Britannia et Hibernia: Somersetshire* (1720–31), p. 745.

2. George Sherburn (ed.), *Correspondence of Alexander Pope* (Oxford, 1956), vol. IV, p. 201.

3. Captain Woodes Rogers, *A Cruising Voyage Round the World*, ed. G. E. Manwaring (New York and London, 1928), p. 8.

4. Robert C. Davis, *Christian Slaves, Muslim Masters* (London, 2003), pp. 3–26.

5. Rogers, *A Cruising Voyage Round the World*, ed. G. E. Manwaring, p. 18.

6. The major developments for calculating longitude accurately were John Hadley's reflecting quadrant of 1731; the publication of Maskelyne's *Nautical Almanac* of 1767; and the series of chronometers invented and perfected by John Harrison, notably the large watch known as H4 which he completed in 1759 and which won him the Longitude Prize in 1773.

7. Capt. Edward Cooke, *A Voyage to the South Sea, and Round the World* (London, 1712), vol. 1, p. 33.

8. Pascoe Thomas, *A True and Impartial Journal of a Voyage to the South Seas and Round the Globe in His Majesty's Ship the Centurion* (London, 1745), p. 142.

9. On their arrival at Juan Fernández, Rogers notes that Selkirk supplied the sick men with an excellent broth of goat meat mixed with turnip tops and greens. He later notes the effect of this on 'our sick men, by which with the help of the greens and the goodness of the air they recovered very fast of the scurvy'. *A Cruising Voyage Round the World*, ed. G. E. Manwaring, p. 74.

Chapter Four: A Man Clothed in Goat-Skins

1. It is named 'Windy Bay' on William Hack's map of 1685, and in an illustration in Edward Cooke's book *A Voyage to the South Sea, and Round the World* (London, 1712) it is called 'Duke and Dutchess Bay'. According to Tim Severin in *Seeking Robinson Crusoe* (London, 2002), p. 32, it was named 'Cumberland Bay' by the commanding officer of a Royal Navy expedition.

2. Cooke, *A Voyage to the South Sea*, vol. 2, p. xx.

3. Ibid.

4. See 'Excavation at Aguas Buenas, Robinson Crusoe Island, Chile of a gunpowder magazine and the supposed campsite of Alexander Selkirk, together with an account of early navigational dividers' by Daisuke Takhashi, David H. Caldwell, Ivan Caceras, Mauricio Calderon, A. D. Morrison-Low and Jim Tate, in *Post Medieval Archaeology*, vol. 41, no. 2 (December 2007), pp. 270–304. My thanks to David Caldwell for supplying me with a copy of this excavation report.

5. Captain Woodes Rogers, *A Cruising Voyage Round the World*, ed. G. E. Manwaring (New York and London, 1928), p. 92.

6. It is interesting to note that in the first volume of his book Cooke only wrote a few sentences describing the rescue of the castaway but so great was the public interest in Selkirk engendered by Rogers' excellent account in his *A Cruising Voyage Round the World* which came out three months later that Cooke produced his own extended account in the second volume of his book.

7. Rogers, *A Cruising Voyage Round the World*, ed. G. E. Manwaring, p. 94.

8. Ibid., p. 117.

9. Ibid., p. 131.

10. Ibid., p 141. The courteous treatment of prisoners by Rogers and his men is in stark contrast to the methods of some of the earlier buccaneers who frequently subjected prisoners to torture, rape and death.

11. Rogers, *A Cruising Voyage Round the World*, ed. G. E. Manwaring, p. 173.

Chapter Five: The Manila Galleons

1. According to the royal treasurer at Manila the galleon carried 2,300 marks of gold, as well as pearls and silks, and the total value of her cargo on arrival at Acapulco would have been over 2 million pesos. William Lytle Schurz, *The Manila Galleon* (Manila, 1985), p. 250.

2. Schurz, *The Manila Galleon*, p. 207.

3. Ibid., pp. 205–6.

4. Captain Woodes Rogers, *A Cruising Voyage Round the World*, ed. G. E. Manwaring (New York and London, 1928), p. 214.

5. Ibid., p. 215.

6. Capt. Edward Cooke, *A Voyage to the South Sea, and Round the World* (London, 1712), vol. 1, p. 347.

7. Rogers, *A Cruising Voyage Round the World*, ed. G. E. Manwaring, p. 217.

8. Cooke, *A Voyage to the South Sea*, p. 351.

9. Ibid., p. 349.

10. Rogers, *A Cruising Voyage Round the World*, ed. G. E. Manwaring, p. 220.

11. Rogers to Alderman Batchelor and Company, California, 31 December 1709. PRO: C.104/160.

12. Rogers, *A Cruising Voyage Round the World*, ed. G. E. Manwaring, p. 228.

13. Ibid., p. 230.

14. Rogers to Alderman Batchelor and Company, Batavia, 25 July 1710. PRO: CO.104/160.

15. Rogers, *A Cruising Voyage Round the World*, p. 286.

16. Rogers to Alderman Batchelor and Company, Cape of Good Hope, 8 February 1710/11. PRO: 104/160.

17. East India Company: *Minutes of Court of Directors, 1710–1712*. British Library: Asian & African Studies, B/15, f. 450.

18. Admiral Hardy to John Batchelor, 9 October 1711. PRO: CO.104/160.

Chapter Six: The Voyagers Return

1. From captain's log of HMS *Essex*, 23 September 1711. PRO: ADM.51/317.
2. *Daily Courant*, London, Thursday 4 October 1711.
3. Giles Batchelor and Edward Acton to John Batchelor, Sheerness, 6 October 1711. PRO: CO.104/160.
4. B. M. H. Rogers, 'Woodes Rogers's Privateering Voyage of 1708–11', *Mariner's Mirror*, XIX (1933), p. 199.
5. Ibid., p. 198.
6. The total sum received in 1710 from sales of the prize goods was £147,975 12s. 4d. See B. M. H. Rogers, *Mariner's Mirror*, XIX (1933), p. 203. According to the National Archives currency converter this would be worth £11,333,405 in 2010.
7. Ibid., p. 205.
8. Ibid., p. 209.
9. For information about Dampier's last days see entry by Joel Baer in Oxford DNB; Anton Gill, *The Devil's Mariner: William Dampier Pirate and Explorer* (London, 1997), p. 364; and Diana and Michael Preston, *A Pirate of Exquisite Mind . . . The Life of William Dampier* (New York, 2004), pp. 322–3.
10. R. L. Mégroz, *The Real Robinson Crusoe: Being the Life and Strange Surprising Adventures of Alexander Selkirk of Largo, Fife, Mariner* (London, 1939), p. 171.
11. PRO: CO.104/160.
12. B. M. H. Rogers, *Mariner's Mirror*, XIX (1933), p. 208.
13. *London Gazette*, Saturday 10 January to Tuesday 13 January 1712.
14. *Post Boy*, London, Thursday 27 March 1712.
15. Brian Little, in *Crusoe's Captain: Being the Life of Woodes Rogers, Seaman, Trader, Colonial Governor* (London, 1960), pp. 156–8, makes a strong case for Defoe's involvement in Rogers' Introduction but can produce no evidence to support his theory.
16. See Glyndwr Williams, *The Great South Seas: English Voyages and Encounters, 1570–1750* (London and New Haven, 1997), pp. 172–3.
17. The number was made up of 959 prizes and 726 ransoms. See David J. Starkey, *British Privateering Enterprise in the Eighteenth Century* (Exeter, 1990), p. 86.
18. *The Boston News-Letter*, 24–31 August 1713.
19. Quoted in Felix Barker and Peter Jackson, *London: 2000 Years of a City and its People* (London, 1974), p. 173.
20. The veracity of this interview has been questioned by R. W. Lovett in 'Sir Richard Steele's "frequent conversations" with Alexander Selkirk', *English Language Notes*, 25/1 (1987), pp. 49–50. But Steele mentions a number of facts which were not included in the accounts of Woodes Rogers and Cooke, such as the great

quantities of turtles on Juan Fernández; the numerous sealions with their dreadful howlings; Selkirk's laming of young goats so that he could catch them when they grew up; and the useful and entirely credible information that Selkirk on his return to London was 'now worth eight hundred pounds . . .'. Steele's comments on Selkirk's appearance also ring true. Steele's article was published in *The Englishman*, 1–3 December 1713.

21. Quoted by Mégroz, *The Real Robinson Crusoe*, p. 149, from details published by W. H. Hart in *Notes and Queries*, 2nd series, XI, 30 March 1861.

22. The two wills of Selkirk are quoted in full by Mégroz, *The Real Robinson Crusoe*, pp. 153–8.

23. Quoted by Mégroz, *The Real Robinson Crusoe*, p. 212, from Chancery Proceedings 1714–1758, *The Petition of Sophia Selkirke widow of Alexander Selkirke late of Largo in the Sheir of Fife in North Brittain Marriner deceased*, 6 December 1723. PRO: C.11/297/61.

24. Captain's log of HMS *Enterprise*, March 1719–October 1720. PRO: ADM.51/312, part 3.

25. The entry in the register is quoted by Mégroz, *The Real Robinson Crusoe*, p. 160.

26. Mégroz, *The Real Robinson Crusoe*, p. 161.

27. Quoted by Mégroz, *The Real Robinson Crusoe*, p. 173, from *The Monthly Repository*, V, 1810, p. 531.

28. David Cordingly, *Heroines and Harlots: Women at Sea in the Great Age of Sail* (London, 2001), pp. 171, 181–2.

29. East India Company: *Correspondence 1712–13*. British Library, India Office records: D/93, f. 511.

30. Captain Charles Johnson, *A General History of the Pyrates*, ed. Manuel Schonhorn (London, 1972; edn. cited New York, 1999), p. 61.

31. East India Company: *Minutes of Court of Directors, 1716–18*. British Library, India Office records: B/54, f. 22.

32. Rogers to Sir Hans Sloane, 7 May 1716. British Library, Sloane collection, no. 4044, f.155.

Chapter Seven: Sugar, Slaves and Sunken Treasure

1. Hugh Thomas, *The Slave Trade: The History of the Atlantic Slave Trade 1440–1870* (London, 1997; edn. cited 1998), p. 92.

2. Ibid., p. 226. Thomas takes his figures from the source he regards as most accurate, which is Philip Curtin, *The Atlantic Slave Trade: A Census* (Madison, 1969), p. 119.

3. Ralph Davis, *The Rise of the English Shipping Industry in the 17th and 18th Centuries* (Newton Abbot, 1962), p. 275.

4. Ibid., pp. 419–21.

5. Richard Sheridan, 'Caribbean Plantation Society, 1689–1748' in *The Oxford History of the British Empire: The Eighteenth Century*, ed. P. J. Marshall (Oxford, 1998), p. 400.

6. Davis, *The Rise of the English Shipping Industry*, p. 280.

7. Peter Earle, *Sailors: English Merchant Seamen, 1650–1775* (London, 1998), p. 42.

8. Captain Charles Johnson, *General History of the Pyrates*, ed. Manuel Schonhorn (London, 1972; edn. cited New York, 1999), p. 35.

9. Governor Handasyd in Spanish Town to Council of Trade and Plantations, London, 25 March 1710. PRO: CO.137/8, no. 80, i–iii.

10. Lieutenant Governor Hodges of Montserrat to Council of Trade and Plantations, 4 February 1710. CSPC, vol. 1710–1711.

11. Lieutenant General Hamilton of Antigua to Council of Trade and Plantations, 5 April 1711. PRO: CO.152, no. 70. The privateers and pirates were no different from other Europeans in treating African slaves as saleable commodities. Governor Parke of St Christopher (St Kitts) wrote on 9 December 1706: 'The privateers used to plague us by taking off our negroes in the night.' He instituted a system of guards all around the island to prevent the thefts taking place. PRO: CO.152/6. no 75.

12. Ibid.

13. Jonathan Dickenson of Antigua to John Askew in London, March 1710. PRO: CO.152/9, no. 27.

14. Mr Dummer to Mr Popple, 17 January 1709. PRO: CO.323/6, no. 74.

15. Mr Dummer to Mr Popple, 31 January 1710. PRO: CO.323/6, no. 96.

16. Mr Dummer to Mr Popple, 1 April 1709. PRO: CO.137/8, no. 35.

17. See report from Governor Lord Hamilton to Council of Trade and Plantations, 28 April 1712. CSPC, vol. 1712–1714, no. 94.

18. The survivor quoted here was the chaplain of the *Hampton Court*, and the quote is taken from records in the Mel Fisher Museum, Key West, Florida.

19. The *Hampton Court* was originally built at Deptford Dockyard in 1678 but in 1701 she was completely rebuilt at Blackwall. She was captured by Forbin's Dunkirk squadron in 1707 but in 1711 she was sold to the Spanish and renamed *Nuestra Señora Del Carmen Y San Antonio*. See David Lyon, *The Sailing Navy List* (London, 1993), pp. 12, 20.

20. Quoted by Colin Woodard, *The Republic of Pirates: Being the True and Surprising Story of the Caribbean Pirates and the Man Who Brought Them Down* (New York and London, 2007), p. 207, from Captain Balchen's letter to the Admiralty, PRO: ADM.1/147, f.24.

21. For the details of the ten vessels given privateering commissions by Lord Hamilton in 1715 see PRO: CO.137/12, no. 78, i–v. In addition to Jennings and Wills,

the named commanders of these vessels include Captain Jonathan Barnet, who captured Calico Jack Rackam and the female pirates in 1718.

22. There is a detailed description of this incident in Woodard, *The Republic of Pirates*, pp. 126–34.

23. Quoted by Woodard, *The Republic of Pirates*, p. 130, from a letter of Captain D'Escoubet to Lord Hamilton, 4 April 1716.

24. Johnson, *General History of the Pyrates*, ed. Manuel Schonhorn, p. 37.

Chapter Eight: Governor of the Bahamas

1. Deposition of John Vickers, late of the Island of Providence, sworn before Thomas Nelson, Virginia, July 1716. PRO: CO.5/1317, f.247.

2. Alexander Spotswood to Harry Beverley, 15 June 1716. PRO: CO.5/1317.

3. Alexander Spotswood to Council of Trade and Plantations, 3 July 1716. PRO: CO.5/1317.

4. Captain Howard to Mr Burchett, Admiralty Office, 15 October 1716. PRO: CO.137/12.

5. R. Methuen to Council of Trade and Plantations, 30 November 1716. PRO: CO.137/12.

6. *Memorial from the Copartners for carrying on a trade and settling the Bahama Islands*, 19 May 1721. PRO: CO.23/1, part 2.

7. The company or corporation they formed had the title of 'The CoPartners for Carrying on a Trade & Settling the Bahama Islands'.

8. *Remarks of the most material transactions relating to the Bahama Islands from their original settlement to this time*, 1717. PRO: CO.5/1265, ff.159–62.

9. Woodes Rogers to the Lords Proprietors of the Bahama Islands, July 1717. PRO: CO.5/1265, f.151.

10. Petition of Woodes Rogers to the King, 19 July 1717. PRO: CO.5/1265, f.149.

11. The humble petition of sundry merchants to the King, July 1717. PRO: CO.5/1265, f.155.

12. Memorial to Joseph Addison from sundry merchants, July 1717. PRO: CO.5/1265, f.157.

13. Mr Secretary Addison to the Council of Trade and Plantations, 3 September 1717. CSPC, vol. 1717–1718, no. 64.

14. In London alone 1,242 men and women were hanged between 1703 and 1772. See Peter Linebaugh, *The London Hanged: Crime and Civil Society in the Eighteenth Century* (London, 1991), p. 91.

15. *Post Boy*, London, Saturday 19 October 1717.

16. The pirate attacks of Bellamy, Vane, England, Teach, Moody etc. at this period are recorded in numerous depositions of merchant sea captains and sailors (PRO:

CO.37/10) and in the *Calendar of State Papers, Colonial America and West Indies* for 1717–18, and in reports in *The Boston News-Letter*.

17. Peter Heywood to Council of Trade and Plantations, 21 December 1717. CSPC, vol. 1717–18, no. 271.

18. Memorial from the Copartners for carrying on a trade and settling the Bahama Islands to the Lords Commissioners of Trade and Plantations, 19 May 1721. PRO: CO.23/1, part 2.

19. Ibid.

20. *Remarks of the most material transactions relating to the Bahama Islands from their original settlement to this time*, 1717. PRO: CO.5/1265, f.159.

21. Ibid.

22. Lieutenant Governor Bennet of Bermuda to the Council of Trade and Plantations, 29 October 1708. CSPC, vol. 1708–1709, no. 176.

23. Lieutenant Governor Pulleine to Council of Trade and Plantations, 22 April 1713. CSPC, vol. 1712–1714, no. 651.

24. Colin Woodard, *The Republic of Pirates: Being the True and Surprising Story of the Caribbean Pirates and the Man Who Brought Them Down* (New York and London, 2007), p. 89.

25. Deposition of John Vickers, late of the Island of Providence, sworn before Thomas Nelson, Virginia, July 1716. PRO: CO.5/1317, f.247.

26. Deposition of Henry Bostock, 19 December 1717. PRO: CO.152/12, no. 67 (iii).

27. Quoted by Angus Konstam, *Blackbeard: America's Most Notorious Pirate* (Hoboken, 2006), from a letter sent to the Council of Trade and Plantations. CSPC, vol. 1716–1717.

28. Captain Charles Johnson, *General History of the Pyrates*, ed. Manuel Schonhorn (London, 1972; edn. cited New York, 1999), p. 72.

29. *The Boston News-Letter*, 11 November 1717.

30. See Konstam, *Blackbeard*, p. 81.

31. Research on the wreck and its artefacts has been carried out by Dave Moore of the North Carolina Maritime Museum and his colleagues. For an excellent summary of the excavation and the artefacts recovered see Konstam, *Blackbeard*, pp. 286–93.

32. *The Boston News-Letter*, 3–10 March 1718.

33. Deposition of Henry Bostock, 19 December 1717. PRO: CO.152/12, no. 67 (iii).

34. Ibid.

35. The details of the visit to Nassau of Captain Pearce are taken from the logbook of HMS *Phoenix*. PRO: ADM51/690; and letters from Pearce to the Admiralty, 4 February, 4 March, 3 June 1718. PRO: ADM.1/2282.

36. Captain Pearce to Admiralty, 3 June 1718. PRO: ADM.1/2282.

37. Deposition of Nathaniel Catling, 17 May 1718. PRO: CO.37/10, no. 10 (v). See also the depositions of John Tibby, 24 May 1718, PRO: CO.37/10; and of Samuel Cooper, 24 May 1718, PRO: CO.37/10.

38. Deposition of Edward North, 22 May 1718, PRO: CO.37/10, no. 10 (ii). See also the deposition of Nathaniel North, 22 May 1718, CO.37/10.

39. Deposition of Joseph Bossa, 28 May 1718, PRO: CO.37/10.

40. Johnson, *General History of the Pyrates*, ed. Manuel Schonhorn, p. 142.

41. Ibid.

Chapter Nine: Welcome to Nassau

1. The details for the arrival of Woodes Rogers and his squadron at Nassau are taken from: log of HMS *Milford*, PRO: ADM.51/606, part 4; log of HMS *Rose*, ADM.51/801, part 4; log of HM sloop *Shark*, ADM.51/892, part 2; letter from Captain Pomeroy to Admiralty, 3 September 1718, PRO: ADM.1/2282; Memorial from Samuel Buck, 3 December 1719, *The state of the Island of Providence*, PRO: CO.23/1, part 1; Woodes Rogers' first report to Lords Commissioners for Trade and Plantations, Nassau, 31 October 1718, PRO: CO.23/1, part 1; and the Appendix to Captain Charles Johnson, *General History of the Pyrates*, ed. Manuel Schonhorn (London, 1972; edn. cited New York, 1999), pp. 615–18.

2. Log of HMS *Rose*, Friday 25 July 1718. PRO: ADM.51/801, part 4.

3. A letter received from on board HMS *Milford* at New York, and published in the *Whitehall Evening Post*, 18–21 October 1718.

4. Johnson, *General History of the Pyrates*, ed. Manuel Schonhorn, p. 616.

5. *The state of the Island of Providence and other Bahama Islands*: Memorial from Samuel Buck, 3 December 1719. PRO: CO.23/1, part 1.

6. To the King from the General Officers of the Army, Horse Guards, 15 July 1726. *The Case of Captain Woodes Rogers, late Governor of the Bahama Islands*. PRO: CO.23/12, part 2, f.56.

7. Log of HMS *Milford*, 6 to 13 August 1718, PRO: ADM.51/606, part 4.

8. Minutes of Assembly of Several of the Principal Inhabitants of the Bahama Islands, 1 August 1718; and subsequent reports on the Councils held between 5 August and 28 September 1718. PRO: CO.23/1, part 1.

9. *An Estimate of what is wanting and necessary for the Fortifications here, Nassau on Providence*, 31 October 1718. PRO: CO.23/1, part 1, f.40.

10. Governor Woodes Rogers to Rt Hon James Craggs, 24 December 1718. PRO: CO.23/13.

11. Woodes Rogers to Council of Trade and Plantations, 31 October 1718. PRO: CO.13/1, part 1.

12. *The Boston News-Letter*, 13–20 October 1718.

13. Johnson, *General History of the Pyrates*, ed. Manuel Schonhorn, p. 137.

14. The protest of Captain King, commander of the *Neptune*, Hagboat, sworn before Woodes Rogers, 5 February 1719. Reproduced in Johnson, *General History of the Pyrates*, ed. Manuel Schonhorn, pp. 144–7.

15. Ibid., p. 145.

16. For details of the capture, trial and execution of Charles Vane, see pages 182–3 and Chapter 12, note 17.

17. Woodes Rogers report to Council of Trade and Plantations, 31 October 1718. PRO: CO.23/1, part 1.

18. Rogers to Craggs, 24 December 1718.PRO: CO.23/13.

19. *A Private Consultation held on Friday the 18 November 1718 at the Secretary's Office in the City of Nassau*. PRO:CO.23/1, no. 18, f.75.

Chapter Ten: Hanged on the Waterfront

1. The full text of the 'Act for the more effectual Suppression of Piracy' (11 Gul. III, chapter VII, AD.1698–9) can be seen in *Statutes of the Realm*, vol. VII, pp. 590–4.

2. *Remarks on the condition of the fortifications at New Providence when Governor Rogers arrived the 25th August 1729*. PRO: CO.23/14, item 71, f.141.

3. *Trial and Condemnation of Ten Persons for Piracy at New Providence, Nassau*. PRO: CO.23/1, no. 18, ff.75–82. A transcript of the trial is reprinted in Captain Charles Johnson, *General History of the Pyrates*, ed. Manuel Schonhorn (London, 1972; edn. cited New York, 1999).

4. Johnson, *General History of the Pyrates*, ed. Manuel Schonhorn, p. 648.

5. Ibid., p. 653.

6. Ibid., p. 657.

7. Ibid., p. 659.

8. Woodes Rogers to James Craggs, 24 December 1718. PRO: CO.23/13, f.22 verso.

9. The full transcript of the trial (like that of the trial of Bartholomew Roberts' pirates) was reproduced in later editions of Johnson, *General History of the Pyrates*.

10. See David Cordingly, *Life among the Pirates: The Romance and Reality* (London, 1995), pp. 207, 233–4.

11. Johnson, *General History of the Pyrates*, ed. Manuel Schonhorn, p. 85.

12. Ibid., p. 84.

13. Angus Konstam, *Blackbeard: America's Most Notorious Pirate* (Hoboken, 2006), p. 142.

14. Governor and Council of South Carolina to Council of Trade and Plantations, 21 October 1718. CSPC, vol. 1717–1718, no. 730.

15. Most of the trial of Bonnet and his crew is reproduced in Johnson, *General History of the Pyrates*, ed. Manuel Schonhorn, pp. 103–10.
16. Ibid., p. 111.

Chapter Eleven: Blackbeard's Last Stand

1. This chapter has an abbreviated account of Blackbeard's last days. For a more detailed account see Angus Konstam, *Blackbeard: America's Most Notorious Pirate* (Hoboken, 2006), pp. 239–65, and Colin Woodard, *The Republic of Pirates: Being the True and Surprising Story of the Caribbean Pirates and the Man Who Brought Them Down* (New York and London, 2007), pp. 288–98.
2. For a useful biography of Spotswood see Oxford DNB.
3. Lieutenant Governor Spotswood to Council of Trade and Plantations, 22 December 1718. CSPC, vol. 1717–1718, no. 800, p. 431.
4. See *The present Disposal of all His Majesties Ships and Vessels in Sea Pay*, issued by the Admiralty Office, 1 May 1718. PRO: ADM.8/14.
5. Lieutenant Maynard's log of HMS *Pearl*, entry for 17 November 1718. NMM: ADM/L/P22.
6. *The Boston News-Letter*, Monday 23 February to Monday 2 March 1719.
7. Ibid.
8. Captain Charles Johnson, *General History of the Pyrates*, ed. Manuel Schonhorn (London, 1972; edn. cited New York, 1999), p. 82.
9. Letter from Lieutenant Maynard to Mr Symonds, Lieutenant of HMS *Phoenix*, written from North Carolina, 17 December 1718. Reproduced in Robert E. Lee, *Blackbeard the Pirate: A Reappraisal of His Life and Times* (Winston-Salem, 1974; edn. cited 1995), p. 234.
10. Lieutenant Maynard's log of HMS *Pearl*. Hicks evidently took over Maynard's duties and his logbook while he was away at Ocracoke. Entry for 3 January 1719. NMM: ADM/L/P32.
11. Spotswood's proclamation of 24 November 1718 is reproduced in full by Johnson in *General History of the Pyrates*, ed. Manuel Schonhorn, pp. 78–9.
12. Ibid., p. 84.
13. Rogers to Craggs, 24 January 1719. PRO: CO. 23/13.
14. Rogers to Craggs, 3 March 1719. PRO: CO.23/13.
15. Captain's log of HMS *Flamborough*, 24 February 1720. PRO: ADM.51/357, part VIII.
16. Ibid.
17. Richard Farrell and W. Nicholson writing to Woodes Rogers from Moore Castle, Havana, 4 April 1720. PRO: CO.23/1, f.127.

18. Captain Edward Vernon to the Admiralty, from Port Royal, 17 June 1720. PRO: ADM.1/2624, part 6.

19. Rogers to Council of Trade and Plantations, 20 April 1720. PRO: CO.23/1.

20. *The humble petition of Samuel Buck of London, merchant, one of the undertakers for settling the Bahama Islands to the Lords Commissioners of Trade and Plantations,* 3 December 1719, which is accompanied by *The state of the Island of Providence and other Bahama Islands: memorial from Mr Samuel Buck.* PRO: CO.23/1, part 1.

21. CSPC, Volume 1720–1721, No. 167, p. 74.

22. Ibid., No. 167 iii, p. 75.

Chapter Twelve: Calico Jack and the Female Pirates

1. *The Boston Gazette,* Monday 10 to Monday 17 October 1720.

2. Anne Chambers, *Granuaile: The Life and Times of Grace O'Malley c.1530–1603* (Dublin, 1979), p. 150.

3. Captain Charles Johnson, *General History of the Pyrates,* ed. Manuel Schonhorn (London, 1972; edn. cited New York, 1999), p. 153.

4. Lawes to Council of Trade and Plantations. CSPC, vol. 1719–1720, nos. 34 and 132. Johnson gives a detailed but rather different description of the capture and recovery of the *Kingston.* See Johnson, *General History of the Pyrates,* ed. Manuel Schonhorn, pp. 620–2.

5. Johnson, *General History of the Pyrates,* ed. Manuel Schonhorn, p. 620. Calico is a type of cotton cloth which originated in India. It is finer and thinner than canvas. In American English 'calico' refers to a cotton fabric with a small, all-over, colourful pattern. In Britain the word describes a plain white or unbleached cotton cloth.

6. *The Tryals of Captain John Rackam, and other pirates.* Printed by Robert Baldwin, Jamaica, 1721. PRO: CO.137/14, p. 17.

7. Ibid., p. 19.

8. Ibid., p. 18.

9. Commission and instructions for Captain Jonathan Barnet, commander of the snow *Tyger,* issued by the Governor of Jamaica, 24 November 1715. PRO: CO.137/12, no. 78 (i), ff.231–5.

10. Governor Lawes to Council of Trade and Plantations, 13 November 1720. CSPC, vol. 1720–1721, no. 288.

11. The description of the finding of Rackam's sloop by Bonnevie and Barnet, and the subsequent action, is taken from the witness statement of James Spatchears, a mariner of Port Royal, who appears to have been a member of Barnet's crew. *The Tryals of Captain John Rackam.* PRO: CO. 137/14, p. 10.

12. Ibid., p. 19.

13. Clinton Black, *Pirates of the West Indies* (Cambridge, 1989), p. 117. Clinton Black was for many years chief archivist of Jamaica.

14. For further reading on women at sea and in the army see: Linda Grant Depauw, *Seafaring Women* (Boston, 1982); Margaret S. Creighton and Lisa Norling, *Iron Men, Wooden Women: Gender and Seafaring in the Atlantic World* (London, 1989); David Cordingly, *Women Sailors & Sailors' Women* (New York, 2001); Diane Dugaw, *Warrior Women and Popular Balladry* (Cambridge, 1989); Marcus Rediker, *Villains of all Nations: Atlantic Pirates in the Golden Age* (Boston, 2004); Jo Stanley, *Bold in her Breeches: Women Pirates across the Ages* (London, 1995); Suzanne J. Stark, *Female Tars: Women aboard Ship in the Age of Sail* (London, 1996); Marina Warner, *Monuments and Maidens: The Allegory of the Female Form* (London, 1985); Julie Wheelwright, *Amazons and Military Maids* (London, 1989).

15. See Rediker, *Villains of all Nations*, p. 119.

16. The theory that Defoe was the real author of Captain Charles Johnson's *General History of the Pyrates* was first put forward by the American scholar John Robert Moore in 1932 but in 1988 it was convincingly challenged by P. N. Furbank and W. R. Owens in their book *The Canonisation of Daniel Defoe* (New Haven, 1988).

17. See letter from Jamaica, 31 March 1721: 'Several pirates have been lately taken and brought in here and on trial most of them found guilty and executed, among them Chas. Vaine and one Racum, two notorious commanders of pirate vessels suffered and died most profligate impudent villains.' CSPC, vol. 1720–1721, no. 295.

18. Johnson, *General History of the Pyrates*, ed. Manuel Schonhorn, p. 144.

Chapter Thirteen: Great Debts and Bills

1. Woodes Rogers to Lords of Trade and Plantations, 20 April 1720. PRO: CO.23/1, f.123.

2. Woodes Rogers, William Fairfax and seven others to Mr Secretary Craggs, New Providence, 26 November 1720. PRO: CO.23/13.

3. John Lloyd to Secretary Craggs, 2 February 1720. CSPC, vol. 1720–1721, no. 372, p. 252.

4. Captain Hildesley to the Admiralty, 25 March 1720. PRO: ADM.1/1880, part 10.

5. Ibid.

6. Ibid.

7. Captain Whitney to the Admiralty, 26 October 1719. PRO: ADM.1/2649, part 11.

8. Woodes Rogers to Craggs, from South Carolina, 20 December 1720. PRO: CO.23/13.

9. Woodes Rogers to Lords of Trade and Plantations, 25 February 1721. PRO: CO.23/1, part 2.

10. CSPC, vol. 1720–1721, no. 455, p. 287.

11. *The Case of Captain Woodes Rogers, late Governor of the Bahama Islands*. Petition to the King from G. Macartney and seven other General Officers of the Army, Horse Guards, 15 July 1726. PRO: CO.23/12, part 2, f.56.

12. The information about the South Sea Company is based on: Julian Hoppit, 'The Myths of the South Sea Bubble' in *Transactions of the Royal Historical Society*, 12 (2002), pp. 141–65; Basil Williams, *The Whig Supremacy 1714–1760* (Oxford, 1939), pp. 169–71; *Chronicle of Britain and Ireland*, ed. Henrietta Heald (London, 1992), pp. 665–7.

13. Quoted by Julian Hoppit from M. Macdonald and T. R. Murphy, *Sleepless Souls: Suicide in Early Modern England* (Oxford, 1990), pp. 276–8.

14. See the entry on John Aislabie in Oxford DNB.

15. Woodes Rogers to Craggs, CSPCS, vol. 1720–1721, pp. 217–18, no. 327.

16. *Historical Register*, 5 (1720), p. 382.

17. Petition to the King from General Officers of the Army, 15 July 1726. PRO: CO.23/12, part 2.

18. The author has conducted extensive searches among the prison records in the Public Record Office, Kew (including the records for the Fleet, King's Bench, Queen's Bench and Marshalsea prisons listed under PRIS/1 to PRIS/10) as well as the records in the London Metropolitan Archives and the Guildhall Library. No record was found to indicate which prison Rogers was confined in, nor is it known exactly when and for how long he was confined.

19. Petition to the King from General Officers of the Army, 15 July 1726. PRO: CO.23/12, part 2.

20. Woodes Rogers to Lord Townshend, 26 November 1726. British Library, Add. MSS. 32748, ff.317–18.

21. British Library, Add. MSS. 4459, ff.101–2.

22. Ibid.

23. PRO: CO.23/14, ff.45–52.

24. PRO: MPG.1/254.

25. Plan of Fort Nassau in New Providence, 24 December 1723. PRO: MPG.1/256.

26. Bahamas correspondence 1728–46. PRO: CO.23/14, f.141.

27. The painting became the property of Woodes Rogers' daughter Sarah. She died in 1743 and according to her will she bequeathed to 'Mr Sergeant Eyre, the picture of her father, brother and herself in one frame'. The painting was engraved by W. Skelton in 1799.

Chapter Fourteen: Death on the Coast of Guinea

1. John Atkins (1685–1757) joined the navy as surgeon's mate of the *Charles Galley* in 1701, and subsequently served on the *Somerset*, the *Tartar* and the bomb ketch *Lion*. His entry in the Oxford DNB was compiled by the naval surgeon Vice-Admiral Sir James Watt.
2. John Atkins, *A Voyage to Guinea, Brazil, and the West Indies* (London, 1735), p. 46.
3. Ibid., p. 139.
4. Jean Barbot, *A Description of the Coasts of Guinea*, quoted by Hugh Thomas in *The Slave Trade: The History of the Atlantic Slave Trade 1440–1870* (London, 1997; edn. cited 1998), p. 346.
5. Captain Herdman to Admiralty, from Barbados, 3 August 1722. PRO: ADM.1/1880, part 3.
6. Atkins, *A Voyage to Guinea, Brazil, and the West Indies*, p. 139.
7. Captain Herdman to Admiralty, 8 April 1723. PRO: ADM.1/1880, part 3.
8. Captain Ogle to Admiralty, from Cape Coast Road, 5 April 1722. PRO: CO.ADM.1/2242.
9. Captain Charles Johnson, *History of the Pyrates*, ed. Manuel Schonhorn (London, 1972; edn. cited New York, 1999), p. 205.
10. Ibid., p. 223.
11. CSPC, vol. 1720–1721, no. 463, III.
12. Ibid.
13. Johnson, *History of the Pyrates*, ed. Manuel Schonhorn, p. 228.
14. Captain Chaloner Ogle to the Admiralty, 5 April 1722, HMS *Swallow* in Cape Coast Road. PRO: ADM.1/2242.
15. For details of the *Swallow*'s actions against the pirates see: Captain Ogle's letter to the Admiralty of 5 April 1722, 26 July 1722 and 8 September 1722, PRO: ADM.1/2243; Captain Ogle's log of the *Swallow*, PRO: ADM.51/954, part 7; log of Lieutenant Edward Chaloner of the *Swallow*, NMM: ADM/L/S564; Proceedings of Court held on the coast of Africa upon trying of 100 pyrates taken by HMS *Swallow*, PRO: HCA.1/99.3; Atkins, *A Voyage to Guinea, Brazil, and the West Indies*, pp. 147, 191–4; Johnson, *History of the Pyrates*, ed. Manuel Schonhorn, pp. 237–87.
16. Captain's log of HMS *Swallow*, 5 February 1722. PRO: ADM.51/954, part 7.
17. Ibid.
18. These figures are taken from Captain Ogle's letter to the Admiralty. Johnson, *General History of the Pyrates*, ed. Manuel Schonhorn, p. 240, notes that the French *Ranger* was manned with sixteen Frenchmen, twenty Negroes and seventy-seven Englishmen.
19. Johnson, *History of the Pyrates*, ed. Manuel Schonhorn, p. 269.

20. Captain Ogle to the Admiralty, PRO: ADM.1/2242.

21. Johnson, *History of the Pyrates*, ed. Manuel Schonhorn, p. 244.

22. These figures are from Captain Ogle's letter to the Admiralty. Johnson, *General History of the Pyrates*, ed. Manuel Schonhorn, p. 245, notes that the *Royal Fortune* had a crew of 157, of whom forty-five were Negroes.

23. Atkins, *A Voyage to Guinea, Brazil, and the West Indies*, p. 192.

24. Ibid., p. 147.

25. Ibid., p. 98.

26. See Marcus Rediker, *Between the Devil and the Deep Blue Sea: Merchant Seamen, Pirates, and the Anglo-American Maritime World, 1700–1750* (Cambridge, 1987), pp. 12, 260; N. A. M. Rodger, *The Wooden World* (London, 1986), p. 114.

27. PRO: HCA.1/99.3.

28. Peter Linebaugh, *The London Hanged: Crime and Civil Society in the Eighteenth Century* (London and New York, 1991), pp. 80, 216–18, 244; and reports in London newspapers of this period such as the *Daily Courant*, the *Post Boy* and *Applebee's Original Weekly Journal*.

29. PRO: HCA.1/99.3.

30. These figures are taken from a list drawn up by Captain Ogle which is headed 'An acct. of the men taken in the Royal Fortune and Great Ranger, Pyrate ships, by his Majtys ship Swallow under my command'. PRO: ADM.1/2242.

31. Captain Chaloner Ogle to the Admiralty, 8 September 1722. PRO: ADM.1/2242.

32. Ibid.

33. The *London Gazette* of 4 December 1722 carried reports of the hurricane received from Kingston, Port Royal, and from HMS *Falkland*.

Chapter Fifteen: Back to the Bahamas

1. Rogers to Council of Trade and Plantations, 12 November 1729. CSPC, vol. 36, 1728–1729, no. 965.

2. *Remarks on the condition of the fortifications at New Providence when Governor Rogers arrived the 25th August 1729*, prepared by the lieutenant, gunner and sergeant of the garrison. PRO: CO.23/14, f.141.

3. *Queries from the Board of Trade for the year 1728*. PRO: CO. 23/14, f.66.

4. Taken from the census figures sent home by Woodes Rogers on 14 October 1731. PRO: CO.23/2 and quoted by Michael Craton and Gail Saunders in *Islanders in the Stream: a History of the Bahamian People* (Athens, Georgia, USA, 1992), vol. 1, pp. 119–121.

5. Estimated population of the English Sugar Islands in 1713, from Richard S. Dunn, *Sugar and Slaves: The Rise of the Planter Class in the English West Indies, 1624–1713* (London, 1973), p. 312.

6. Richard Sheridan, 'Caribbean Plantation Society, 1689–1748', in *The Oxford History of the British Empire: The Eighteenth Century*, ed. P. J. Marshall (Oxford, 1998; edn. cited 2001), vol. II, p. 401.

7. Quoted by Brian Little, *Crusoe's Captain: Being the Life of Woodes Rogers, Seaman, Trader, Colonial Governor* (London, 1960), pp. 214, 215.

8. *Bahamas Correspondence, 1728–1746*. PRO: CO.23/14, ff.121. See also Harcourt Malcolm, *A History of the Bahamas House of Assembly* (Nassau, 1921).

9. CSPC, vol. 38 (1731), nos. 419, 526.

10. These figures are taken from Marcus Rediker, *Villains of All Nations: Atlantic Pirates in the Golden Age* (Boston, 2004), p. 29. They are based on detailed studies made by Rediker and are confirmed by many contemporary estimates made by colonial governors, merchants and others.

11. Peter Earle, *The Pirate Wars* (London, 2003), p. 206.

12. Marcus Rediker, *Between the Devil and the Deep Blue Sea: Merchant Seamen, Pirates, and the Anglo-American Maritime World, 1700–1750* (Cambridge, 1987), p. 283.

13. *The Boston Gazette*, 1–8 June 1724.

14. Governor Sir Nicholas Lawes to Council of Trade and Plantations, 12 June 1721. CSPC, 1720–1721, no. 523.

15. Governor Lawes, 18 May 1722. CSPC, 1722–1723, no. 142.

16. Governor Burnet to Lord Carteret, 25 June 1723. CSPCS, vol. 1722–1723, no. 606.

17. *The present Disposal of all His Majesties Ships and Vessels in Sea Pay*. PRO: ADM.8/14.

18. See Earle, *The Pirate Wars*, p. 269, n.14.

19. *Bahamas Correspondence, 1728–1746*. PRO: CO.23/14, f.157.

20. Lewis Bonnett to Charles Delafaye, New Providence, 10 February 1730. PRO: CO.23/14, f.183.

21. Woodes Rogers to Council of Trade and Plantations, 10 February 1731. CSPC, vol. 38, 1731, no. 47.

22. *Bahamas Correspondence*, PRO: CO.23/14, f.225.

23. *Gentleman's Magazine*, September 1732, p. 979.

24. For details of the will of Woodes Rogers and the fate of his son William, see Brian Little, *Crusoe's Captain* (London, 1960), pp. 199, 210, 219, 222, and G. E. Manwaring's Introduction to Captain Woodes Rogers, *A Cruising Voyage Round the World* (London and New York, 1928), pp. xlv, xlvi.

Epilogue

1. The reference to pirates was dropped when the Bahamas achieved independence in 1973 and adopted the new motto 'Forward, upward and onward together' to go

along with a fine coat of arms which celebrates the sun, the sea and the fauna and flora of the islands.

2. The following works were consulted for this chapter: Paula R. Backschreider, *Daniel Defoe: His Life* (Baltimore, 1989); Peter Earle, *The World of Defoe* (London, 1976); David Fausett, *The Strange Surprising Sources of Robinson Crusoe* (Amsterdam, 1994); John Robert Moore, *Daniel Defoe: Citizen of the Modern World* (Chicago, 1958); John Richetti, *The Life of Daniel Defoe* (Oxford, 2005); Pat Rogers, *Robinson Crusoe* (London, 1979); Arthur W. Secord, *Studies in the Narrative Method of Defoe* (Illinois, 1924); Tim Severin, *Seeking Robinson Crusoe* (London, 2002); James Sutherland, *Daniel Defoe: A Critcal Study* (Harvard, 1971); Ian Watt, *The Rise of the Novel: Studies in Defoe, Richardson and Fielding* (London, 1957).

3. *Coleridge's Miscellaneous Criticism*, ed. Thomas Middleton Raysor (London, 1936), pp. 194, 300.

4. Richetti, *The Life of Daniel Defoe*, p. 185.

5. Secord, *Studies in the Narrative Method of Defoe*, p. 31.

6. Glyndwr Williams, *The Great South Sea: English Voyages and Encounters, 1570–1750* (London and New Haven, 1997), p. 179.

7. Quoted by Rogers in *Robinson Crusoe*, p. 142.

8. Moore, *Daniel Defoe: Citizen of the Modern World*, p. 223.

9. Daniel Defoe, *The Compleat English Gentleman*, ed. K. D. Bulbring (London, 1890), p. 225.

10. Secord, *Studies in the Narrative Method of Defoe*, p. 49.

11. Rogers, *Robinson Crusoe*, p. 22.

12. Captain Charles Johnson, *General History of the Pyrates*, ed. Manuel Schonhorn (London, 1972; edn. cited New York, 1999), p. 6.

13. Ibid., p. 62.

14. Ibid., p. 141.

15. Ibid., p. 143.

16. Ibid., p. 143.

17. Professor Schonhorn notes that Rogers probably contributed certain details to Johnson's book. See Johnson, *General History of the Pyrates*, ed. Manuel Schonhorn, p. 673.

Bibliography

Andrew, Kenneth, *The Spanish Caribbean: Trade and Plunder, 1520–1630* (New Haven, 1978)

Atkins, John, *A Voyage to Guinea, Brazil, and the West Indies* (London, 1735)

Backschreider, Paula R., *Daniel Defoe: His Life* (Baltimore, 1989)

Baer, Joel H., 'Captain John Avery and the Anatomy of a Mutiny', in *Eighteenth Century Life*, Johns Hopkins University Press for the College of William and Mary, vol. 18, February 1994

—— 'William Dampier at the Crossroads: New Light on the "Missing Years," 1691–1697', *International Journal of Maritime History*, 8 (1996)

Barker, Felix, and Jackson, Peter, *London: 2000 Years of a City and its People* (London, 1974)

Black, Clinton, *Pirates of the West Indies* (Cambridge, 1989)

Bradley, Peter, *The Lure of Peru: Maritime Intrusions into the South Sea, 1598–1710* (London, 1989)

Burl, Aubrey, *That Great Pyrate: Bartholomew Roberts and his Crew, 1718–1723* (Port Talbot, 1997)

Callander, John, *Terra Australis Cognita: or Voyages to the Terra Australis or Southern Hemisphere* (Edinburgh, 1768)

Chambers, Anne, *Granuaile: The Life and Times of Grace O'Malley, c.1530–1603* (Dublin, 1979)

Cooke, Capt. Edward, *A Voyage to the South Sea, and Round the World* (London, 1712)

Cordingly, David, *Life among the Pirates: The Romance and the Reality* (London, 1995). Published in the USA as *Under the Black Flag: The Romance and the Reality of Life among the Pirates* (New York, 1995)

— *Heroines and Harlots: Women at Sea in the Great Age of Sail* (London, 2001)

Cox, Thomas, *Magna Britannia et Hibernia . . . or a New Survey of Great Britain* (London, 1720–31)

Craton, Michael, *A History of the Bahamas* (London, 1962)

Craton, Michael, and Saunders, Gail, *Islanders in the Stream: A History of the Bahamian People* (Athens, Georgia, 1992)

Creighton, Margaret S., and Norling, Lisa, *Iron Men, Wooden Women: Gender and Seafaring in the Atlantic World* (London, 1989)

Curtin, Philip, *The Atlantic Slave Trade: A Census* (Madison, 1969)

Dampier, William, *A New Voyage Round the World* (London, 1697)

— *Voyages and Descriptions* (London, 1699)

— *A Voyage to New Holland, &c. in the year 1699* (London 1703)

— *Dampier's Voyages*, ed. John Masefield (London, 1906)

Davis, Ralph, *The Rise of the English Shipping Industry in the 17th and 18th Centuries* (Newton Abbot, 1962)

Davis, Robert C., *Christian Slaves, Muslim Masters* (London, 2003)

Defoe, Daniel, *An Essay on the South-Sea Trade* (London, 1711/12)

— *The Life and Strange Surprising Adventures of Robinson Crusoe, of York, Mariner* (London, 1719)

— *A Tour through the Whole Island of Great Britain* (London, 1724–6)

Depauw, Linda Grant, *Seafaring Women* (Boston, 1982)

Dugaw, Diane, *Warrior Women and Popular Balladry* (Cambridge, 1989)

Dunn, Richard S., *Sugar and Slaves: The Rise of the Planter Class in the English West Indies, 1624–1713* (London, 1973)

Earle, Peter, *The World of Defoe* (London, 1976)

— *The Sack of Panama* (London, 1981)

— *Sailors: English Merchant Seamen, 1650–1775* (London, 1998)

— *The Pirate Wars* (London, 2003)

Edwards, Philip, *The Story of the Voyage: Sea-Narratives in Eighteenth-Century England* (Cambridge, 1994)

Evelyn, John, *The Diary of John Evelyn*, ed. E. S. De Beer (Oxford, 1959)

Exquemeling, John, *Bucaniers of America* (London, 1684). First published in Dutch as *De Americaensche Zee-Roovers* by A. E. Exquemeling (Amsterdam, 1678)

Fausett, David, *The Strange Surprising Sources of Robinson Crusoe* (Amsterdam, 1994)

Funnell, William, *A Voyage Round the World* (London, 1707)

Furbank, Philip N., and Owens, W. R., *The Canonisation of Daniel Defoe* (New Haven, 1988)

Gilkerson, William, *Boarders Away II: Firearms of the Age of Fighting Sail* (Lincoln, Rhode Island, 1993)

Gill, Anton, *The Devil's Mariner: William Dampier Pirate and Explorer* (London, 1997)

Hacke, William, *A Collection of Original Voyages . . . published by Capt. William Hacke* (London, 1699)

Harcourt, Malcolm, *A History of the Bahamas House of Assembly* (Nassau, 1921)

Heald, Henrietta (ed.), *Chronicle of Britain and Ireland* (London, 1992)

Howse, Derek, and Thrower, Norman (eds.), *A Buccaneer's Atlas: Basil Ringrose's South Sea Waggoner* (Berkeley and Oxford, 1992)

Johnson, Captain Charles, *A General History of the Robberies and Murders of the Most Notorious Pyrates* (London, 1724). There are numerous editions of this book. I have used the most comprehensive edition edited by Manuel Schonhorn under the title *A General History of the Pyrates* (London, 1972), with the author's name given as Daniel Defoe, but I have cited the Dover Publications edition (New York, 1999).

Konstam, Angus, *Blackbeard: America's Most Notorious Pirate* (Hoboken, 2006)

Lavery, Brian, *The Arming and Fitting of English Ships of War, 1600–1850* (London, 1987)

Lee, C. D., 'Alexander Selkirk and the last voyage of the *Cinque Ports* Galley', *Mariner's Mirror*, vol. 73 (1987)

Lee, Robert E., *Blackbeard the Pirate: A Reappraisal of His Life and Times* (Winston-Salem, 1974; edn. cited 1995)

Linebaugh, Peter, *The London Hanged: Crime and Civil Society in the Eighteenth Century* (London and New York, 1991)

Little, Brian, *Crusoe's Captain: Being the Life of Woodes Rogers, Seaman, Trader, Colonial Governor* (London, 1960)

Lovett, R. W., 'Sir Richard Steele's "frequent conversations" with Alexander Selkirk', *English Language Notes*, 25/1 (1987)

Lyon, David, *The Sailing Navy List: All the Ships of the Royal Navy, Built, Purchased, and Captured, 1688–1860* (London, 1993)

Macky, John, *A Journey through England* (London, 1722)

Marley, David, *Pirates and Privateers of the Americas* (Santa Barbara, California, 1994)

Marx, Jennifer, *Pirates and Privateers of the Caribbean* (Malabar, Florida, 1992)

Masefield, John (ed.), *Dampier's Voyages* (London, 1906)

Mégroz, R. L., *The Real Robinson Crusoe: Being the Life and Strange Surprising Adventures of Alexander Selkirk of Largo, Fife, Mariner* (London, 1939)

Moore, David D., 'A General History of Blackbeard the Pirate, the *Queen Anne's Revenge*, and the *Adventure*', *Tributaries*, vol. VII, 1997 (North Carolina Maritime History Council)

Moore, John Robert, *Daniel Defoe: Citizen of the Modern World* (Chicago, 1958)

Morgan, Kenneth, *Bristol and the Atlantic Trade in the 18th Century* (Cambridge, 1993)

Oldmixon, John, *The British Empire in America* (London, 1741)

Parry, J. H., *The Spanish Seaborne Empire* (London, 1966)

Pawson, Michael, and Buisseret, David, *Port Royal, Jamaica* (Oxford, 1975)

Pitman, Henry, *A Relation of the Great Sufferings and Strange Adventures of Henry Pitman* (London 1689)

Pope, Dudley, *Harry Morgan's Way: The Biography of Sir Henry Morgan* (London, 1977)

Preston, Diana and Michael, *A Pirate of Exquisite Mind: Explorer, Naturalist and Buccaneer: The Life of William Dampier* (New York, 2004)

Rediker, Marcus, *Villains of all Nations: Atlantic Pirates in the Golden Age* (Boston, 2004)

— *Between the Devil and the Deep Blue Sea: Merchant Seamen, Pirates, and the Anglo-American Maritime World, 1700–1750* (Cambridge, 1987)

Richetti, John, *The Life of Daniel Defoe* (Oxford, 2005)

Riley, Sandra, *Homeward Bound: A History of the Bahama Islands to 1850* (Nassau, 2000)

Ritchie, Robert C., *Captain Kidd and the War against the Pirates* (Cambridge, Massachusetts, and London, 1986)

Rodger, N. A. M., *The Command of the Ocean: A Naval History of Britain, 1649–1815* (London, 2004)

— *The Wooden World*, (London, 1986)

Rogers, B. M. H., 'Woodes Rogers's Privateering Voyage of 1708–11', *Mariner's Mirror*, vol. XIX (1933)

Rogers, Captain Woodes, *A Cruising Voyage Round the World* (London, 1712). I have used the edition with an introduction and notes by G. E. Manwaring (London and New York, 1928)

Rogers, Pat, *Robinson Crusoe* (London, 1979)

Schurz, William Lytle, *The Manila Galleon* (Manila, 1985)

Secord, Arthur W., *Studies in the Narrative Method of Defoe* (Illinois, 1924)

Severin, Tim, *Seeking Robinson Crusoe* (London, 2002)

Sharp, Bartholomew, *The Voyages and Adventures of Capt. Barth. Sharp, and Others in the South Sea* (London, 1684)

Sheridan, Richard, 'Caribbean Plantation Society, 1689–1748', in *The Oxford History of the British Empire: The Eighteenth Century*, ed. P. J. Marshall (Oxford, 1998)

Snelgrave, William, *A New Account of Some Parts of Guinea and the Slave Trade* (London, 1734)

Spate, O. H. K., *The Spanish Lake* (London, 1979)

Stanley, Jo, *Bold in her Breeches: Women Pirates across the Ages* (London, 1995)

Starkey, David J., *British Privateering Enterprise in the Eighteenth Century* (Exeter, 1990)

Sutherland, James, *Daniel Defoe: A Critical Study* (Harvard, 1971)

Thomas, Graham A., *Pirate Hunter: The Life of Captain Woodes Rogers* (Barnsley, 2008)

Thomas, Hugh, *The Slave Trade: The History of the Atlantic Slave Trade 1440–1870* (London, 1997)

Thomas, Pascoe, *A True and Impartial Journal of a Voyage to the South Seas and Round the Globe in His Majesty's Ship the Centurion* (London, 1745)

Uring, Nathaniel, *The Voyages and Travels of Captain Nathaniel Uring*, ed. A. Dewar (London, 1928)

Wagner, Kip, *Pieces of Eight: Recovering the Riches of a Lost Spanish Treasure Fleet* (London and New York, 1966)

Watt, Ian, *The Rise of the Novel: Studies in Defoe, Richardson and Fielding* (London, 1957)

Williams, Basil, *The Whig Supremacy, 1714–1760* (Oxford, 1939)

Williams, Glyn, *The Prize of all the Oceans: The Triumph and Tragedy of Anson's Voyage Round the World* (London, 1999)

Williams, Glyndwr, *The Great South Sea: English Voyages and Encounters, 1570–1750* (London and New Haven, 1997)

Williams, Neville, *The Sea Dogs: Privateers, Plunder and Piracy in the Elizabethan Age* (London, 1975)

Woodard, Colin, *The Republic of Pirates: Being the True and Surprising Story of the Caribbean Pirates and the Man Who Brought Them Down* (New York and London, 2007)

Index

Acknowledgments

The idea for this book was first suggested to me by my writer friend Richard Platt, who thought that it was time for a fresh look at the adventurous career of Captain Woodes Rogers. My thanks to him and to Bill Swainson, my editor at Bloomsbury, who took on the book and, as usual, had shrewd advice on how to deal with a subject which proved to be more complex and wide ranging than a straightforward biography.

The book is based on the Colonial Office and Admiralty documents held by the National Archives (Public Record Office) in London, and on material in the Library of Congress in Washington, D.C., and the National Maritime Museum in Greenwich. The writings of William Dampier, Captain Charles Johnson, Daniel Defoe and Woodes Rogers himself have been an essential resource, while *Crusoe's Captain*, a well-documented biography of Rogers by Brian Little which was published in 1960, proved a most useful starting point. I have also made use of a considerable number of more recent books and would like to acknowledge my debt to the following in particular: *The Pirate Wars* by Peter Earle, *Blackbeard* by Angus Konstam, *Villains of All Nations* by Marcus Rediker, *Seeking*

Robinson Crusoe by Tim Severin, *British Privateering Enterprise in the Eighteenth Century* by David J. Starkey, *The Great South Sea* by Glyn Williams, and *The Republic of Pirates* by Colin Woodard.

Fifteen years ago I organised an exhibition entitled *Pirates: Fact and Fiction* at the National Maritime Museum in London. This led to the writing of *Life Among the Pirates* (entitled *Under the Black Flag* in the United States), which has done remarkably well over the years and resulted in my acting as consultant for an exhibition based on the book at the Mariners' Museum in Newport News, Virginia, and a small exhibition on pirates at the South Street Seaport Museum in New York. I was also involved in the creation of a museum of piracy at Nassau in the Bahamas, and was historical consultant for the first of the *Pirates of the Caribbean* movies, as well as for several documentary films on pirates. These and other ventures resulted in visits (some under sail) to many West Indian islands as well to Key West, Florida, and several museums on the east coast of North America. During the course of these visits my wife and I received generous hospitality from many people and would especially like to thank Peter and Mary Neill, William and Kerstin Gilkerson, Claudia and Craig Pennington, Madeleine Burnside, Julie McEnroe, Benjamin 'Dink' Bruce, John Hightower, Simon and Robin Robinson, Tom Goodwin and Ellen, and Orjan and Amanda Lindroth.

I would also like to thank Gill Coleridge, my literary agent, for her constant support over the years, and to thank her assistant, Cara Jones, for fielding a steady stream of queries on pirates and other maritime subjects. The staff of Bloomsbury, my publishers, have been as helpful and efficient as always and, in addition to Bill Swainson, I would like to thank Nick Humphrey and Anna Simpson for their valuable input, and Laura Brooke for handling the publicity. Thanks also to John Gilkes for the beautifully drawn maps, and to Richard Dawes, the copy editor, for spotting and correcting numerous errors, inconsistencies, and misspellings. Of course I remain responsible for any that remain.

As in the past my greatest debt is to my family. My son Matthew has taken a keen interest in the subject and has been a constant source of ideas and practical suggestions; my daughter Rebecca has helped me sort out my thoughts over coffee in the British Library on many occasions; and, in addition to her advice and encouragement throughout the writing of this book, my wife has shouldered most of the responsibility for family and grandparent duties so that I could get the book finished. It is to her, therefore, that this book is affectionately dedicated.

D.C.
Brighton, Sussex
January 2011